Marketing Professional Services

Marketing Professional Services

Edward W. Wheatley

Prentice-Hall, Inc., Englewood Cliffs, New Jersey 07632

Library of Congress Cataloging in Publication Data
Wheatley, Edward W., (date)
   Marketing professional services.

   Includes bibliographical references and index.
   1. Professions—Marketing.   I. Title.
HD8038.A1W48   1983   658.8   82-10190
ISBN   0-13-557462-5

Editorial/production supervision by Kim Gueterman
Cover design by Diane Saxe
Manufacturing buyer: Ed O'Dougherty

© 1983 by Prentice-Hall, Inc., Englewood Cliffs, N.J.   07632

All rights reserved. No part of this book may be reproduced in any form or by any means without permission in writing from the publisher.

Printed in the United States of America

10 9 8 7 6 5 4 3 2 1

ISBN 0-13-557462-5

Prentice-Hall International, Inc., *London*
Prentice-Hall of Australia Pty. Limited, *Sydney*
Editora Prentice-Hall do Brazil, LTDA, *Rio de Janeiro*
Prentice-Hall Canada Inc., *Toronto*
Prentice-Hall of India Private Limited, *New Delhi*
Prentice-Hall of Japan, Inc., *Tokyo*
Prentice-Hall of Southeast Asia Pte. Ltd., *Singapore*
Whitehall Books Limited, *Wellington, New Zealand*

To Betty, Sarah, Lisa, and Richard

Contents

Foreword xi

Preface xv

1 Modern Marketing: Perspective and Challenge 1

What marketing is—and what it isn't 2
Marketing's evolution 6
The marketing concept 8
Meta marketing 14
Professionals and marketing 16

2 Marketing Professional Services 20

What's different about service marketing? 21
Do you feel like a traffic cop? 26
What do you sell? What does your client buy? 27
You've been very patient 31

3 The MPS Audit: A Self-Administered Diagnostic Test 32

What is a marketing professional services audit? 32
What makes a good marketing audit? 33
Some words of warning 35
Taking your MPS audit 37
Your practice environment 38
Client analysis and opportunities 40
Philosophy, positioning, and targeting 41
Your service mix 41
Professional fees 42
Personal communication 43
Written communication 44
MPS control and evaluation 45
We're under way! 45

4 Developing Your Marketing Program 46

What is an MPS plan? 47
The importance of an MPS plan 48
Increase your probability for success 51
Organizing for marketing: Who should do it? 53
The quicksand of marketing planning: Generalizations 58
How to structure your marketing plan 60
MPS implementation and control 62

5 Analyzing Your Practice Environment 70

Economic variables 71
The political environment 75
The legal environment 76
Ethics 78
The natural and cultural environment 79
The competitive environment 81
Technology 86
The managerial environment 89

6 Client Analysis and Targeting 92

You the analyst 92
Client identification, segmentation, and targeting 100
Marketing research and the professional 104

Contents ix

7 **How to Position Your Services 111**

What is positioning? 111
Positioning: Some familiar examples 113
Positioning: Expanding the concept 114
Your MPS positioning statement 116

8 **Your Written Communication Program 122**

Your image 123
Have you seen our logo? 126
Institutional communication: The VIP approach 129
Competitive communication 136
Advertising 136
Other competitive communication 147
Administrative communication 152

9 **Promoting Your Practice: Personal Communication 154**

Image: The mirror that doesn't reflect 156
Components of your professional image 156
The client interview or consultation 165
External communication programs 171

10 **Your Professional Fees 177**

Establishing fee objectives 178
Fee strategies 180
Fees for new services 186
Determining professional fees 188
Communicating fees 190
Getting paid! 192
Ethical and legal issues 194

Notes 196

Index 199

Foreword

The last 20 years have brought significant and permanent changes to nearly every profession. Certified public accountants, architects, health care specialists, attorneys, engineers, consultants—all have been affected. If you are a practicing professional, you have had to adjust to these changes to survive and prosper. If you are relatively new to professional practice, these changes will shape your current practice and future potential.

How has the environment of the professional changed? Quantum leaps in knowledge and technology have outmoded former practice methods and techniques. Staying current, learning, adapting, changing, even pioneering change are ever-growing responsibilities of the modern professional. Regulations, accountability, and liability demand increased vigilance and control over the quality and consistency of our work. Competition has intensified—no longer can most professionals hang out their shingle and assume the clients will be standing in line. Today, clients are better informed and more demanding than they used to be. Their level of expectation is high. Long-term client loyalty must be nurtured and protected, never taken for granted. When all of these changes are added to shifts in the economic, social, cultural, political, and international environment, the scope of change is almost revolutionary. Change has not only been dramatic, but dynamic as well—coming upon us at ever increasing rates.

How have professionals and professional firms coped with these fundamental changes? Unfortunately, some have not done too well, trying to stay afloat on the good ship "tradition" not realizing that the hull is beginning to fill up with water from the waves of change. The more astute professional has adapted by "professionalizing" practice management and using many of the modern management practices that are used by commercial firms. This is a healthy development for both the client and the professional. After all, professional talent is a resource. Like other resources, its use must be planned and managed to yield maximum return. For a professional, of course, "to yield maximum return" is to serve clients knowledgeably and effectively. The application of modern marketing management techniques to the professions is a natural evolutionary development in practice management. *Marketing Professional Services* is an important addition to modern practice management.

The benefits of this book can be direct and immediate. It begins with a brief, yet thorough, introduction to the field of marketing, what it is, how it is done in the commercial arena, how product and service marketing differ. After you've finished Chapter 2, you'll be ready to test yourself and your firm as to your marketing strengths and weaknesses. It will help you to determine whether you are using the marketing revolution to your advantage, or are you already losing ground to your competitor. Ed Wheatley offers you a self-administered marketing professional services audit, which you will find not only challenging, revealing, and instructive, but will also serve as a springboard for your leap into the modern world of marketing.

Next, the book gets down to cases. Step by step, it provides a structured approach to developing your own marketing plan. Each chapter is enriched with concrete suggestions and examples based on actual professional and organizational experience. I'm sure you'll see yourself or your colleagues reflected in many of the situations presented.

In addition to its content, several features make this book particularly useful to professionals. Because of their own training and disciplines, professionals can more fully appreciate its philosophy, breadth, actionability, and adaptability which make it a thoroughly practical and versatile guide.

Philosophy. This book reflects Ed's—and my—firm belief that in marketing, as in all other areas, professionals need not and should not engage in unethical practices. We can effectively and aggressively market professional services with both dignity and high regard for professional ethics.

Breadth. No matter what your professional field, this book's managerial approach helps you evaluate your current marketing efforts and provides the tools to better integrate marketing into your practice management system. It is flexible enough to adapt to whatever your field of professional practice happens to be.

Actionability. From the marketing audit through the development of a written communication program, you'll be able to use the material in your everyday practice activities.

Adaptability. This book offers suggestions for professionals and firms in various stages of marketing development. Whether you are just entering practice or are part of a large, successful firm, *Marketing Professional Services* can help improve your client service and retention, market your services to potential new clients, strengthen your firm's organization, and provide guidelines for improved profitability.

Norman S. Rachlin, CPA
Managing Partner
Rachlin & Cohen
Coral Gables, Florida

Preface

HOW WILL THIS BOOK HELP YOU?

The professional service marketing program and techniques presented in this book can be applied and utilized in your practice and firm to increase your "top line" and your "bottom line." Of course, client service and satisfaction come first. But in order to maintain and improve service and quality, your practice must grow. Your professional gross income (top line) and your net profit (bottom line) should show steady improvement. This book will show you how to achieve that objective. It is not a book of theories. It is a book that will take you step by step through the application of modern marketing to your professional activities. How will you benefit by reading this book?

- You'll be up to the minute in the rapidly developing field of professional service marketing.
- You'll take a candid, revealing, and instructive self-administered diagnostic test that will pinpoint areas of weakness in your client development and retention activities.
- You'll learn what steps should be taken to bring modern marketing into your practice.
- You'll be given a step by step formula to follow that shows you not only what to do, but how to do it.

As you study and adopt these proven methods and techniques, client retention, development, and profitability will improve. Present clients will note the positive changes in your image and practice. That wonderful perpetual motion machine of recommendations and referrals will be put into motion.

What are the challenges and opportunities for you in professional service marketing? Chapter 1 defines modern marketing and the marketing concepts underlying professional service marketing. You'll learn how and why successful consumer and industrial product firms have made marketing an integral part of their operation. In other words, you'll learn how professional marketers market.

Adjusting modern marketing techniques for your service environment. Chapter 2 shows you how to translate the success of modern marketing from the manufactured product marketplace to the professional service environment. The key differences are pinpointed for you and their application enriched by examples.

How effectively are you marketing your professional services? In Chapter 3 you'll take a candid, comprehensive, and revealing diagnostic test—I call it an MPS audit. This self-administered exam will pinpoint your weaknesses and strengths in professional marketing. This is an eye-opening experience for professionals and professional firms.

How can professional service marketing be integrated into my firm? By now you'll be considering several specific actions. Chapter 4 presents alternative ways to organize the MPS function. Evaluative criteria are presented to help you select the best formula. Now you are ready to proceed. But how do you put all the pieces together in a complete, systematic, and controllable formula? The remainder of the chapter provides the answer. It lays out a complete, practical, and proved planning formula step by step.

Now that you have a planning formula to follow, subsequent chapters show you how to "fill in the blanks" by developing your own MPS plan. These chapters not only tell you what to do, but are filled with tips, examples, and recommendations covering scores of topics, including competitive positioning, strategy and tactics, client specialization, selecting a logo, institutional and competitive advertising, preparing advertising that sells, personal communication, proposal and report preparation and presentation, image building, community relations, publicity, and fees.

A PERSONAL NOTE

I'm a marketing person—pure and simple. I'm enjoying a career timing pattern that puts me in the thick of the developing field of professional service marketing. My education, experience, and interests have made it possible to apply the principles and practice of modern marketing management to the rapidly changing, challenging, and exciting professional environment. As a university professor and practicing consultant, I also consider myself a professional. I will readily admit to one philosophical bias: Professional service marketing can and should remain "professional." We don't have to hide our light under a bushel. We don't have to be stodgy. We can inform and persuade effectively while maintaining professional dignity and respect for the intelligence of our current and prospective clientele. It is my sincere belief that this book will help you achieve that result. At the same time you, your associates, and your clientele will benefit from a growing and financially strong professional practice.

ACKNOWLEDGMENTS

Many persons and organizations played a role in the development and production of this book. Walter Beran, former partner in charge of client relations, Ernst & Ernst and currently vice chairman, West Coast Region, Ernst & Whinney, provided early career opportunity and experience for the author in the professional arena. Norman S. Rachlin and Stanley L. Cohen, founding senior partners of Rachlin & Cohen, CPAs, provided invaluable insight and input. Harry Payton and Richard Rachlin (Payton & Rachlin, PA), Richard Lyons (Lyons & Smith, PA), John Tramontine (Fish & Neave), Don Feldman and Chuck Levey (Feldman, Abramson, Smith, Magidson, and Levy, PA) all provided exposure and experience in the law firm environment. The Florida Institute of CPAs and the Dade County Chapter of CPAs were extremely helpful. Zeljka Bilbija contributed an architect's perspective.

Ted Jursek, my Prentice-Hall editor, assisted greatly with guidance, patience, and substantial input. Production editor Kim Gueterman fine tuned the manuscript. Graduate research assistants Patricia Bright and Jim Johnson diligently and creatively assisted in manuscript research. Deborah and Gary Jones typed and revised the manuscript with due allowances for the author's handwriting and deadlines. Carol Ott, marketing staff coordinator, made the "final" corrections to the manuscript.

I especially appreciate the constructive criticism of manuscript reviewers. Finally, my deepest professional debt is owed to the scores of professionals I have worked with over the years in organizations, associations, seminars, conferences, workshops, and as clients or students.

I intend to keep learning.

Edward W. Wheatley

Chapter 1
Modern Marketing: Perspective and Challenge

Most professionals probably have a negative reaction when they hear the word "marketing." Perhaps you are one of them. This negative bias toward marketing is usually an emotional reaction to generalizations and stereotypes the professional associates with marketing activities, not a reaction based on knowledge or experience. But today's increasingly well-managed and competitive business environment makes this attitude not only inaccurate, but dangerously unproductive.

The purpose of this chapter—and of this book—is to permit you to examine your own understanding of modern marketing and to help you make a more objective appraisal of the potential role of marketing in the development and management of your own professional activities. You owe it to yourself, to your colleagues, and to your clients to develop this understanding, for the knowledge will prepare you to make a more informed decision about whether, when, and how the management of your professional activities should be broadened to include the marketing function. Fortunately, the field of marketing professional services has not developed in a vacuum; the function and field of marketing has grown and prospered over the last forty years. Today, marketing departments are found in consumer and industrial goods and service companies as well as in manufacturing corporations. About 50 cents of every consumer dollar goes to pay for marketing costs associated with products and services we all use. Fifteen to 20 percent of students in colleges and schools of business administration pursue degrees in the field. Hundreds of books and thousands of periodical articles dealing with marketing topics fill business libraries. There are scores of professional associations in marketing and related specialties. Finally, marketing is no longer limited in its application to products or services. As we will see, the application of marketing has been expanded to include persons, places, politics, organizations, causes, and professions.

What does all this mean? Does it mean "they know something that we don't"? Have manufacturing and service companies, political parties, celebrities, resorts, and other private and public sector organizations found a new way of conducting their affairs that works? The answer is simply yes, they have. Well-managed enterprises put every managerial concept to the test of fire. If an approach works, they use it. Marketing works. Now people in the professions are asking, what *is* marketing? Does the marketing approach have any value in the professional service field? The pages that follow will give you the basis for an answer.

I urge you, regardless of your impressions of the field, to let this book work for you. As a professional, your typical approach to a client problem is to listen and gather all available data relevant to that problem. You then evaluate this information carefully, and using your training, knowledge, and creativity analyze the client's situation. Then you prepare and recommend a solution you feel is in the client's best interest. As a marketing professional, I am simply asking you to be as good to yourself as you are to your clients. But before we discuss the application of modern marketing approaches to the professional service field, we need to develop a careful definition of marketing and find out what professional marketers do.

WHAT MARKETING IS— AND WHAT IT ISN'T

The field of marketing is broad and complex. Is advertising marketing? No. Is the use of discounting and other sales promotion and pricing gimmicks marketing? No. Is the use of personal sales representatives delivering carefully prepared sales presentations marketing? No. Is the conduct of client surveys marketing? No. The correct answer to these questions is that all of these activities—and many more—are *part* of a modern marketing operation. As consumers we are bombarded with persuasive communications varying in quality from highly informative and useful to misleading and annoying. Many of us equate these attempts at persuasive selling with marketing. The leading professional association in the field, The American Marketing Association, defines marketing as ". . . the performance of business activities that direct the flow of goods and services from producer to consumer or user." Philip Kotler, a well-known marketing scholar and writer, defines marketing as ". . . that human activity directed at satisfying needs and wants through exchange processes." Various authors in the field offer several additional versions of a definition.[1]

However, perfect recall of these definitions doesn't really provide us with an answer to the question, "What is marketing?" The reason is simple: It's not possible to develop a quick and simple, yet meaningful definition of marketing that has any communicative power or utility. So, let's move from the abstract to the applied. Operating on the premise that marketing is what it does, we can say that a modern marketing department has five basic functions:

1. Understanding the needs and desires of current and prospective customers.
2. Assisting in the development of need- and desire-satisfying products and services.
3. Developing informative and persuasive communication flows between the marketing organization and the appropriate audiences.
4. Ensuring that the products and services are provided at the right time, the right place, in the right form, and at the best price.
5. Keeping the customer satisfied and loyal after the exchange.

How does the modern business corporation bring this definition to life? How do businesses do marketing? Let's briefly examine these five aspects of marketing and specifically identify how modern businesses get the job accomplished.

Understanding Customer Needs and Desires

Marketing research programs are conducted on an ongoing basis by modern corporations. These investigations take several forms. In-depth discussion, led by a skilled moderator and later carefully interpreted by experienced professionals, are generally referred to as *focused group research. Experimental groups* of past, current, or potential customers may be established and subjected to a variety of experiences. As in all experiments, the researcher is attempting to find some possible cause and effect relationships. *Observation techniques* might also be employed to film, tape, and/or count certain types of behavior which could then serve as inputs for decision making. In addition to focus groups, experimental research, and observation techniques, *survey research* is widely employed.

Research is conducted by internal research departments, external market research firms, and individual consultants. The ultimate objective of market research is to reduce the uncertainty and risk in deciding what products and services should be marketed and how they should be presented. It's important for professionals to note that consumer and industrial firms carefully analyze at least two dimensions of their market. Remember we talked about learning consumer wants and needs. A consumer may need an automobile to get to work each morning and to fulfill the basic need of transportation. This is clearly a functional requirement. Yet which car a consumer purchases will depend partly on the intangible and emotional aspects of the purchase. In the professional setting, a young father may need a will, clearly a simple functional requirement. Yet the satisfaction of emotional needs through all the stimuli provided by the law firm may determine whether he will become a long-term client and gradually expand his utilization of the firm's services.

How much do you really know about your clients? Does this knowledge extend beyond the scope of your limited professional involvement? It is ironic that the Burger King Corporation has devised elaborate consumer behavior models concerning how various market segments seek, evaluate, and patronize a fast food restaurant, while a large CPA firm may never have even considered making a systematic study of the composition of its current and potential clients or their perceptions of the functional and emotional aspects of the client-firm relationship.

Development of Need-Satisfying Products and Services

In industrial and technical firms it is common to find research and development departments. Their activities include everything from basic to applied research. What is learned in the lab is applied directly to the development of new products or services and the modification of existing offerings. In other firms, particularly consumer product companies such as Procter & Gamble, General Foods, and McDonalds, there are new product departments or product development departments. These marketing staff activities lead to new product and service development, modification, and/or deletion. The marketing staff relies on input from a variety of sources and specialists. With data developed from marketing research activities, the marketing department is in an excellent position to coordinate product and service development. Good product and service development, modification or termination decisions are most effectively made when the probable reactions of the market have been carefully studied.

Are you, as a professional, systematically evaluating your service offerings? On what basis do you or your organization make decisions to add, modify, or delete client services?

Development of Informative and Persuasive Communication Flows

Business firms need to make customers aware that their products and services exist. They do this through informative communication. This type of communication stresses product and service features, specifications, price, availability, terms of sale, and so on. In addition, firms seek to persuade customers to switch to their products or services, or to try a new product or service. In addition, persuasive communication seeks to maintain customer loyalty by reinforcing the purchase decision in a positive way. Business firms use four major types of communication to pursue this aspect of marketing: advertising, personal selling, sales promotion, and publicity. In addition, organizations engage in ongoing public relations programs directed at building a positive image with all their publics, not just with customers. These publics include employees, investors, suppliers, the financial community, the community in which the firm is located, regulators, and others. *Advertising* is the communication of a series of messages to a mass audience utilizing mass media (newspapers, radio, television, magazines). *Personal selling* involves the preparation and delivery of individually tailored presentations to an individual prospect or decision-making group in a potential client organization. *Sales promotion* refers to short-term and intensive activities used to spark interest and support ongoing promotional activities. *Promotions* familiar to most of us include special sales, grand openings, contests, games, demonstrations, samples, free trials, and couponing.

Unlike advertising, *publicity* is a nonpaid form of communication utilizing mass media. However, the communication is usually prepared and controlled by media personnel rather than the advertiser. To be worthy of this coverage, a firm's activities must have news value to some segment of the media's audience.

What do you do to make clients aware of your services? What promotional techniques have you employed to persuade potential clients to utilize your talents?

Delivering Products and Services

In today's competitive business environment, with so many satisfactory product alternatives available, price is becoming a more important decision-influencing variable. As the inflation rate continues to rise, even the more affluent consumer is becoming price conscious. Marketing specialists work carefully with individuals in the firm involved with the cost side of product and service development. These include both technical and financial specialists. It is the job of marketing to advise management concerning consumer's economic and emotional perceptions of price as well as probable competitive reactions to new pricing strategies. In a manufacturing firm, getting products to consumers involves the selection of a system of middlemen, including transportation, warehousing, wholesaling, and retailing institutions. Jantzen bathing suits do the manufacturer little good sitting in the California plant. The suits must be moved through channels of distribution and into retail stores throughout the country if the consumer is to have the opportunity to compare and purchase. In a service business such as Burger King, great attention is given to the selection and development of restaurant location, decor, staffing, and operations. The service system, which results in the speedy delivery of food products, is constantly evaluated and streamlined.

How are your professional fees set? What does a professional do to adjust fee structure to differing clients and competitive conditions? How often do you review your service system? What is involved in the location, decor, and staffing of your professional offices? How are location or expansion decisions analyzed?

Keeping Customers Satisfied after the Sale

We all have one thing in common. We are all consumers. As consumers, we each have scores of war stories to tell about the individual firms with which we have done business. This fifth role of marketing is probably the weakest link in the development of the field. Many marketing-oriented organizations seem more interested in adding new clients or making new sales than in continuing to satisfy existing customers. Unfortunately, consumer experience is often typified by the sign I saw recently hanging in the service department of an automobile dealership. It said: I'd like to help you out—which way did you come in?"

Maintaining customer loyalty through providing good ongoing service is a particularly demanding problem in the consumer and industrial durable goods field. Consumer appliance companies like RCA and Whirlpool pride themselves on the operation of their service departments. They see service as an extension of the marketing effort. Their experience is common to many firms that are working to give equal emphasis to postpurchase customer relationships. Indeed, a whole new field of consumer affairs has developed rapidly since 1970. There now exists a Society of Consumer Affairs Professionals whose membership is composed primarily of corporate executives charged with the responsibility of postpurchase consumer satisfaction.

What steps do you or your firm take to measure the satisfaction of your current clients? How much of your client-development effort is geared toward maintaining existing clients and expanding the scope of services provided? Are there policies and systems that identify, analyze, and solve client problems promptly? Consumer affairs specialists tell me that company loyalty is enhanced when postpurchase problems are handled promptly and intelligently. One of my friends in the field puts it this way:

> Consumers are used to being ignored, lied to and hassled when they seek to solve a purchase problem with a business organization. They expect bureaucratic red tape, excuses, the filling out of endless forms and challenges to their intelligence and integrity. In our company (a large consumer appliance manufacturing firm), customers are pleasantly surprised to find they are listened to, treated courteously and responded to promptly and fairly. The fact that they had a problem with our product but that we handled it in an efficient way, makes them even more loyal to us. I guess it's because our performance is the exception to the rule these days.

MARKETING'S EVOLUTION

By now you can see that marketing is much more than advertising or personal selling: rather, it is a field that has evolved by putting an umbrella over a variety of business activities that affect customer satisfaction. This was not always so. The very firms that today operate highly sophisticated and effective marketing departments were once in the same position as the professions are today. If we are to understand the potential application of modern marketing to professional services, we must briefly examine the evolution of marketing as an accepted functional area in business. Voltaire has said, "All generalizations are bad, including this one." It will be necessary to generalize as we leapfrog quickly through decades of time. However, this brief historical journey will help explain why professionals are currently evaluating, debating, and discussing the application of marketing to the management of their practices.

Revolutions, Robber Barons, and Model-Ts

An economic historian once told me that our Industrial Revolution was led by individuals who pursued and found the answers to the following four questions: How to make it, how to make it faster, how to make it cheaper, how to make more of it. A critical peripheral issue was how to get the resources to accomplish the first four objectives. As our nation was expanding westward, industrial and individual consumers needed every conceivable product and service. Business energies were turned toward the technical problems of product design and production. Income levels were not high, yet our growing population produced huge potential markets for an unending list of products. The energy of business was focused on the development of mass production capabilities.

Power in American business quickly gravitated to those individuals and firms who were successful in developing adequate capital and applying it to successful mass production technology. Competition was nonexistent or minimal. Little if any market research was conducted: Manufacturing firms decided what to produce and how to produce it. The emphasis was on distributing and selling the output of our economic system. The highest-ranking person in a marketing-related activity was the sales manager. There was little if any organized input or feedback from the marketplace. Decisions were made based on what was convenient for the company and what was prudent financially. The selling function was seen as a necessary evil. The peddlers, or puffers, as they were called, had little if any input in policy making. American business was being run by production- and finance-oriented executives.

This period was climaxed in the late 1800s when the spoils of industrial and financial success went to a relatively few individuals and families. These so-called Robber Barons frequently appeared more interested in enhancing their monopolistic power and incomes than in the long-run interests of consumers and society. The managerial philosophy that exemplified this period most colorfully is attributed to Henry Ford. One of his staff suggested that consumers might prefer a choice of colors in the automobiles produced by his company. Ford is alleged to have replied, "Give them any color they want as long as it's black." Economists refer to this approach as bending the will of demand to meet the will of supply.

The Sales Era

Through the latter part of the nineteenth century and the early part of the twentieth century, American business did indeed become proficient in mass producing just about everything. Competition became more intense at all levels. Consumers had more discretionary income and became more selective. Businesses found they could no longer easily sell everything they could produce. The passion to sell, to get rid of output, to increase volume, was a major motivating factor of the sales era. In several market categories, there was an abundance of supply over demand. Salespeople were instructed to "get rid of" the output. Some managements didn't look too closely at the practices that were utilized to achieve that objective. Sales-oriented organizations sometimes used high-pressure sales tactics and techniques, false and misleading advertising, bait and switch pricing, payoffs, phoney promotional allowances, and other economic dirty tricks. Today the field of marketing still suffers from the negative stereotypes that became so firmly rooted in the public's mind during the sales era.

Modern Marketing

No one can say precisely where or how the marketing philosophy was developed. It has probably always existed in one form or another from the time economic transactions have been part of human history. However, as the twentieth century rolled along through the period of the Roaring Twenties and the Depression years of the thirties, many corporate managements began to be as interested in the long-run survival and success of their enterprises as in the short-run attainment of sales volume and profits. Companies like General Electric, Westinghouse, and Borden are often mentioned by research scholars as having managements that were pioneers in the marketing approach. This approach involved the careful analysis of current and potential markets to gain a better understanding of what consumers wanted and needed. The information was then used to help develop and shape the products and services offered by the firm. The motive was not humanitarian; rather, companies believed they would have the best competitive edge and the highest probability of developing and maintaining long-term customer loyalty if their products and services more closely met consumer needs and desires.

Did this philosophy work? The answer is an unqualified "yes." It is difficult to find a successful American company that does not have a full-time marketing department. The departments may vary in size, depending on company sales and operations. However, the power base at the decision-making level has shifted. Production and finance are still critical, but now marketing is also a top-level functional area.

Figure 1-1 illustrates the typical organization of a manufacturing company operating in the modern marketing era. Please remember that the term "marketing era" does not imply that marketing runs modern corporation, or that it is the single most important area. What has happened and is continuing to happen is that marketing is gaining a position of power and influence in corporate affairs, operations, and decision making.

Figure 1-2 shows the organization of a marketing department for a large fast-food franchising firm. Note how complete this organization is. Each job to be done according to the modern definition of marketing has its counterpart in this rather typical departmental organization chart. Of course, no single organizational chart can be a model for how best to organize every marketing function. An organization chart for a CPA firm, law firm, consulting engineering company, or most other professional service organizations would certainly be different. These charts are offered to show you how the marketing function is organized and how it fits into the typical business organization. Later, we will use this background material as a basis for discussing how to introduce marketing into the professional service firm.

THE MARKETING CONCEPT

Are you interested in developing your professional service practice to include the marketing function? Perhaps you feel your practice or your organization is already

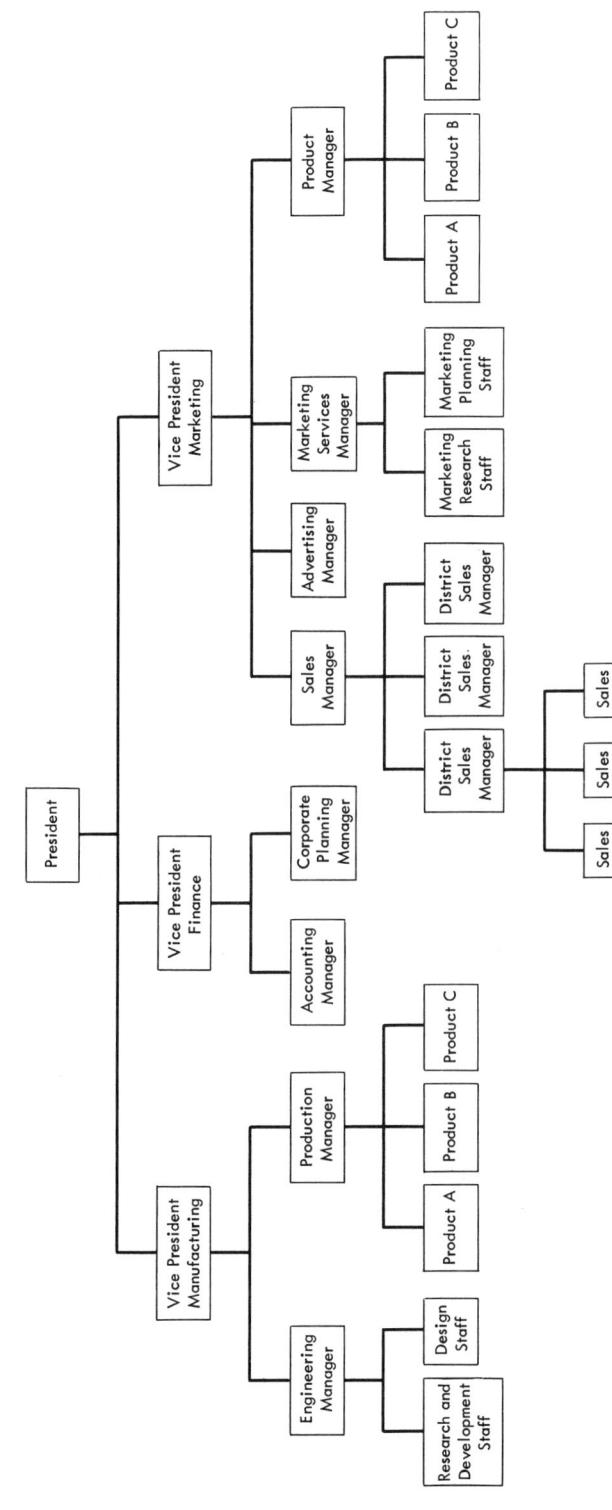

FIGURE 1-1 Marketing's role in the overall organization

Source: Martin L. Bell. *Marketing, Concepts and Strategy*, 2nd ed. (Boston: Houghton Mifflin, 1972), p. 147.

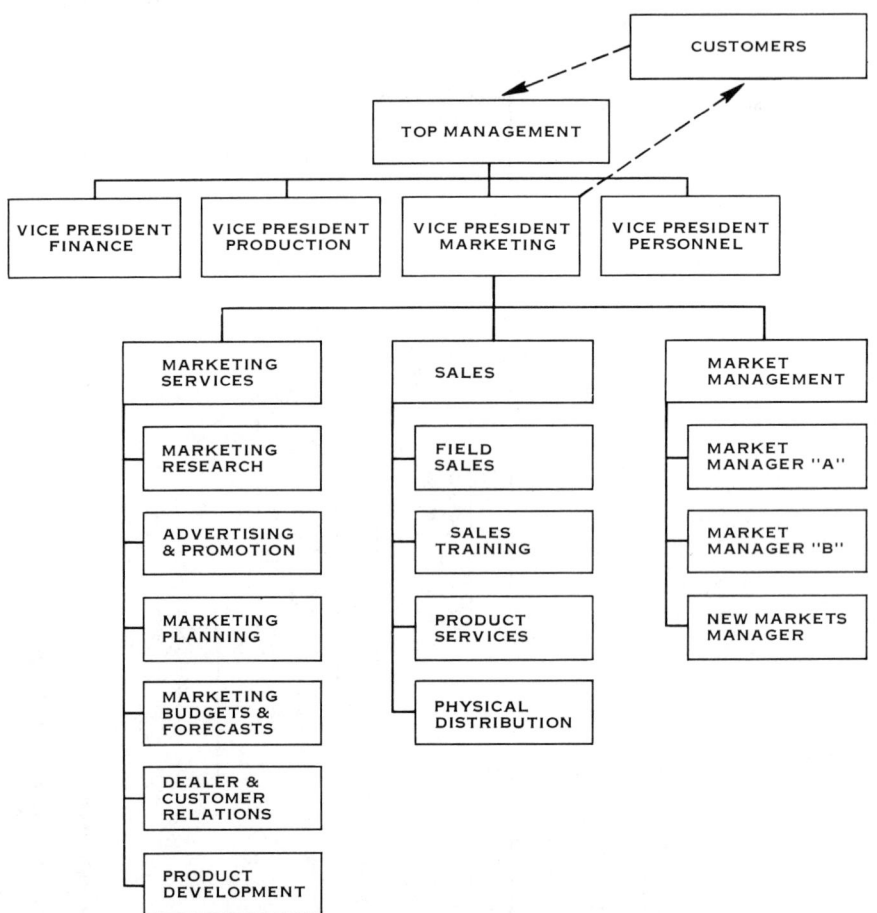

FIGURE 1-2 Marketing in a consumer service firm

operating with a marketing orientation. Before we address these questions directly, I'd like to acquaint you with the criteria that must be met for a consumer or industrial product or service firm operating under the marketing concept. The purpose of this chapter is to acquaint you with the role and operations of marketing in American business; however, I'm sure you've already begun comparing the business sector to your professional environment. The marketing concept is really a philosophy of management that can be applied with appropriate modifications to almost any situation in which organizations or individuals are serving clients or customers. To operate under the modern marketing concept, four basic criteria must be satisfied. We'll briefly examine each from the business point of view and provide examples.

Consumer Orientation

Any significant decisions must be made considering the positive and negative effects on consumers, giving these equal weight with other types of decision variables. Of course, every business and professional service feels it is consumer- or client-oriented. The real test comes in analyzing how important decisions are actually made. I knew the chief executive officer of a large chain of full-service department stores. About $100,000 was needed to develop better staff training programs for store sales employees, and it was possible to generate this money by streamlining store credit and billing procedures and shifting to descriptive billing. With descriptive billing, the customer would not receive copies of invoices he or she had signed when making a charge purchase. Rather, the customer would receive a single computer-prepared bill that briefly described the items purchased, the dates, and the amounts owed the store. The personnel people loved the idea. They'd get their training program money. The financial and accounting people loved the new system. It was more streamlined and more accurate.

The chief executive officer, however, made a very difficult decision. He refused to approve the project because "our customers won't like it." His experience and research had shown him that customers felt more secure about the bills if they could see copies of the actual sales invoices they had signed in the store. This was especially true when cards were held by families and several individuals were using the card to make purchases. This was a difficult and unpopular decision, and an excellent example of this chief executive's consumer-oriented decision-making style, which was largely responsible for the phenomenal growth and success of this quality department store group. The essence of this first criterion is orienting the business first to consumer's needs and desires, within the constraints imposed on all organizations by resources.

A Highly Placed Marketing Executive

A quick glance at the organization chart can answer this question. If we're talking about a business corporation, is the marketing executive on a level with other functional area executives? If, for example, the marketing executive were a subordinate of the vice-president of production, we could not say that the company was operating under the modern marketing concept. Rather, this would be a clue that the company was still production-oriented. Professional firms represent quite an enigma in this area. Some large accounting and law firms of which I'm personally aware have partners who spend the vast majority of their time in client relations activities. Yet if you were to see an organization chart of the firm, you would have no inkling that the marketing function was a high level, full-time activity. In other cases, such firms may have a partner in charge of client relations, or a partner in charge of practice development. In other professional service firms, the managing partner's job description includes practice development and client relations.

That the position is present is of course important. It is equally important that the individual or individuals involved in the marketing function are on a level with other decision makers within the organization. It's quite possible to have a "token" marketing executive. I'm aware of one *Fortune* top 100 company which operates in just that fashion. The top consumer affairs executive has a staff of six—six secretaries! This person's responsibility is to travel around the world giving speeches and entertaining. He is very good at both. His message is that his company really cares about customers and dealers, and I'm sure it does in its way. His secretaries' primary responsibilities are to make his travel arrangements, set up cocktail parties, and keep him on track on his incredibly busy and complex itinerary. The other bits and pieces of the marketing function are performed in various other departments. Based on competitive pressures, I doubt it will be very long before this man is out of a job. But his company is very late in evolving from the production into the marketing era.

**Complete Authority
and Responsibility for the Marketing
Function**

As you can see from the preceding example, having a top-ranking marketing executive is not enough. That executive must have the authority and responsibility for the activities necessary to implement and operate the marketing function. Marketing professionals refer to these activities as the *marketing mix*. It includes such things as marketing research, product and service research and development, distribution, dealer relations, pricing, advertising, personal selling, sales promotion, marketing planning, and sales forecasting. Please glance back to Figure 1-2. In this well-known national fast-food franchising firm, the vice-president of marketing indeed has the tools needed to do the marketing job. Correspondingly of course, that individual is held strictly accountable for marketing budgets and results. Salary, fringe benefits, and promotions depend on the achievement of goals set out in annual marketing plans. I'm reminded of the story of a corporate president heading a group of high-quality men's specialty clothing stores in Texas. The business had been built by his father and grandfather. The current president was not young or inexperienced: he simply was unwise. His greatest weakness was in delegating and using the talents of specialists.

When I looked at his organization and evaluated it under the marketing concept, he was proud to tell me: "Ed, sure marketing is represented in this organization. I have a sales manager." When I remarked that the corporation had gone through three different advertising agencies in four years, he shook his head and smiled: "I can never get an ad agency to do what I want them to do. I think we can really increase business if we start selling three-piece suits made in the Orient at $39.95 and advertise the hell out of them." Unfortunately, his advertising counselors were right. The business had been built on a gold-plated clientele of executives and professionals. The clothing was expensive and very conservative. The promotional campaigns the president wanted had begun to ruin sales and drive away prestige clients. His reply: "No matter, Ed, I solved that problem. I now pay 51 percent of the salary of the creative director on my account, who works for the new agency. You'd better believe they do what I tell them!"

In this instance, the corporate president had demoted the vice-president of marketing to the position of sales manager and stripped this capable individual of the tools needed to operate the marketing function. He had taken personal control over advertising and was flying in the face of the unanimous advice of several different advertising specialists. The company was successfully turned around in a year by "promoting" the president to chairman of the board, reorganizing the management structure, and implementing the marketing concept. The board chairman now spends his time in community affairs and public relations activities. He's a great asset to his company in this capacity, and fortunately this story has a happy ending.

Coordination with All Functional Areas

Marketing is important, but I'm always suspicious of my marketing colleagues who say that marketing is the most important function in any organization. I simply don't believe it. We spent a year and a half in executive development seminars attempting to bring back together a company that had been blown apart by a marketing professional. This firm was a leader in the medical equipment and diagnostic field. Its strength had been its research and development and manufacturing capabilities. During a reorganization, an outside president was named. This person was a marketing specialist. Rather than carefully welding together the highly technical and scientific R&D and manufacturing team with the growing marketing function, the president saw to it that marketing immediately dominated the organization. In spite of repeated and enlightened attempts by the owners to integrate the marketing and the R&D functions, destructive conflict developed. Over the next 18 months the company experienced serious problems. Several key technical people and some of the administrative staff resigned. Ironically, some of the technical people went into business for themselves and were almost immediately in direct competition with their former organization.

Certainly marketing is important, but so is production, research and development, manufacturing, finance, and all the other areas in the modern business organization. It is the job of every functional area specialist to work effectively and cooperatively with every other functional area. Of course, natural conflicts do exist. Marketing people like new products, product changes, more liberal warranties, and so on. Production specialists like standardization and long production runs. Financial people and legal people like limited warranties and minimal financial and legal risk and exposure. In a CPA firm, for example, there will always be different points of view among audit specialists, tax and estate planning personnel, management service staff, and client relations executives. No one function is any more important than the other. Constructive conflict based on sincere professional differences and points of view means a healthy business and professional environment.

META MARKETING

Now you are up to date concerning the evolution of marketing in the modern business organization. We've developed a working definition of the term, traced the growing importance of marketing in a brief historical review, examined the organization of marketing departments and how they fit into business corporations, and looked at the philosophical foundations of marketing in the marketing concept. Although I've raised some questions about marketing in the professional service environment, you still might be wondering, "why am I reading this book?" If the evolution of marketing had stopped when it reached its full flowering— in the business setting—most professionals would still not be aware of and interested in the field. However, a bridge between the traditional application of marketing and the unknown future dimensions and influence of the field began to develop in the 1950s. This extension of marketing is called *meta marketing*. From the Greek, it means simply "beyond the traditional marketing." The field of marketing developed and matured in consumer and industrial product manufacturing firms. Marketing principles and practices began to be adopted and adjusted for service organizations. Today, marketing principles and techniques are used in the marketing of organizations, people, places, and causes. This gradual broadening in the application of marketing is illustrated in Figure 1-3. The success of this approach in other than the consumer and industrial product business setting is largely responsible for professionals' current interest in the adoption, modification, and implementation of the marketing concept. In essence, meta marketing brings us to where we are in the decade of the 1980s.

The settings for new applications of marketing concepts are sometimes quite surprising. Being an Army veteran, I was surprised to learn that one of my MBA students was an infantry major. In chatting with him, I found he had recently been assigned as a faculty member at West Point. "Why, may I ask, are your pursuing an MBA degree with an emphasis on marketing?" He replied that his next regular duty assignment would be the Army Recruiting Command, and his responsibility would be the development of a recruiting program (marketing plan). That same year, a university colleague of mine left his teaching position to begin a two-year assignment with the Department of Defense. His assignment was to do the necessary market research and analysis to improve the recruiting success rate for an all-volunteer Armed Forces.

Figure 1-4 somewhat humorously illustrates another application. This print media ad, prepared for the American Cancer Society, is part of its antismoking campaign. It never fails to elicit strong reactions from smokers and nonsmokers alike.

Finally, we may have seen marketing come full circle in the energy business. Those of us who drove the gas-hungry, high-horsepower chariots of the 1950s and 1960s can remember EXXON's "Put a tiger in your tank," Shell Oil Corporation's "the presidents' game," and American Oil's "Super pro contest." Power companies fought to get us to "live electrically." These firms cooperated with appliance

```
                              MARKETING

                    CONSUMER & INDUSTRIAL PRODUCTS
                                  ⬇
                          ┌─────────────────┐
                          │      CARS       │
                          │    CLOTHING     │
                          │   APPLIANCES    │
                          │  PAPER PRODUCTS │
                          │    COMPUTERS    │
                          │ CAPITAL EQUIPMENT│
                          └─────────────────┘
                                  ⬇
                    CONSUMER & INDUSTRIAL SERVICES
                                  ⬇
                          ┌─────────────────┐
                          │    EDUCATION    │
                          │  ENTERTAINMENT  │
                          │     TRAVEL      │
                          │ VEHICLE REPAIR  │
                          │   MAINTENANCE   │
                          │    DAY CARE     │
                          └─────────────────┘
                                  ⬇
                            METAMARKETING
```

ORGANIZATIONS	PEOPLE	PLACES	CAUSES	PROFESSIONS
⬇	⬇	⬇	⬇	⬇
GOVERNMENTS CHURCHES COMPANIES POLITICAL PARTIES	JIMMY CARTER FRANK SINATRA RONALD REAGAN BILLY GRAHAM	THE BAHAMAS CANADA ATLANTIC CITY EUROPE MIAMI BEACH	ENVIRONMENTAL PROTECTION PUBLIC HEALTH FUEL CONSERVATION RACIAL UNDERSTANDING	PUBLIC ACCOUNTING LAW HEALTH CARE ARCHITECTURE CONSULTING

FIGURE 1-3 Marketing to metamarketing
Source: Adapted from E. J. Fox and E. W. Wheatley, *Modern Marketing*, (Glenview, Ill.: Scott, Foresman, 1978), p. 13. Reprinted by permission.

manufacturers to show us how we could enjoy the labor-saving benefits of everything from dishwashers to trash compactors. The energy crisis of 1973-74 changed all that and introduced a new term into the vocabulary of marketing. "Demarketing" involves the use of marketing techniques to encourage attitudes and behaviors of conservation. On a tangential but related issue, firms whose activities have come under closer public scrutiny are seeking to improve their image and acceptability. Citgo is telling us that there are only so many dinosaurs down there which dissolve into oil, but they remind us that they are doing their very best all over the world to uncover new petroleum sources and are also exploring alternative energy possibilities. Caterpillar Tractor reminds the opinion leaders and well-educated members of the National Geographic Society that there are no easy answers, only intelligent choices. Caterpillar wants us to know that although its products are used to change the landscape and to perform strip-mining and other environmentally dangerous operations, the company is doing its best to ensure minimum damage and restoration of the environment wherever possible.

FIGURE 1-4 Social marketing

PROFESSIONALS AND MARKETING

Are You a Professional?

"What's in a name? That which we call a rose by any other name would smell as sweet." We're all familiar with the quotation from Shakespeare, and it embodies the spirit of the next several paragraphs. It's impossible for anyone to confer the professional designation on anyone else. The American concept of the professions has its roots in Europe, and the European tradition still influences whom we refer to as professionals and whom we do not. In the broadest sense of the word, a "professional" is anyone who can earn a living by rendering services. In that sense, Franco Harris, Donna Summers, and Julia Child are professionals. Of course, using this broad definition, so were Willie Sutton and John Dillinger! In the more rigorous sense, professionals are those in a field which (1) is clearly defined and delineated; (2) is guided by a formal ethical code accepted by its members; (3) is policed by professional peers, including adjudication and expulsion from the profession for violation of the ethical code or professional practice standards; (4) has detailed criteria for membership, including educational experience, periods of training or apprenticeship, and performance standards; (5) recognizes membership by formal certification; and (6) the interests of clients or patients are placed before selfish interests.

Not too many decades ago, going into a profession meant one of three things: medicine, law, or accounting. Since the 1960s, the term professional has been applied to more and more specialty fields. These include architecture, engineering, financial and investment counseling, management, marketing, educational and many other forms of consulting, speech therapy, the clergy, career military, and health care administration. Indeed, the current campaign of a large national franchised real estate group, Century 21, reminds us that members are "real estate professionals." While the real estate professional does not ease other people's pain and suffering, real estate people would argue that they do have a well-defined and limited area of specialization. Their field requires training, apprenticeship, and the passing of examinations at various levels. They point to real estate boards and codes of ethics that prescribe conduct and performance. They also point to a number of their colleagues whose licenses have been removed for breaches of ethics or negligent performance. If it gets to a real shootout, they challenge doctors, accountants, and attorneys to produce their scores for the enforcement and removal of undesirable or marginal practitioners. The fact is that a professional is as a professional does. A good electrician can perform in a professional manner, just as a CPA can perform in a nonprofessional manner. The word "profession" has become a generic term in our vocabulary.

While this is an interesting mental exercise, it probably does us very little good to continue analyzing and theorizing concerning what constitutes professional standing. The current interest and controversy over the application of marketing to professional services is having its greatest visibility and impact in the fields of law, accounting, and the medical and related professions. The organizations and individuals falling under the broader definition are also interested in and experimenting with marketing approaches. The objective of this book is to introduce you to and make you operationally proficient with the principles and practices of marketing in a professional service setting. To that end, a narrow definition of the term "profession" is unnecessarily restrictive.

Should Professionals Market?

This question is moot. In my opinion, almost all professionals have marketed since time began. If you define marketing as "hard-sell" media advertising, then of course most professionals have not marketed. Now, however, you know that marketing encompasses much more than advertising or sales promotion. True, advertising is one ingredient in the marketing mix, *but it is not marketing*. The fact that most professionals already engage in some form of marketing and "protest too much" is eloquently expressed by the British consultant and author Aubrey Wilson. Speaking of certain restraints concerning the selling or advertising of professional services, Wilson says that these

> . . . restraints, legal and self-imposed, are restraints on methods, not restraints on marketing. Even the most rigid and pompous of medical practitioners or barristers finds nothing objectionable in having their services "referred" by existing patients or clients. The "change of address notice", which announced the opening of a private practice by a medical consultant, and were sent to every GP who ever referred a patient to him, may have been dispatched as a result of mixed motives. Indeed, the sender may have difficulty in identifying the marketing content of what is claimed to be purely communication of information: the conference attendees, learned papers, and TV appearances of medical practitioners and lawyers are not always motivated by the simple desire to impart knowledge. Are large or discreet window lettering, entrance signs, or sight notice boards directed entirely to identifying the architect's location? Are the detailed stockbrokers' circulars designed solely for the purpose of providing information for investors?"[2]

Perhaps the question "Should professionals market?" needs to be rephrased to "Should you market?" That is to say, should you develop an integrated, ongoing marketing function as a regular part of your client development and retention activities? In other words, should marketing become an integral part of your management system? As you've guessed by now, my position is that one way or another professionals have always marketed.

Legal Issues

The question of "is it legal" for professionals to market is no longer valid. The 1970s Supreme Court decision permitting attorneys to advertise in spite of various bar association prohibitions reminds us that there never has been anything illegal about marketing in the professions. The regulation of marketing and specific subactivities has largely been self-imposed. In fact, at the federal level, regulators seem to consider it illegal *not* to market.

In October 1979, the Federal Trade Commission ordered the American Medical Association (AMA) to remove its ban against physician advertising. This regulation, according to the FTC, had hindered and restricted competition, resulting in injury to the market and the public's opportunity to make informed decisions. In July 1980, The American Medical Association's member house of delegates passed a new code of ethics. The former code had been in existence for over twenty years. The new code was shorter and simpler. The profession's response to the Federal Trade Commission's finding was clearly evident. Missing from the new code was the statement that a physician "should not solicit patients." In addition, the prohibition that a physician should not associate with other medical professionals who do not make use of a "scientific basis" of healing was repealed. These two examples should make it clear to all professionals that self-imposed prohibition of marketing activities is, at best, a fading idea. It is also, in my judgment, short-sighted.

Economic Issues

Professionals most often raise the following economic questions: (1) Can I afford a full-time marketing program? (2) Exactly what will it cost? (3) Exactly what will it return? The answers depend upon how you define marketing. If marketing means massive media advertising expenditures, then surely a new dentist joining a group of practitioners cannot afford the expense. If marketing is defined in the proper way, that same dentist, seeking to gain visibility and awareness of the new practice, could engage in many activities which are inexpensive and normally part of the conduct of the professional practice. In this sense, the dentist could easily afford to market and is probably already incurring marketing expenses.

The cost of marketing depends upon the specific plan adopted. It also depends upon how costs are allocated in the professional service firm. For example, the careful redecoration of a pediatrician's office to make it an attractive place for kids and parents is a marketing expense. The membership of the pediatrician's husband or wife in local clubs or organizations is a marketing expense. The information brochure the pediatrician might produce concerning immunizations is a marketing expense. A well-managed pediatric practice would normally be engaged in all these activities. This raises two points: First, that professionals do market and that marketing costs are normally absorbed under the categories of practice management or administrative expenses. In a proprietary business, money spent to enhance the company's image, impress its clients, develop awareness, and persuade are clearly designated in the marketing budget. As I hope you will see, the cost of developing and implementing a marketing program is not as high as you might imagine. If the professional service firm is large, a client relations department or a community relations executive might be established. In such cases, the expenses could be considerable. The costs depend on the way in which the professional seeks to allocate them, the nature of the specific marketing activities, and the size and scope of the program.

There are no data publicly available to substantiate the return on investment of professional marketing budgets. Ideally, before you invest in marketing, you'd like to know how it will increase the number of clients or how it will increase the profitability of your client mix. While there may be many intermediate objectives in a marketing program, the bottom line still has to add up to acceptable revenue and profit figures. The fact that marketing does yield a return to many professional service firms is best shown by the presence of the marketing function in such organizations. Consulting, securities, and public accounting firms were among the first to integrate marketing as a full-time managerial function. The "Big 8" accounting firms carefully segment, target, profile, and plan to pursue and penetrate certain industries. Their professional communications are generally well done. Proposal writing is considered an art, and the professional who brings in the largest number of new accounts finds quick promotion and compensation. This isn't to say that a fully developed and integrated marketing approach is recommended for every individual practitioner or every firm: The theme of this book is that you cannot afford *not* to consider professional service marketing.

Chapter 2
Marketing Professional Services

In Chapter 1 we traced the development of managerial philosophies beginning with the production and finance orientation to the present marketing orientation. We discussed the definition of modern marketing, the marketing concept, and the marketing mix. Individuals familiar with consumer and industrial product marketing would be very comfortable with the discussion in Chapter 1. Why? Marketing, as a field, got its start and developed in the consumer product manufacturing firms as well as firms that made goods for industrial use. Companies like Borden, General Electric, General Foods, Procter & Gamble, and Westinghouse developed and implemented the marketing concept. Today marketing has parity with other functional areas in most modern business corporations. The function is no longer subordinate to production or finance. Marketing executives are intimately involved with major policy and decision making.

Since its founding, the greater proportion of our country's gross national product has been composed of agricultural and industrial products—things we grew or made for each other. As we move into the second half of the twentieth century, services have become a major component of the gross national product. Today it is estimated that approximately two-thirds of our labor force is involved in services—in doing things for us rather than making things for us.

The growing importance of our service sector is due to more than entrepreneurial creativity. Rising levels of affluence have given people the income to "hire it done." The increased utilization of services has spread to everything from the architect who designs a home to the exterminating firm that keeps household pests under control. Increases in the divorce rate and the number of working women have increased the demand for everything from the day care centers to fast food restaurants. The fields of travel, entertainment, hospitality, and recreational services have grown as individuals and families make more creative use of leisure time. Educational services have exploded as a whole generation of individuals in their middle and later years flock to continuing education programs. Finally, as a result of more specialization within the professions, client utilization of professional services continues to grow.

Marketing as a managerial specialty grew up in the manufacturing milieu. It is now being applied to services, and in your case to professional services. In this chapter we will illustrate the critical differences between product and service marketing. We will identify and discuss the differences between service marketing and professional services marketing. The objective of the chapter is to help you make the transition from traditional marketing management, applied in the product context, to service marketing, which will more closely fit your needs. Finally, you will walk a mile in the service client's shoes. You will exchange roles with your clients and see the sometimes revealing difference between what you "sell" and what professional service clients really buy.

WHAT'S DIFFERENT ABOUT SERVICE MARKETING

The principles of modern marketing management can and are being broadly applied across a spectrum of activities. However the practice of marketing must be carefully tailored to fit the environment to which it is being applied. Figure 2-1 illustrates a typical marketing system for an organization manufacturing consumer products. Note the elaborate series of specific sequential steps which typifies the development of a new product from concept until the consumer acquires and uses it. Most marketing scholars and practitioners would have their own version of this process, but all would encompass comparable steps. Now that marketing has been institutionalized as part of the corporate managerial system, it becomes involved early in the development process. Please note that marketing research can also be performed after the sale to measure consumer attitudes and satisfaction. Such data provide an early warning system for problems that might indicate product or marketing redesign and revision.

Figure 2-2 indicates key differences in the overall process for service marketing. For example, it would be quite unusual for the professional individual, small group, or firm to engage in market research prior to determining exactly what profession to enter and or what professional services to offer. In the professions one "becomes a professional" and then sets about marketing professional services. In the marketing of consumer products, on the other hand, market research is utilized to determine what new products or services consumers might need and be willing to pay for. These products and services are carefully developed, priced,

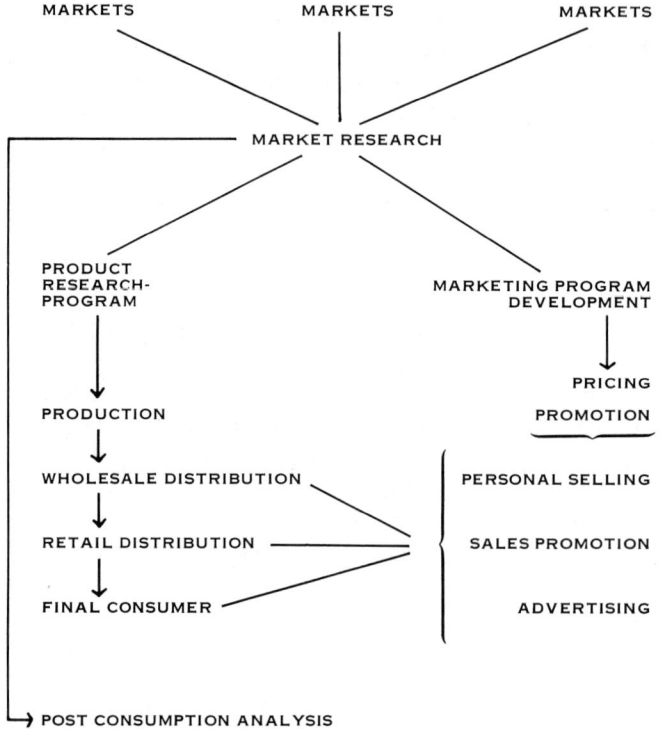

FIGURE 2-1 Consumer goods—The typical marketing process

FIGURE 2-2 Services—The typical marketing process

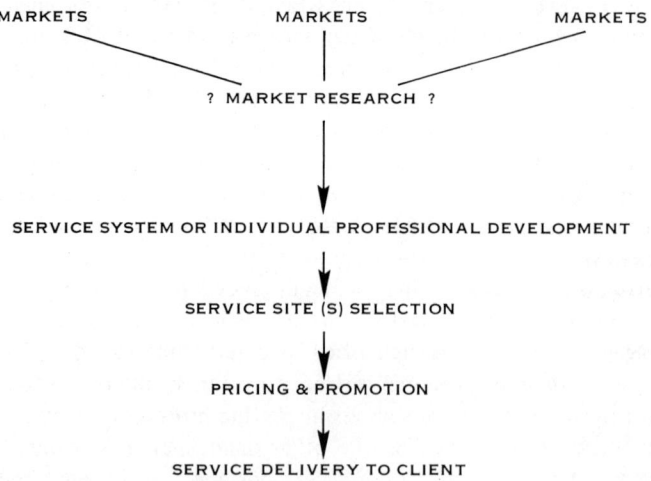

distributed and promoted. In contrast to professional services, in consumer and industrial goods promotion, advertising, personal selling, sales promotion, publicity, community relations, and public relations have long been a regular part of the marketing manager's competitive arsenal. The utilization of promotion in the marketing of professional services is not only relatively new but is a heavily questioned and often questionable activity in the minds of many professionals.

Let's examine some of the specific differences between products and services. These differences will help develop a clear understanding of the problems and opportunities facing the service marketer. This discussion will also help explain the significant differences in the product versus professsional service marketing processes illustrated in Figures 2-1 and 2-2. The following list is not exhaustive or mutually exclusive. The many interrelated aspects of service marketing will become clearer as you read. Perhaps the easiest way to identify with the discussion is to place yourself for the moment in the role of both a service supplier and a consumer of professional services.

Heavy Emotional Component

In Service purchasing, awareness needs and motives carry a high emotional component. Purchase decisions and repurchase behavior depend partly on the consumers perception of the emotional fit between the consumer's self-concept and the supplying professional. Where a high degree of congruence exists, purchase loyalty will be high. Where incongruence exists, consumers will continue to try other professionals until their emotional needs are satisfied. Certainly the development of an international tax trust is an extremely complex technical matter. But the CPA who does not minister to the client's emotional needs may not be utilized again, even though the technical work was flawless.

Intangibility

When we deal with consumer or industrial products, we have an item that can be seen, felt, smelled, weighed, touched, analyzed, and modified in a variety of ways. Service marketing presents a different problem. What does the consumer purchase when he or she spends $300 for an annual medical physical? Information and, hopefully, peace of mind. Certainly the apparatus, chemicals, and processes involved in an examination and tests are tangible, but the consumer is not buying these items. Rather, the purchase involves information that leads to knowledge about the consumer's present physical condition. Intangibility makes services more difficult to describe and also results in problems in measuring consumer satisfaction.

Durability

In addition to being tangible, a suit of clothing may last a consumer for several years. During its lifetime, a consumer has a much longer exposure to the positive and negative results of the purchase decision. An effective product continues to market itself long after the sale has been made. Most services are more short-lived. Once the contact with the service provider has taken place, the experience begins to evaporate from the consumer's mind. Developing and maintaining client loyalty is made more difficult.

The Inventory Problem

Products can be stockpiled; services cannot. The makes and models of automobiles driven by Americans are staggering in number, yet Midas Mufflers, through careful analysis, has developed a stock and inventory plan that permits it to maintain an adequate supply of mufflers, tailpipes, clamps, and other automobile accessories. The majority of customers will find exactly what they need, no matter when they drive in or what they are driving. If for some reason the dealer is out of stock or the consumer's need is unique, a phone call brings same-day delivery of the required part from an area warehouse. In the service field a considerable amount of the resource base is personnel-related. A small law firm receiving a large case cannot simply go to a "warehouse" for ten attorneys to provide the service. Major shifts in demand patterns create severe service marketing problems for many professional organizations.

The Demand Estimation Dilemma

In the Midas example, inventory can be built up prior to periods of historically heavy demand. Peak-load demand periods and unforecast demand do cause problems in a product marketing firm, but these problems are not as severe as in the service organization. In the service marketing situation, handling demand variations can be facilitated through the cross training of personnel, the use of part-time labor, and attempts to shift demand to slower periods through promotional or price incentives. Service industry marketers are beginning to take advantage of some of these approaches. The use of paraprofessionals and preplanning and scheduling regular services are examples.

The Peak-Load Problem

Service marketers are faced with another unique problem. If unforecasted service demand clusters within a short time period and the service supply system cannot expand, one of two things happens. In the first scenario, the service provider reduces the amount of time and attention given to each individual client in order to serve the large client demand. If careful quality control is not part of this adjustment, the long-run result of such a strategy will be negative. The probability of dissatisfied clients increases. Even though the service provider made every attempt to assist clients with their problems, many clients will not be satisfied with the level of service received. In the second scenario, the peak-load problem is handled by refusing to take on the additional clients. New demand is satisfied only to the extent that the professional can still provide full service to all clients. The theory in this approach is that often during peak-load periods the service quality level for regular, existing clients goes down. In this zero-sum game not only do new clients receive inferior service, but existing clients also suffer. Professionals following the second scenario should always couple their behavior with a carefully developed and sincerely presented set of referral alternatives for the inquiring new clients.

In my experience, many professionals let demand manage them. We will discuss this in the market targeting and segmentation chapters. There is one bona fide reason professionals feel compelled to handle any and all peak-period business: There is a probability that a temporary or a drop-in client may become a regular.

The Personal Component

As a result of production proficiency, wide distribution, mass media, pre-selling, self-selection, and self-service retailing, consumer product marketing is becoming more depersonalized. Many retail clerks are not salespersons in the true sense of the word. Rather, they are order takers and exchange processors. If you purchase a portable radio to take with you on a vacation, you really purchase its technical features and the functions it performs. On the other hand, if you are considering the services of an architect to help you design a new home, the personal sensitivities of that professional to your personality, life style, sense of esthetics, taste, and a host of other emotional dimensions have a direct bearing on whether the architect will indeed get the commission. In a divorce proceeding, for example, the way in which the attorney interacts with the parties often has as much to do with the progress of the case as what the attorney does. The importance of the personal element in service marketing is one of the most critical and unique differentiating factors in the field.

Personnel Carryover

The personal component of service marketing is not just a function of the interpersonal skills of the individual professional directly serving the client. In addition, every human being who works with the professional's organization has a material emotional and functional impact on the client. If a potential client is poorly handled over the phone or in the reception area, that individual may never become a client. Indeed, many professionals who are terrible at human relations are made tolerable by their staff. On the other hand, the very best professional can quickly be ruined by insensitive staff personnel.

Elusiveness of Evaluation

Consumers need not know the intricacies of an internal combustion engine to understand whether the automobile is performing well. They are either happy with it or they are not. How, on the other hand, does a consumer evaluate the long-run success of a hernia operation? Similarly, a law client is in a poor position to judge whether or not the attorney has performed to the maximum professional degree. Professional service clients normally do not have the technical expertise to make accurate evaluations of the professionals they utilize. Professionals are more often evaluated on the basis of their reputations, the way in which other professionals and lay individuals describe them, and how well they satisfy the emotional and functional needs of the client.

Information flows between client and professional are also unique in the marketing sense. A physician may examine and prescribe for a patient. The patient leaves to begin a period of self-administered treatment. Seldom does a patient report back to the physician concerning the success or failure connected with the particular medical problem unless the problem is serious or prolonged. Similarly, consultants furnish their reports and recommendations. Shortly thereafter, they leave the organizations with which they have become so intimately involved, and often have little further client contact. Feedback concerning their recommendations is often missing. In the consumer and industrial goods markets, firms frequently set up elaborate tracking mechanisms to stay in touch with customers after a purchase has been made. Warranty programs, marketing research surveys, focus groups, and consumer panels are routinely used to monitor ongoing consumer experience and satisfaction with the product.

Directness of Distribution

Glance back at Figures 2-1 and 2-2. In the product marketing areas there is frequently an elaborate series of middlemen who assist in moving the product from the producer to the consumer. These institutions, such as wholesalers and retailers, are supported by promotional programs that include personal selling, display, sales promotion activities, and advertising. Specialists exist in all these areas. They comprise the marketing team and help move goods and services through the channel of distribution. Professional service marketing has a "short" distribution channel compared to the longer channels in the consumer products area. The professional is the direct distributor. It is asking too much to expect all technically qualified professional specialists to also be expert administrators and marketers. It is important that professionals recognize their strengths and weaknesses in client relations and practice management. The service delivery system can be designed around the unique differences that abound in the professional world. Service support personnel, facilities, and procedures can supplement the professional who is not interested or expert in management and marketing.

DO YOU FEEL LIKE A TRAFFIC COP?

As a professional, you have daily and direct experience with unique marketing situations peculiar to your field. Christopher H. Lovelock, a professor at the Harvard Business School, has identified several roles marketers play as they deliver services to their clients.[1] Do any of these roles fit you?

1. Admissions officer. Many professionals make the decision as to whom they can and will serve. This filtering or screening effect has little similarity to the marketplace for products.
2. Club secretary. Professonals frequently develop long-term relationships with

clients. As part of the arrangement, some professionals keep in touch by regular mailings, including information releases, brochures, and newsletters. Client organizational and personal special occasions are remembered by cards. Workshops and seminars may be held to maintain contact.
3. Police officer. Under some conditions, professionals also play police officer. Clients must be disciplined if they "misbehave"—don't follow the professional's advice. Clients often share facilities in doctors, denists, or optometrists offices. They must cooperate by being on time, waiting their turn, and so on.
4. Teacher. Often the client must be instructed concerning various aspects of the problem, treatment, or cure. Effective results depend on the teaching abilities of the professional and/or staff, especially where extensive client involvement or cooperation is required.
5. Dramatist. To gain client cooperation, satisfaction, and loyalty, professionals often act as stage managers and dramatists. They set the stage (professional office and systems), costume (themselves and staff), and choreograph the exchange transaction (service delivery and follow-up).

You can probably add several of your own product-service marketing differentiators to this list. An attorney friend, for example, believes that satisfaction is the key reason why people buy products and consumer services. On the other hand, people turn to professionals for the solution of problems. An individual may be quite happy to spend $50,000 for a new yacht. That same individual will be most unhappy to spend $50,000 to pursue or defend a lawsuit. A physician friend gives an even more dramatic example of this difference. "Yes," he says, "the consumer may indeed be very happy to spend $50,000 on the boat, but let me send that same consumer a $500 bill for a thorough physical and all hell breaks loose!" In discussing this problem orientation with a dentist friend, another variation was noted: "Consumers can postpone the consumption of consumer goods or services, but if they've been in an accident and need emergency dental work they need it now!"

I suspect there are cases like this in many of the professional areas. While there is no shortage of challenges for marketing professionals in the consumer and industrial product and service fields, the preceding discussion illustrates some of the unique differences and difficulties in the professional services area. Later in the book, I am going to recommend a marketing programming process that can help you deal more effectively with these unique circumstances.

WHAT DO YOU SELL?
WHAT DOES YOUR CLIENT BUY?

To someone uninitiated into the field of marketing, the preceding two questions may seem a bit ridiculous. So, I'd better clarify the marketing perspective on these issues. Peter Revson said, "We don't sell cosmetics—we sell hope." Stop and think about it.

Does the user of cosmetics really care about the chemical and molecular structure of a particular foundation makeup? Does the consumer worry about the care and sanitary measures that went into the production and quality control of a substance which is going to be placed around the mouth and the eyes each working day for perhaps forty or fifty years? Does the customer really care about the technology of fixing the various colors so that they will not fade, run, or deteriorate in various conditions of heat and humidity? The answer to all these questions is apparently "no." If customers cared, I suspect you would find cosmetics manufacturers carefully explaining these details and attempting to differentiate their products from competitors. Instead, you find cosmetic marketing based on the romantic appeals and attraction of the opposite sex. Headlines like "Look your loveliest," "You'll look younger," "The new you," and "Tempt him tonight" present the possibilities of eternal youth, sexual adventure, and romance, not hygiene or chemistry breakthroughs.

If you're a technician and all this romantic stuff bores you, then let's use an example on the more practical side. Theodore Levitt, noted marketing teacher, scholar, and author, is credited with a statement often used by marketing professionals. Levitt said: "Consumers do not buy quarter-inch drills, they buy quarter-inch holes." Once again, the implication is that consumers are not aware of, nor do they particularly care, how a quarter-inch electric hand drill is cast, wired, grounded, or assembled. Rather, the consumer wishes to hang a picture. This task requires the drilling of a quarter-inch hole to mount a stud for a picture hanger. There may be some consumers who are technologically oriented. These few will take considerable pleasure in shopping for and selecting a particular quarter-inch drill based on its technical specifications and performance. For most consumers, however, there is little if any interest in anything but the price and the ability to perform the basic function for which the product is intended.

The God Syndrome

As professionals, we often tend to get wrapped up on our own string. The required professional training and education we undergo somehow makes it necessary for us to inflict the details of our wisdom on our clients. What we are selling frequently is a technically complicated specialty filled with nuances and the opportunity for creative approaches. To the professional this is exciting, to the professional this is life. To the consumer it may be a pain in the neck. Performing intricate oral surgery involving both tooth and gum in a thoroughly correct and successful manner is a source of great professional pride and satisfaction for the oral surgeon. The client could care less. The clients assumes that the professional is qualified or he or she would not be permitted to practice. What the clients wants is to have the problem solved, to have a sense of security while the solution is under way, and to return to his or her normal life as quickly as possible, with no intention of ever seeing the surgeon again!

I'm aware of one professional, a close personal friend as a matter of fact, whose favorite word is "problem." Each client was told "I see problems here," no matter what the situation. The professional then went to great pains to study the situation and to explain precisely how the problem would be solved. What this professional was really doing is loosely referred to as the "God thing." In this particular variation, the professional enlarges upon the client's problem, makes the client feel insecure, and then miraculously provides the solution.

Unsophisticated users of professional services may find this style acceptable. The regular user of professionals soon recognizes what is going on and is turned off. Fortunately for the professional in question, and unfortunately for his constituents, he was in the semi-public sector, where his tenure was guaranteed and his manner inflicted on a restive but captive audience.

The Do It Youself Syndrome

Everett B. Turner, a consulting engineer with experience as a marketing executive in a professional services firm, provides some penetrating insights concerning the do it yourself syndrome:

> Basically, many problems associated with the marketing of professional services grow out of the "do it youself" syndrome, a common affliction among professionals with a technical background. This syndrome is defined as the tendency of the technically oriented professional to consider himself an expert in all the disciplines in which he is involved when, in fact, he may possess only superficial knowledge in all except the technical aspects.
>
> Unfortunately, this do it yourself syndrome has reached full maturity in the marketing discipline as it applies to professional services. Almost all professionals consider themselves to be experts when it comes to selling their own services. The result is that professionals within a service firm tend to give lip service to the marketing concept. . . .
>
> . . . most professional service firms with a technical background tend to think of their services as consisting of a particular mix of expertise, knowledge, background, and experience. Hence, the professional with the do it yourself syndrome describes services in terms of his own capabilities rather than in terms of the clients' needs. The prospective client is called upon for a great deal of interpretation which, in fact, the professional should be providing. The client is being asked to recognize his own needs, to translate these needs into technical terms, and further, to sort out the capabilities of the service firm as they are applicable to the problem. In other words, by laying the burden of interpretation on the prospect, the professional effectively reduces the chances that there will be an opportunity to sell a service.[2]

Understanding Client Needs and Desires

Although we have been analyzing certain differences between service and product marketing, it's important to note that these differences create opportunities as well as problems. We can use Everett Turner's comment as a catalyst to bring product and service marketing closer together. All marketing planning, implementation, and control begins with developing an understanding of client needs and desires. This understanding is focused on functional as well as emotional motivation. Built on this foundation, the marketing program for a specific professional individual, group, or organization can then be adjusted as opportunities and resources require.

In a classic *Harvard Business Review* article, Warren J. Wittreich analyzes what clients look for in evaluating potential professional service suppliers. Wittreich feels that the reduction of uncertainty is one of the fundamental motives for consumers of professional services:

> In the most general and fundamental sense, what the professional service organization really has to offer to corporate clients is the reduction or minimization of uncertainty. Other terms may be used: confidence, peace of mind, increased certainty, and so forth. Regardless of the terminology, the fact is that independent of the services offered, the professional service organization holds out the promise of introducing more certainty in a particular area in which the client feels uncertain.
>
> The feeling of uncertainty will not neccessarily be overtly articulated by very many clients. But it is there. Three kinds of uncertainty can be distinguished:
>
> (1) There is the basic uncertainty of knowing with whom to deal and on whom to rely. In other words, the client who is interested in getting some assistance via a professional service is faced with the problem of where to get it. He has a number of alternatives open to him.
>
> (2) Because of the large sums of money involved in the purchase of the services themselves, there is uncertainty as to whether these monies are being wisely spent. I am referring to such expenditures as those for large-scale research undertakings, costly consultants, or commissions or fees paid for services. In most instances the amounts eventually at stake are still larger.
>
> (3) There is even more uncertainty in the problem itself. This problem is why the buyer of professional services is seeking advice or assistance in the first place. Whether the problem is in marketing, finance, personnel, research and development, or what, it is without question the single most important of the three sources of uncertainty.
>
> Recognition of this particular concept of uncertainty, plus recognition of the three different sources of uncertainty, is the first step toward clearly defining the considerations that should apply to the sale of purchase of a professional service.[3]

Wittreich accurately observes:

> . . . goods are not the same as services, and the buying and selling of goods is not the same as the buying and selling of professional services. These differences in turn call for the use of evaluation and sales concepts different from those usually employed in the case of products.[4]

Service marketing is different, but it is important to stress that the differences in service marketing also present the professional with a host of competitive marketing opportunities.

The next milestones in modern marketing management will occur in the service marketing area, with professional service marketing in for a large share of the action. Bell and Appel have identified the "service gap" as marketing's most important crisis of the 1970s. They point out that in spite of significant accomplishments in the production and distribution of goods, the entire area of services has not kept pace. They forsee unlimited opportunity for improvement in the service area. Further, the firms that move quickly to remedy these problems will be the big winners in terms of growth and profits: "In the future, greater affluence, moderate gains in population, and increasing specialized products and services will attest to an enlarged demand for services. If, as predicted by Nelson Foote, the customer in year 2,000 has as his first constraint time, not money, marketers face the need to substantially readjust their operating premise. Service may now function as a catalyst for needed change. Because similar deficiencies are found in service offerings of competing organizations, significant advantages will likely occur to firms correcting such deficiencies. Importantly, service has the potential to provide the differential capable of propelling firms into niches in the marketplace where eroding effects of retaliation are minimized. Moreover, frustrated consumers appear financially and psychologically ready to use service as an important basis for selecting suppliers."[5]

YOU'VE BEEN VERY PATIENT

You are reading this book to learn more about marketing your professional services. You won't be disappointed. From Chapter 3 on, this book is directed specifically to that objective. But before you take your self-administered marketing professional services audit (Chapter 3), review Chapters 1 and 2. If you are to profit from the application of the modern concept of marketing, you should understand what marketing is and what it isn't. You should also review and consider the unique characteristic of the service marketing environment—your environment.

Has this side trip into the history, development, and current structure of marketing been necessary? Yes, not only necessary, but vital. Many professionals have little business background or orientation. Their primary contact with marketing has been as a consumer of industry's products and services. Media advertising and personal selling *is* marketing as far as these professionals are concerned. In Chapter 1 we presented a more complete definition and explanation of marketing. The professional services marketing audit and professional service marketing program presented in subsequent chapters have evolved from strategies and tactics successfully employed in business. As professionals, we can learn and profit from these experiences.

You can significantly enhance the value of this book and the application of marketing to your field in several ways. These include taking courses, attending seminars and conferences, and supplementary reading in introductory marketing management texts. You'll not be surprised when I suggest *Modern Marketing—Principles and Practice* by E. J. Fox and E. W. Wheatley as appropriate background reading.

Chapter 3
The MPS Audit — A Self-Administered Diagnostic Test

How well are you marketing your professional services? What are your primary areas of strength and weakness? What can you do, what should you do, what might you do to improve client retention, growth, and profitability? In this chapter you'll be given the opportunity to evaluate yourself, your staff, your practice. Your responses to these and many other questions will be facilitated by a self-administered diagnostic marketing audit. Before you start turning pages to find the questions and see how you rate, it is important that you take a few minutes to become familiar with what a marketing audit is, how it fits into a practice management audit, and the benefits and limitations of this diagnostic tool. When viewed from this perspective, you'll find the marketing audit and its results to have meaningful application to your practice.

WHAT IS A MARKETING PROFESSIONAL SERVICES AUDIT?

A marketing audit is a "systematic, critical, and impartial review and appraisal of the total marketing operation, of the basic objectives and policies of the operation and the assumptions which underlie them as well as of the procedures, personnel, and organization employed to implement the policies and achieve the objective."[1] Although the marketing audit you are about to take will not be quite as comprehensive as this definition implies, there are two important terms you should remember: the key words are "critical" and "impartial." Your own enlightened self-interest should produce candid responses to the audit questions. For you to get the most out of the exercise, I will suggest some additional approaches a bit later. In addition to the definition just cited, Kelly and Lazer suggest some key advantages to the use of the marketing audit technique. In identifying the basic purposes of the marketing audit activity, they note that the aim of the audit is prognosis as well as diagnosis. It is a search for opportunities and a means of exploiting them as well as for weaknesses and means for their elimination. Finally, the marketing audit is the practice of preventive as well as curative marketing medicine.[2]

Is the marketing audit like a financial audit? Yes and no. The practice of financial auditing has been widely accepted during the twentieth century. The theories, principles, and practice of accounting have been well established and documented. The data base is quantitative, and the units of measurement rather precise. But the financial audit is limited to assuring the users of financial information, including investors and the government, that your financial statements fairly and accurately represent the financial condition of your practice in accordance with the generally accepted accounting principles. So, while a financial audit does satisfy the requirements of a systematic, critical, and impartial review, it is limited to one aspect of your operation. This is in no way intended to diminish the importance of the function. In fact, over the last ten years most CPA firms have given increased emphasis to expanding the scope of their review beyond strictly accounting matters. Such firms now routinely furnish "management letters" in which they comment on their client's internal control procedures as well as suggest other ways in which the organization could be improved.

As a professional, you are undoubtedly aware of organizations and individuals that do consulting for practice management. These consultants specialize in everything from setting up a professional practice to evaluating existing professional organizations and recommending areas for improvement. The typical management review or evaluation has not dealt in any detail with the marketing professsional services area. Why? There are two basic reasons. First, MPS is a new and rapidly developing field; second, the expertise and orientation of these consultants has been more in the area of operations and systems management.

WHAT MAKES A GOOD MARKETING AUDIT?

Author, practitioner, and scholar Phillip Kotler suggests that marketing audits should meet at least four criteria. Kotler's criteria apply to the professional as well as to the business and public sector environment.[3]

Periodic Basis

Many organizations carry out marketing audits only under crisis conditions; for example, when sales level off or fall, or when competitive or market situations change drastically. To gain the full benefit of the technique, it should be applied annually or at least on some periodic basis. Deteriorating conditions can be noted and checked while new opportunities can be identified and appropriate responses developed.

Comprehensive Scope

A narrow review of your professional service marketing activities may focus on only one or two symptomatic problem areas, such as community involvement. Perhaps the community involvement of your professional staff is excellent; perhaps it can be improved. However, if your practice has a negative image, it could be due to an entirely different source, such as insensitive staff, fee structure, or billing policies. Lack of comprehensiveness in the audit procedures can lead to treating symptoms rather than identifying and dealing with causal factors.

Systematic Procedures

Two optometrists will probably conduct a vision examination in more or less the same manner. Two marketing consultants may differ considerably in their approach to assessing and diagnosing the marketing function in a particular organization. A systematic, written procedure is recommended. Such a procedure allows the professional and the marketing specialist to communicate clearly as to what is going to be reviewed and what is not. In addition, if the recommendations for periodic review are followed, then some sort of learning curve can develop. As professional service marketing is integrated into your organization, the marketing audit can be an invaluable learning experience. Marketing audits in future periods can be done more quickly and more efficiently and provide comparative data if a systematic approach is utilized over time.

Objectivity

Ideally, your marketing audit should be conducted by an individual who has sufficient objectivity to be candid in the evaluation of your practice. The audit you will soon take is self-administered, but I suggest that if and where possible, you obtain additional outside or objective input. Can an attorney, for example, objectively evaluate the client relations strengths and weaknesses of a receptionist who may be a relative? Even if the answer to the objectivity part of that question was "yes," would it be likely that the attorney's criteria and perspective would be truly representative of the average law firm client? Kotler recommends an outside evaluator who has had broad experience in marketing audits so that the review of your practice does not take place in a vacuum.

SOME WORDS OF WARNING

Before you take your MPS audit, I would like to present a few cautionary thoughts. Although, I am an enthusiastic supporter and user of the marketing audit approach, the technique does have some limitations. A clear understanding of these limitations will help you to get the most from your marketing review. Naturally you and I have never been guilty of any of the examples we'll use—but I assure you they do come from the real world, and I have been involved in several situations dealing with each type. As you take your MPS audit, keep the following problems and limitations in mind.

The Panacea Syndrome

The successful conduct of a marketing audit will not prevent or solve all practice management problems. Professional service marketing is only part of the total practice management system. In fact, an effective marketing audit may uncover areas outside the marketing function that will require additional attention. For example, there was a successful Midwestern professional practice whose client lists, revenues, and profits seemed to plateau. The firm was facing a threat from a national organization aggressively marketing its services. The local firm appointed a committee of partners and retained a marketing consultant. The engagement was aborted when the committee learned that the majority of the partners planned to take no action on the consultant's recommendations. In fact, the majority of the senior partners were hostile to even the most conservative marketing approach. They expected "someone else" to develop the practice for them. They somehow believed that the development and documentation of a marketing program could solve all their problems without any involvement on their part.

No Trespassing Territory

An effective marketing audit must be broad. All areas that impinge on client satisfaction, retention, growth, and profitability must be open for review and evaluation. Even though the typical marketing audit follows a set format, both the auditor and the client must be willing to branch into new areas of investigation suggested by the findings of a specific evaluation. For example, I was involved in the review of a large professional firm in the Southeast. It soon became apparent that serious problems existed in the recruiting, motivation, and retention of younger professionals in the organization. This was verified in interviews at all levels and by outside input from clients. When remedial activities addressed to this problem were recommended as part of the marketing plan, the management group acted defensively: "This has no relationship to marketing," they stated; "the marketing consultant should be concerned about our external relationships and leave the internal operation of the practice to us!"

Certainly, marketing consultants are not experts in practice mangement. However, the placement of "off-limits" signs on areas of the practice not only reduces the effectiveness of the audit, but also the opportunity to develop competitive advantages. Although the major thrust of the marketing review is in marketing and marketing related areas, the convoluted logic in the preceding example could result in the development of superior marketing practices to market an inferior organization. Let the marketing review branch and probe. After all, it's still your practice, and you will make the final decision as to which recommended activities are desirable and appropriate and which are not.

Selective Perception

We sometimes hear what we want to hear or what our background, education, and environment have conditioned us to hear. In the first instance, we are deluding ourselves. In the second, we are attempting to be objective. Indeed, we think we are. But we are not. That's why it's important to solicit other viewpoints and input as you evaluate your organization's MPS potential or activities. In the smaller organization, the marketing audit could be completed by several individuals independently and then the results compared. In a larger organization, the management committee, managing partner, or partner in charge of client relations could conduct the review.

Ideally, the audit should be conducted by an outside independent professional with the cooperation, involvement, and support of everyone involved in the professional practice. Wherever possible, client input should be sought or at least sampled. Nothing is more revealing, sobering, and helpful than to compare our self-concept to the way in which others view us. I once asked a practice partner to describe himself and his relations with clients. He indicated that he was highly professional, diplomatic, firm but fair, and well liked by his clients. Several clients, however, painted an entirely different picture. They viewed him as impersonal, aloof, and too busy. Although they respected him, they felt that he did not spend enough time with them, that he was detached and really didn't care. Beware of selective perception as you engage in your self-administered audit.

Confidentiality

One of the keystones of professionalism is the confidential relationship between practitioner and client. If the individual conducting your MPS audit is able to gain your trust and confidence as the review is performed, the opportunity for candid and helpful input at all levels is greatly enhanced. In one professional service organization, many of the staff were critical of the way in which their organization's exhibits at professional conventions and meetings were structured and operated. Feedback from conference participants was also negative. These findings led to several specific recommendations regarding conference and convention exhibition procedures. Unfortunately, the senior professional in the organization was responsible for these activities and manned many of the exhibits. This senior person placed great pressure on the consultants to reveal the identity of the critics. For several weeks there was total preoccupation with finding out who the culprits were. Finally, and only because of the overwhelming odds, some of the recommended changes were grudgingly made. This organization continues periodically to utilize a marketing review, with good success. Had the confidences of the staff professionals been breached, the effectiveness of the audit technique would have come to a hasty end.

The Intuitive Leap

In reviewing your own marketing practices and those of your organization, your tendency may be to accept verbal input or secondary data as the literal truth. As you review your organization's strengths and weaknesses or as you assist an outside reviewer in the process, remember that the audit is a data collection process, not a conclusion and decision process. Guard against being guilty of "my mind is made up, please don't confuse me with the facts." Stay in the tentative mode. Be patient if you're utilizing the services of an outside expert; give this person the time and opportunity to collect, ingest, and reflect upon a wide variety of stimuli and information. As a professional, you know the importance of carefully and objectively developing all the evidence before reaching a conclusion.

TAKING YOUR MPS AUDIT

The MPS audit that follows is divided into eight sections:

1. Your practice environment
2. Client analysis and opportunities
3. Practice philosophy, positioning, and targeting
4. Your service mix
5. Professional fees
6. Personal communication
7. Written communication
8. MPS control and evaluation

Before you respond to the questions in each section, please review the brief introductory comments. In fact, you may wish to read the introductions to the eight sections prior to beginning the question and answer activity. In this way you'll gain an overview of the entire process. This will help your responses to be direct and useful, as well as eliminate possible duplication.

In addition to answers, the audit questions will stimulate further questions. This is to be encouraged. These questions will be of two types—branches and probes. Branching questions will arise when a basic audit question suggests a second or third question related to the first. Branching may occur when the audit question does not exactly fit your circumstances but stimulates a question or series of questions that do. Probing questions usually develop when an audit question is directly related to your practice or to an area of interest involving your practice. In a probe you get deeper and deeper and usually more specific in the level of detail than called for in the basic audit question.

For example, one audit question asks if you are aware of the boards, agencies, or committees that have significant regulatory potential for your practice environment. In your particular environment, there may be a new ad hoc committee that could be very important. A case in point is an attorney friend of mine who chairs the committee on paralegals in his state. This exposure has great promise for generating referrals. You may wish to branch and initiate a question or two directly related to the area of inquiry of the basic audit question. Another audit question asks you how alternative future economic scenarios might affect your practice environment. Let's say that your practice is not generally affected by overall economic conditions, but the condition of a particular industry, for example furniture manufacturing, is extremely critical since you not only serve industry clients, but are also affected by the economic situation of individuals employed in furniture and related industries. You may wish to develop two or three probing questions that pinpoint forecasted economic conditions for that specific industry.

The mechanics of taking the audit vary from professional to professional. Some individuals may prefer to make marginal notes directly on the book pages. Most people, however, need a lot more room. I suggest you copy the questions, then cut them out and paste them to the type of writing surface most comfortable to you—a medical pad, a legal pad, or a looseleaf notebook. Personally I prefer the looseleaf format. It permits expansive analysis, space for branching and probing questions, and space to record input from any other individuals involved in the process. Not every audit question will apply to every professional or every organization, but beware of the "NA" (not applicable) syndrome. An easy way to avoid critical self-evaluation is simply to say, "Well that's not applicable in our case." The real question is could it be applicable, and should it be applicable? At the very least, every question should be evaluated in the light of the potential contribution it could make to client retention, growth, and profitability.

YOUR PRACTICE ENVIRONMENT

Your practice environment is the real world in which you operate. It includes both macro and micro variables. Macro variables include national and regional governmental policies and regulations, and the national and regional economic situation. Micro variables are those which are more closely and directly related to your everyday opportunities and constraints. They consist of local regulations, local economic conditions, the composition of your practice market, and so on. In consumer and industrial product and service marketing, we refer to this portion of the environment as the external environment or uncontrollable variables. Although each of us has some opportunity to have an effect on our practice environment, the impact on any one individual or firm is usually slight. The importance of understanding your practice environment and keeping up to date concerning changes is that the most successful professionals are usually those who can adjust to and often profit from changes.

1. Do you have a practice management plan?
2. Do you have a marketing professional services plan?
3. Is your practice organized so that a specific individual has the authority and responsibility for practice management operations?
4. Are your practice management operations evaluated on a routine basis? How often, by whom, and with what effects?
5. Are there any laws that have significant regulatory impact on your practice?
6. Are you in compliance with these requirements?
7. What are the current ethical codes of your profession?
8. Do you have copies of the specific ethical codes that affect you?
9. Are you appropriately involved with the key professional associations that affect your practice environment?
10. What specific actions have been taken by you to consider, modify, or enforce your ethical codes?
11. Are there any immediate or future political developments that might significantly affect your professional environment, including those of other professionals, your clients, your staff, and referral sources?
12. What agencies, boards, commissions, committees, and so on have had or could have significant impact on your professional environment?
13. Are you aware of and appropriately involved with any political or public organizations that affect your professional environment?
14. Who are your direct competitors?
15. Who are your indirect competitors?
16. Can you describe the client base of your most significant competitors?
17. What do you know about the fee structure of significant competitors?
18. What do you know about competitors' strengths and weaknesses?
19. Are you in a position to assess size, structure, and potential for future growth for key competitors?
20. Do competitors know what you want them to know about you?
21. Describe the current economic situation and how it affects your practice environment.
22. How might future economic scenarios affect your practice?
23. Have you developed at least one offensive and one defensive strategy to cope with significant economic changes?
24. How does your natural environment (regional location, climate, topography) affect your current and future practice environment?
25. Can you enumerate the key technological advances associated with your profession over the past few years? Include those which directly affect your

clients, such as new medical hardware for physicians, and those which indirectly affect clients, such as minicomputer billing and administrative systems.
26. Which technologies are you using or not using? Why?
27. How are you tracking and evaluating potential future service delivery or administrative technology?
28. Identify any key cultural shifts in your practice environment, such as significant in- or out-migrations.
29. Do you have an operating budget appropriately developed and controlled?
30. Do you receive and review detailed, accurate, and understandable regular reports concerning financial condition of and trends in your practice?
31. Do you have a human resources plan and program that identifies long-range goals, inventories strengths and weaknesses of existing staff, and provides for training and growth, feedback and consultation?

CLIENT ANALYSIS AND OPPORTUNITIES

Now that you have assessed many of the general and specific factors in your professional environment, it is time systematically to consider the nature of your current practice and the opportunities for future expansion and growth. If you are a new professional, these questions are designed to get you thinking in an organized way about client analysis. If you are currently involved in an individual or group practice these questions will help you see where you are and where your practice might develop in a new and interesting way.

1. In addition to your individual working client files, have you established an independent set of client analysis files?
2. Is new client information routinely collected and posted to the client analysis files?
3. Is client information summarized in matrix form by key practice variables, such as client type, size, primary and secondary services provided, billings, collection experience, profitability, growth potential, referral potential, and so on?
4. Does the posting, review, and reporting of client information take place on a routine and regular basis?
5. Are you able to identify high-assay (current and potentially high-profit clients) and low-assay clients?
6. Do high- and low-assay clients fall into any identifiable segments or groups?
7. What discrete segments emerge or seem to be emerging from your client analysis? For example, if you are a CPA, are more of your clients small industrial businesses, self-employed professionals, or commercial firms?
8. Considering your present high-assay client bases and the strengths of your practice, what is the potential client base that you would like to serve? For example, if you are the administrator of a health maintenance organization, do you have a detailed list of potential individual and organizational members?
9. Are any environmental developments forecast that could create opportunities for new client acquisition? An example might be a county or state government program to bring a certain type of industry to your area.

10. Have you developed a client purchasing model? Such a model is a diagram or description of the actions your clients take from the time they are aware of the need for professional service until they actually locate and retain a professional.
11. Do you routinely solicit, record, analyze, and act on client input and evaluation of your professional services?
12. Do you or members of your staff conduct exit interviews with clients who are terminating or have apparently terminated their relationship? Do any patterns exist that might indicate areas of weakness, improvement, or opportunity?

PHILOSOPHY, POSITIONING, AND TARGETING

The questions in this section and the material in the related chapter that follows will assist you in considering how you and your practice can become actively and appropriately involved in marketing your professional services.

1. Have you and/or your staff thoroughly discussed your philosophy concerning marketing?
2. Has this philosophy been reduced to writing and communicated to all professionals and staff?
3. Has a positioning statement been drafted, discussed, reduced to writing, and communicated?
4. Based on your analysis in sections 1 and 2 and the development of an appropriate positioning statement, have you identified specific client targets for service expansion?
5. Based on your analysis in sections 1 and 2 and your position statement, have you identified specific targets for new client acquisition?
6. Are your client targeting plans in actionable form? For example, does detailed information concerning the client target exist?
7. Is a specific individual charged with the responsibility for client development?
8. Are objectives quantified where possible, including time for accomplishment and projected costs and revenues?

YOUR SERVICE MIX

Your service mix refers to the combination of services you offer to clients. These services may include those which are directly professional, such as the preparation of a will by an attorney, and services which are not directly professional, including credit, the mailing of information or news releases, or client parking. Please note that the audit sections are based on the assumption that you have responded to the first three sections. The main thrust of the service mix review is to ensure that you are matching your services to client needs and market opportunities.

1. Is service mix analysis, planning, development, and termination a regular part of your management activities?

2. Do you have a written description of services you currently provide and services you prefer to handle by referral?
3. Are you able to provide clients with written information concerning the services available from your referral sources?
4. How well does your current service mix match the present and potential market opportunities you have identified?
5. Have you objectively assessed your own current level of qualifications to provide the services offered?
6. How often do you assess the level and currency of qualifications of your staff relative to your service mix offerings?
7. Do you have an ongoing program that provides for upgrading service delivery skills?
8. Are continuing professional education and development activities matched to your marketing opportunities and targets?
9. Have you identified areas for potential service expansion for existing clients?
10. Have you identified potential new service offerings for potential clients?
11. Is your staff recruiting and training program matched to service expansion and new service development objectives and opportunities?
12. Do you have a systematized service delivery operation or procedure?
13. How often is your service delivery system reviewed critically?
14. What are the significant strengths and weaknesses of your service delivery system?
15. Which items in your service mix are candidates for deemphasis, sell-off, or termination?

PROFESSIONAL FEES

Marketing professionals are concerned about the economic and emotional components of fees. In the industrial and consumer product and service fields, marketing professionals are intimately involved in establishing and communicating prices. The following questions are designed to help you assess the current fee structure in your own practice.

1. What is the normal fee structure or range of fees in your practice environment?
2. Do you solicit client feedback concerning your fee structure on a regular basis?
3. How do your fees compare with those of direct competitors? with professional fees in general?
4. On what basis do you justify fees that are lower *and* higher than competitive norms?
5. How do you establish fees?
6. What procedures exists for fee structure review?
7. Does your current management system allow you to match costs to revenues by client or engagement?
8. Do you maintain a record of fee-related problems, such as failure to get or retain clients; direct complaints or disputes; billing writedowns, writeups, and writeoffs?

9. How and when are prospective clients made aware of your fee structure and policies?
10. Do clients receive a separate written document discussing fee policies, or is this discussion part of your practice brochure or client information booklet?
11. Does your management system provide for control so that fee proposals, billing, and collection procedures are consistently applied by all staff?
12. Has a fee policy been developed and documented? Would you describe your practice as fee-competitive, competitive on other than fee dimensions, or flexible?
13. How are clients notified of revisions in your fee structure?

PERSONAL COMMUNICATION

The personal communication review includes not only your personal interactions with clients, but also those of your staff. Interpersonal communication provides a unique marketing opportunity and permits confirmation that the client has indeed made the right selection of the professional and the professional organization. Even though the professional may be technically qualified, inappropriate or ineffective interpersonal relationships will quickly send the client looking for an alternative.

1. Do you hold regular staff meetings characterized by open, two-way communication?
2. How often do you meet with your staff individually?
3. Are staff members willing to take you into their confidence on occasions when they have pressing personal problems that have affected or might affect their performance?
4. Are appropriate staff briefed and assisted in carrying out their client, professional, and community relations roles?
5. Has the initial client or prospective client consultation procedure been carefully developed and utilized?
6. Are client contact personnel, from receptionist to paraprofessionals, evaluated and trained in interpersonal relationships?
7. Have you sought objective evaluation of your own interpersonal skills?
8. What areas of strength and weakness do you think exist in your own inventory of interpersonal communication skills?
9. How has your service delivery system been adjusted to compensate for staff strengths and weaknesses?
10. Do you solicit direct client feedback concerning perceptions of your staff on a regular basis?
11. Are current and potential referral sources identified in writing and catalogued by level of referral activity?
12. Does a system exist for personal acknowlegement and follow-up of all referrals?
13. How often do you call/see regular referral sources?
14. Do you maintain a written record of related professionals to whom you refer?

15. How do you follow up your referrals to ensure that your colleagues are aware of your importance to their practice?
16. List the activities you and or your staff conduct to stimulate referrals—seminars, workshops, mailings, luncheons, visits, and so on.
17. Have you prepared or caused to be prepared a written analysis of the community infrastructure, noting relevant clubs, boards, committees, and so on?
18. Have you developed a community relations plan and targeted key organizations for active involvement by you and your staff?
19. Does your benefit and compensation program provide for specific recognition of associates or staff who generate new clients?
20. Does your benefit and compensation program provide for associates and staff whose activities create positive visibility for the practice?
21. Do clear and generous reimbursement policies exist for staff people who participate in approved community and professional activities?
22. Are the policies in numbers 19, 20, and 21 well documented and communicated?

WRITTEN COMMUNICATION

The label "written communication" is being used in the broadest sense. Professionals who are investigating marketing frequently focus on advertising as the primary form of written communication. But typical mass-media advertising may not be at all suited to professional marketing objectives. In this audit section, we will review many other types of written communication that can affect client and prospect perception. Advertising will be discussed in detail in Chapter eight.

1. Have you selected a practice image objective?
2. Is the image you wish to convey congruent with all aspects of your practice, such as client base, service mix, staff, location and facilities, fee structure?
3. Have you selected a practice identifier or logo consistent with your image?
4. Are *all* printed and typed communications centrally reviewed and controlled before release?
5. Does your practice identifier or logo appear on every piece of written communication generated by your practice?
6. Has an appropriate type style been selected to match your image goals?
7. Is this distinctive type style used on *all* printed communication?
8. Have appropriate paper stock and color(s) been selected and used to build practice identity?
9. Identify, collect, and review all current written communication vehicles, such as stationery, envelopes, receipts, invoices, purchase orders, cards, proposals, pamphlets, brochures, appointment cards, billing reminders, client data sheets. Are they consistent in appearance, quality, use of logo?
10. Have you reviewed all self-completion client forms for clarity, diplomacy of questions, and mechanical problems, such as room to write?
11. Has some form of client brochure or information and service document been developed and circulated?

12. If your practice involves proposals, are proposals carefully prepared and reviewed from an objective marketing perspective for form, content, and presentation?
13. Do you publish and distribute useful informational communications to maintain client contact?
14. Is the decision to publish informational communications verified by client, prospect, or referral source need?
15. What printed media such as journals, convention or conference programs, trade or professional magazines, are read by your clients, prospects, referral sources?
16. Are any general or mass newspapers and magazines consistently read by clients, prospects, referral sources?
17. Is media advertising (informational, institutional, or persuasive) congruent with your MPS philosophy and image?
18. Have existing informational pieces such as newsletters and up-dates been critically tested for value to clients and prospects?

MPS CONTROL AND EVALUATION

1. Is the MPS program reduced to a written document that specifies objectives, time frames, resources, expected results, and responsibilities?
2. Are all staff participating in MPS program implementation within their comfort zone?
3. Does a regular, periodic review of MPS program progress take place?
4. Is MPS program contribution part of the total review process for monetary and nonmonetary staff compensation?
5. Do you maintain a concise, permanent record of MPS ideas and activities that failed as well as those that succeeded?
6. Does your management system provide sufficient current data to permit development of an MPS information system isolating MPS program activity costs, client information and analysis data, and profitability analysis?

WE'RE UNDER WAY!

We have now reviewed what you are and are not doing in marketing your professional skills. We will devote the next several chapters to giving you action information and ideas. This information will assist you in considering and taking action in the development of your own MPS program.

Chapter 4
Developing Your Marketing Program

Chapter 3 offered an opportunity to identify many of your strengths and weaknesses as a marketer of professional skills. After completing the diagnostic marketing audit, most professionals find they need the answer to two questions. First, how do I capitalize on my strengths or the strengths of my organization? Second, what can I do to eliminate or reduce the significance of any weaknesses that were noted in the professional service audit? The answer to these questions is simple: develop a detailed and actionable marketing professional services (MPS) plan. Although the answer is simple, the development, implementation, control, and evaluation of effective marketing plans is not, but as they say in the Caribbean, "Not to worry."

This chapter will present alternative structures for use in the development of a marketing program. We will recommend a specific, step-by-step approach that you can adapt to your practice or organization. The chapter will not only show you how to structure your own MPS plan, but also assist you in answering the tough question of who should be involved in the planning process. Subsequent chapters will be devoted to each section of MPS plan development. By the time you have finished reading the remainder of the book, you will have the answer to two other important questions. First, what is MPS all about, and is it for me? Second, how can I proceed to make marketing a part of my regular practice operations?

WHAT IS AN MPS PLAN?

An MPS plan is a written document specifying in detail the professional's/organization's marketing objectives, the action programs that will be utilized to pursue these objectives, the individual(s) who have the authority for implementing the plan and those responsible for carrying out its activities.

Is it possible to "do marketing" without a written plan? A professional organization or practice that operates without a written marketing program may be marketing its professional services. It is not, however, doing so "professionally." How does the MPS plan relate to a written practice management plan? The MPS plan is a component of a practice management plan. The practice management plan concerns *all* managerial aspects of a practice, including marketing, finance and accounting, personnel, and operations management. We are focusing only on the marketing component.

Naturally, practice management plans are not mutually exclusive in coverage. For example, the way in which client visits are scheduled is not only an operations problem, but also has implications for the marketing program. There are very few data that would permit generalization concerning the use of formal practice management programs by professionals. My experience and intuition suggest that a relatively small number of individual professionals and a minority of professional organizations operate under a fully developed practice management program. However, the number of professionals and professional organizations seeking to improve operations management and profitability is increasing. The growing interest in marketing professional services is one reflection of this transfer of the managerial technology explosion.

Should you have a formal practice management plan? It's very easy for me to say "yes," but let's be realistic. Most professional practices and organizations do not evolve in the theoretically correct way. Professionals do not sit down and carefully develop a long-range strategic plan that will govern the behavior and evolution of their practice or organization into the future. Rather, they hang out the shingle, unlock the door, and work like the devil to do the best job they can. If they're good and if they're right and if they're lucky, clients materialize, the client base expands, and their careers are personally and financially rewarding. Take heart, my friends, for this is the way most businesses evolve! Rather than following the textbook approach, most commercial firms in both the consumer and industrial goods and services market get started by running up the flag and seeing who salutes. By that I mean that someone has a new product or service idea, develops the resources to finance its production or delivery, engages in information and persuasive communication, gets it to market, and hopes for the best.

What really happens as individuals and firms, whether professional or commercial, evolve is that they begin to utilize, slowly at first, more and more managerial technology to help them deal with complexity and uncertainty. The development of an MPS program prior to the existence of a full-blown practice management program is a natural process in the order of things. So don't be discouraged; don't feel you are somehow behind the times as a professional because you do not have a formal practice management program. The fact that you are reading this book indicates that you are on your way to evaluating and possibly implementing modern managerial approaches to the nontechnical aspects of your professional practice.

THE IMPORTANCE OF AN MPS PROGRAM

There have been thousands of articles and hundreds of books on the topic of planning. During the 1970s, particular emphasis was given to long-range strategic planning. Indeed, the entire field of management has been neatly summarized by experts as the activities of planning, organizing, and controlling an individual or an organization's activities. Why this emphasis on planning? In my judgment, two words provide the answer: complexity and uncertainty. The life of the professional becomes more and more complex with each passing year. The demands of the professional's constituency increase. These demands come not only from clients, but from colleagues, staff, peers, and the public at large. In addition, regulations proliferate, both within the professions and from external sources. Technology leaps ahead of our ability to cope with it. New methods for professional service delivery, as well as management, damn us to be ever behind in our reading and perhaps always somewhat out of date in our understanding of the cutting edge of theory and practice in our fields. And here we are considering yet another wrinkle in our professional careers, the marketing of professional services!

Planning helps us identify the critical variables in the success of a professional practice. Skillful planners set priorities and allocate human and monetary resources in a manner consistent with opportunities and returns. A written plan helps us focus, helps us get a handle on what's going on and stay on target more of the time. From a strictly humanitarian point of view, careful planning permits the professional to serve a larger number of clients at a more effective level of performance.

The increasing complexity of the professions has come about relatively recently. Changes in regulations, codes, ethics, client expectations, professional liability and responsibility, technology and in other areas have upset the once placid apple cart of predictability. These changes have created a certain amount of insecurity and uncertainty. Furthermore, changes seem to be taking place at an accelerating rate. What is the professional to do? Unfortunately, many of us are reacters and adapters. We spend a great deal of our time modifying our modus operandi to cope with the latest changes. Such behavior detracts from the performance of our professional service and hurts both our own profitability and the clients we serve.

A carefully developed plan considers possible future scenarios, evaluates the best reaction to them, and minimizes the disruption of our practice should they become reality. This is not to say that planning is the solution for all professional management ills. Complexity and uncertainty will continue to frustrate even the best-managed professional organization. What effective planning does is to reduce disruption. Professionals who anticipate change and are ready with alternative action plans can frequently react creatively, productively, and profitably to change. The very existence of a plan and the development of the plan itself seems to reduce anxiety concerning possible future scenarios and the uncertainty they portend.

Let's examine some other advantages to the regular development of a formalized, written MPS plan.

1. Time out. There is seldom enough time to cope with all the day-to-day tasks that must be accomplished. Crises arise, unscheduled problems creep into the day's activities, the practice begins to manage us. If professionals allow this syndrome to continue, they often lose control of their practices. Although they may earn comfortable incomes, they may not be performing the types of service they truly enjoy and for which they are best qualified. The best way to ensure that planning takes place is to require the regular preparation of detailed written plans. The word "regular" is relative. At a minimum, planning should take place on an annual basis. I'm familiar with several CPA firms that annually go into "retreat." These three-day to one-week sessions are devoted exclusively to the development of annual plans as well as the review of past performance. Force yourself to take time out to review the past, analyze the present, and consider the future.

2. Involvement and diversity. Planning frequently involves more than a single professional. In a partnership or small organization several professionals may be involved in the planning session. In a smaller practice, the professional, paraprofessionals, and other staff may be involved. Such involvement creates diversity of input. You'll be surprised how many creative ideas for marketing and for practice management as a whole come out of planning conferences.

3. Participation equals commitment. As your colleagues and staff become involved in the planning process, you will note an increasing level of awareness, commitment, and follow-through to the objectives agreed to in the plan. Marketing is a people activity. In developing and securing good long-term relationships between your organization and your clients, sincere and warm enthusiasm from everyone in the organization is the ideal. Solicit input from anyone involved in client service delivery. Let them know their feedback and concern are very much appreciated. Don't secure cooperation and commitment the way my drill sergeant did in the infantry. He announced: "There will be a volleyball game at four o'clock Sunday afternoon. You will show up, you will participate, you will have fun!"

4. Coordination. In even a two-person practice, such as professional and secretary, it's important that each member of the team know what the other is attempting to do. The planning process promotes coordination. There seems to be

an inverse relationship between successfully coordinated activities and the size and complexity of organizations. In professional firms employing several, scores, or hundreds of people, all affected departments should be involved in the planning process so that maximum coordination and effectiveness are promoted.

5. The learning curve. The first time you develop a marketing professional services plan, you'll normally experience the "fantastic-frustration syndrome." Some of your programs will work out splendidly, while others will not only be disappointing, but may not be cost effective. A colleague of mine who is a specialist in the management of professional organizations likes to remind his clients of the four Ps—to pursue perfection, practice planning. In other words, the more experience we have in planning, the better we become. It's an unfortunate fact that humans tend to learn more from their mistakes. Planning means formalizing our activities to some extent. It also means documenting our behavior so that our mistakes become apparent both in magnitude and in cost. I'm familiar with one professional service organization which believed that professional convention attendance and participation was a key ingredient of its success. Careful tracking of conference activities in a structured marketing planning program revealed that these activities were not only ineffective, but also quite expensive—$50,000 per year in 1982 dollars. The senior members of this organization learned from their mistake, eliminated extensive conference travel and participation, and experimented with local contact activities and informational publications for referral sources. This organization continues to learn how to develop more effective marketing programs.

6. Measurement. Once the professional has enunciated clearly the objectives and tasks necessary in the implementation of a marketing program, it becomes easier to evaluate progress or lack of progress toward goals. In practices where compensation is partially reflective of progress toward practice growth and profitability, more objective measurement of progress can be made. For example, in a West Coast dental clinic, professionals were urged to get out into the community and become known. This rather vague objective was difficult to measure. It was simply not possible for anyone to receive special compensation or recognition for "bringing patients into the clinic." On the other hand, a small law firm with approximately the same number of professionals was also looking for community involvement from its members. However, as part of its written annual marketing program, the firm specified the types of organizations targeted, the types of participation desired, and the minimum amount of attendance at meetings, committee memberships, presentations, and so on that would be acceptable. In addition, the firm help provide professionals with materials that could be used for speeches, with lists of organizations in their area of residence or practice, and with financial support for dues, conference registration, and so on. The specificity that resulted as a by-product of the planning activity made the evaluation and compensation sequence for the management group a good deal more objective and effective.

Well, it's not difficult to see that I am a strong advocate of formal planning. My own approach is that some form of planning should take place in all organizations that depend on client income for their survival. This planning requirement should be met no matter how large or small the professional practice. However, the complexity, level of detail, and breadth of the plan will depend on the size, type, clientele, resources, experience, philosophy, and personality of the professional or professional organization in question.

INCREASE YOUR PROBABILITY FOR SUCCESS

In our book *Modern Marketing*[1] Ed Fox and I devoted an entire chapter to planning. In the experience and research leading up to the development of that chapter, we noted some common characteristics of professionally developed marketing plans. As you begin to think about structuring your own plan, it will be helpful to keep the following desirable characteristics in mind.

Have Feasible, Congruent and Specific Objectives

In 1980, I received a call from a managing partner of a CPA firm. He had just gained this position and felt under self-imposed pressure to create spectacular results. His requirement for the firm's first marketing professional services objective was to double volume within the next 12 months. The MPS audit revealed that the firm was not able to handle the business it already had. The first priority should have been to improve the level of service to existing clients. The objective of doubling volume was not feasible from any perspective.

Congruence refers to the marketing approach and its relationship to the firm's philosophy and positioning. It would not be congruent for a professional or oganization wishing to position itself as the most technically qualified "professional's professional" to engage in massive media advertising. One objective more congruent with the professional's professional image would be to have manuscripts accepted for publication in the leading professional journals, to be appointed chairperson of the certifying board, to be on the research seminar of the annual conference program, and so forth. Finally, the objectives should be stated in as specific terms as possible. The real test is, can the objective be quantified? Quantification simplifies measurement, measurement simplifies the tie-in between effort and reward:

> A precise statement of objectives forces planners to consider what is possible and feasible—and what is needed to achieve that.
> The clearer the objectives, the easier it is to develop plans for achieving them. Progress toward achieving them can be more easily measured, and clear-cut responsibility and authority for obtaining them can be determined. Such statements also enable other practice personnel to respond more specif-

ically and to make their input more helpful.

Finally, specific statements of your objectives give you clear, written records of what you hoped to achieve. Even if something goes wrong, this will help you reduce the likelihood of making similar errors in the future.[2]

Enumerate All the Steps

Feasibility, congruence, and specificity should be hallmarks of the task statements. After objectives have been specified, the activities or tasks necessary to accomplish those objectives are enumerated. Measurement, control, and the assignment of authority and responsibility are greatly facilitated when planners take the time to be as specific as possible about the types of professional service marketing activities required to achieve objectives.

Have an Implementation Schedule

The typical professional planning horizon is one year. Within the one-year framework, monthy or quarterly activity schedules should be developed. In addition to short-term, tactical plans of one year or less, many larger professional organizations utilize a two- to three-year planning horizon. Short-term objectives are sequenced to lead toward longer-term goals. For example, a firm of architects and urban planners with which I'm familiar developed some short-range marketing targets to help get them established and develop revenue in the short run. These targets were selected, however, based on three-year goals for the types of clients and work in which they would like to specialize. Their long range objective was to build a regional reputation. Preparing an implementation schedule is mandatory. In addition to the benefits cited, a written schedule helps produce a logical flow of activities. Problems of coordination are also minimized.

Build in Flexibility

I once asked a friend of mine who was a financial analyst and counselor how he lived with the requirement of giving advice based on a long-term and uncertain future. He replied: "The fact that no one can forecast the future gives the forecaster a certain comfort." An important disclaimer that should be made over and over again is that planning does not guarantee success or certainty. The more sophisticated marketing plan will have flexible objectives that will allow for over or under attainment and provide for a redirection of resources and effort. In a small professional practice or organization, the availability of a large number of contingency options is simply not feasible. The larger professional organization may be able to plan for and act on contingency options. In the individual professional's case or in the case of the small firm, flexibility simply means the willingness to be flexible—that is, to consider and learn from the outcome of the marketing program and to adjust appropriately in future periods.

One example of contingency planning in a large-scale operation involved a health maintenance organization promotional campaign. The HMO marketing group conducted research which indicated an extremely low level of awareness and understanding of specific facts about HMOs in one of the target communities. One of the specific objectives in the marketing plan was to continue advertising until 25 percent of the audience test sample could identify the HMO by name and demonstrate that they understood the HMO concept being explained in the announcements. Once the requisite level of awareness had been achieved, monies were pulled away from media budgets and applied to a program of visual and group orientations and enrollment sessions.

In consumer and industrial product and service firms, contingency objectives frequently deal with anticipated competitive reaction to marketing programs. For example, banks and savings and loan marketing departments typically have a series of flexible objectives based on the types of services, premiums, and costs competitors are promoting during the current period.

Specify Authority and Responsibility

Practice management and administration activities are often looked upon at best as necessary evils by most professionals. Getting professionals and staff to buy into the marketing program and to participate is a challenging task. One requisite for planning success is the involvement and backing of the person or persons who have the top political and financial power in the organization. These individuals must have the authority to delegate and control MPS plan implementation. Those charged with implementing portions of the MPS plan must be given direct authority or have authority by association. Finally, the implementation schedule should specifically fix responsibility for tasks by name or title. Without the backing of top management and the specific fixing of authority and responsibility for plan accomplishment, most MPS activities will become nice to do things that never get done.

ORGANIZING FOR MARKETING: WHO SHOULD DO IT?

I remember asking a woman who was a senior management person in her firm how she was doing. Her reply was entertaining and instructive. She responded: "You know, after I passed age 35, I learned that the answer to most questions is—it depends"! Who should be in charge of MPS plan development, implementation, control, and evaluation? It depends. I'd like to suggest several approaches to organizing for marketing planning. You can then decide which approach or combination of alternatives best suits your professional environment and situation.

The Senior Professional

In many professional organizations, the top political power is in the hands of the senior professional member. In first-generation organizations, this person may be the founding professional. I like to think of this alternative in terms of the senior professional fallacy. It is wrong, in my judgment, to assume that because an individual is the senior professional in the organization, that automatically implies greater interest or superior talent in marketing. Although it is critical that the MPS program have the full support of the power structure, it is not necessary that this individual or individuals have the direct responsibility for plan development, implementation, control, and evaluation. If the senior professional approves the integration of marketing into the regular practice management program and will give it visible support, this may be all that is necessary. I do not favor the senior professional approach unless in an individual case that person is uniquely fitted and interested in the actual development of the MPS program.

The Managing Partner

As professional organizations grow over time, one excellent approach to dealing with the demands for effective practice management is the appointment of a suitable management partner. This individual, almost always a professional, has administrative skills and interests. Managing partners, sometimes called administrative partners, are usually generalists. Their counterparts in firms of financial analysts, brokers, architects, consulting engineers, and so forth may carry the title of president or even executive vice-president.

Title aside, we are talking about the individual who is charged with the management of the day-to-day operation of the organization. Essentially, all operating people report to this individual. His or her responsibilities are broad and typically include approval authority and veto power in almost all areas of the organization's operation. In essence, the managing or administrative partner, executive VP, or whatever, has been delegated full authority to run the firm on behalf of the other professionals. But although it is essential that this individual be involved in the development, communication, promotion, and evaluation of the MPS plan, it may be simply asking too much of an already busy manager to accept full responsibility for plan development and execution.

An MPS Task Force

A task force is generally a group that gets together on a one-time basis to handle a specific situation. Frequently, task forces operate in an isolated fashion. They are appointed to investigate a specific problem or the feasibility of a new market opportunity. They then report back to the appointing authority. Seldom are they given the operational role of implementing, managing, and evaluating the results of their activity. How might the task force be used in conjunction with MPS? Well, as a professional, you might appoint a task force to investigate how MPS could be utilized and integrated into your regular practice.

Typically, a task force would provide information concerning what MPS involves, alternative ways of integrating marketing into the practice, and perhaps make recommendations concerning whether or not this function should be added. For a firm or professional group already utilizing an MPS plan, a task force might be appointed to carry out some specific activity or to make an investigation. These are appropriate and specific assignments that traditionally seem to fit the task force mode. I would discourage the task force approach beyond these limited uses.

The Committee

All disparaging comments concerning committees aside, most professionals are quite comfortable operating in the committee mode. Professional organizations beyond the one- to three-person firm generally have some sort of regular committee meeting. In larger organizations, there are standing committees. Ad hoc committees, those appointed for a specific period of time to acccomplish a specific purpose, are also utilized.

The committee format is one of the more desirable alternatives. It permits input and guidance from senior firm personnel, managing partners, and so on. Key individuals in the organization remain informed, and yet the actual work can be delegated to and performed by someone with more time, talent, and interest in marketing. The key weakness in the committee form is unclear delegation of authority. In one professional firm with which I recently worked, a practice development committee was formed to handle the development of the MPS plan. While coordination and information exchange were excellent as the project got under way, it soon became clear that the committee members were uncertain about their authority and responsibilities in MPS plan development. The administrative partner was a member of this committee and also chairperson. Members who were developing subsections of the proposal were delayed because they had to get decisions from the administrative partner. In addition, the committee, with eight members, was too large. Eventually, I bypassed the committee completely and worked directly with the administrative partner. If you adopt the committee approach, assuming you are not a sole practitioner, I recommend keeping the membership to three individuals, with one individual clearly having the authority to act and the responsibility for MPS plan development and implementation.

The Director of Marketing

This involves the creation of a new position and title and the assignment of an individual to this post on either a part- or full-time basis. Prior to taking such a step it is essential that the organization be committed to implementation of the marketing concept. You cannot change the practice characteristics of professionals simply by creating a new job and letting someone else do it. There is one fundamental truth I have learned, and that is that professionals market their own services. Marketing pros like myself can, have, and will contribute much to assisting professionals in the endeavor. But hiring a hotshot marketer and expecting that person to perform miracles without the support and involvement of the professional simply does not work.

If this approach appeals to you, who should the marketing professional be? Ideally, the individual should be a qualified professional—architect, financial analyst, CPA, physician, medical professional. He or she should also be a generalist, broadly skilled and interested in management and marketing. Is it rare to find such a combination? You bet it is! It may not be cost effective to utilize a professional in the marketing management role. The professional could be earning fees that would more than cover the cost of hiring a marketing person as well as make an overall contribution to the profitability of the firm.

Hiring the marketing professional to work with you or your organization, either on a part- or a full-time basis, is a critical step. Compatibility is the key word. Certainly the marketer may have ideas that are different from yours or those of your professional colleagues. Indeed, that may be why you are hiring the person. However, if this is to be more than an exercise in futility, the marketing pro must be able to relate to, work for, and work with your professional colleagues. While no union is ever 100 percent successful, unless a high degree of compatibility exists, the marketing program is doomed to a cloudy future. To be a full-time marketing manager with a professional organization is simply not in my career plan. However, I enjoy working with professionals and professional firms. I feel comfortable and seem to fit in. There is a good explanation for this.

I spent three years on a general staff in the Army Medical Service Corps working full time with medical professionals. The next three years were spent as a marketing consultant with Ernst & Ernst, now Ernst & Whinney, one of the big eight accounting firms. In addition to working and traveling with accountants and tax attorneys for three years, I also had an opportunity to study accounting and to pass the accounting theory, auditing, and law portions of the CPA exam. My work as researcher, writer, and consultant in the field of marketing has placed me in close contact as an expert witness and researcher with law firms representing various marketers. I've developed a keen appreciation for the inner workings of the legal profession. This general acceptance by professionals, to which there are of course exceptions, has come only after a long period of orientation and experience. If you decide to hire a marketing pro to head your MPS operation, don't just accept the first former brand manager from Procter & Gamble that walks through the door.

Consultants

The use of consultants and consulting organizations in the transfer of all technologies to the professions is widespread. Data-processing consultants come in to set up your payroll or client billing or project management system. Financial consultants come in to assist you in the development of accounting systems, in budgeting and cash management, and to help you consider the tax and estate implications of your financial decisions. Should you consider the use of a consultant in developing your MPS program? The answer is a qualified "yes." Don't expect the consultant to come and work in a vacuum. Don't expect the most beautiful consulting report and carefully developed program to guarantee the program's implementation and success.

The consultant working in isolation on a project basis, at least in this area, usually prepares a beautiful report that quickly gathers dust as it sits in the bottom drawer along with other "nice to do someday" projects. I recall a Midwestern professional firm with nine partners. I was asked by the junior partner to analyze the firm and to prepare a marketing professional services plan. Over a get acquainted dinner I got the feeling that the junior partner was given this "dirty job" and that the senior partners really had no interest in marketing. Rather than accept the assignment, I offered a counterproposal. I asked to meet with the nine partners for a one-day workshop. The objective of the workshop was to give the firm an overview of marketing and its applications in the professional services environment. The latter part of the afternoon would be devoted to a session called "Is MPS for Us." During the day, it became clear that the senior partners were very much against any sort of "marketing" activities, while a minority coalition was strongly in favor. Politically, it just didn't make sense to bring in a consultant. The result was predetermined; the senior partners (and the firm) would ignore the recommendations while attempting to convince the minority coalition that it had at least been given a fair chance.

A more positive case where I was an MPS consultant involved a thirteen-partner, one-hundred-person firm. The managing partner appointed an action committee to consider and coordinate the MPS consulting engagement. Firm members at all levels gave generously of their time for interviews. There was participation at all stages of the marketing audit process. A firm partner was assigned as the project coordinator to act on behalf of the managing partner to solve any problems, provide data, and be a sounding board as program development progressed. Partners and other executives had continuous opportunity for input, and the draft recommendations were carefully edited and reviewed to identify and deal with resistance and problems prior to presentation of the final plan. Finally, the consultant was retained on an as-needed basis to assist in implementation and modification of the plan in action.

The plan was nine months in the development process, and it will probably be a full year or more before details are final and implementation begins. However, once the plan is under way, the firm is assured of commitment and involvement from the majority of its professionals and staff. Ironically, the fee to "write a marketing plan in a vacuum" for the Midwestern professional firm and the fee to evolve a working relationship with the other firm were approximately the same. In the second instance, more work and responsibility were undertaken by the client professional organization. This involvement led to commitment, and the commitment to results. If you select a consultant, do so carefully and let that person become involved in your practice.

Do It Yourself

For the sole practitioner or small organization (two to three individuals), the do it yourself method has many advantages. There are several excellent books and scores of articles on marketing professional services. There are professional development and continuing education courses, as well as seminars sponsored by professional associations that you can attend at little cost. In addition, if your profession requires continuing professional education units, short courses and seminars in marketing will generally receive full credit. There are entrepreneurial groups and consultants who, for a fee, conduct two- and three-day workshops in the marketing of your professional skills. Continuing education divisions of your local college or university may offer such courses conveniently scheduled during evening hours. If no such course is available, your professional group may be able to meet with the dean of the school of business or the dean of continuing studies to demonstrate the need for such a program. There are a number of marketing courses that you could take as a continuing education student in many colleges and universities during special summer terms or in the evening.

Any or all of these activities can lead to discovery of productive ideas and approaches that can help you improve the marketing of your professional skills. This approach is direct and inexpensive if you do not have to compute the opportunity cost for the loss of your professional time. The most significant weakness in this approach is that although individual ideas may be gleaned, frequently the busy professional is unable to integrate these ideas into a total marketing program and implement the program effectively.

The Combination Approach

This approach involves getting some professional assistance to evaluate professsional service marketing and the role it might play in your practice. A small organization can work directly with the marketing professional, who can get it started at a level appropriate for the organization's size, budget, and comfort zone. A larger oganization can utilize the services of an outside marketing pro, and learn all it can during the period of assessment and MPS plan development. The committee might call the consultant in from time to time for an objective review of progress or specific special services. Ultimately, the effective consultant will seek to provide the professional organization with the internal capability of developing and implementing ongoing marketing programs.

Choosing an Approach

Which approach to organizing for marketing is best for you? Well, I've declared a few of my biases, and undoubtedly you feel more comfortable with some of these approaches than with others. Ultimately, the best answer still is—it depends. My best judgment is that you should consider and develop a marketing plan in the way that is most comfortable within your practice environment and that will lead to an effective outcome considering the size, scope, personalities, and politics of your organization.

THE QUICKSAND OF MARKETING PLANNING: GENERALIZATIONS

One sure way to differentiate good marketing plans from bad is to count the number of marketing generalizations present, particularly in the statement of plan ob-

FIGURE 4-1 Tip-Offs to Shallow Planning

1. "Our policy will be to beat (or lead) competition."
2. "Our suggestive advertising campaign will have a high impact through its intensive aggressiveness."
3. "We intend to steadily build our market."
4. "We will offer a better (or quality) product."
5. "Our plan is to satisfy the consumer."
6. "Our packaging will stand out from all others."
7. "We plan to penetrate the high-class market."
8. "We will develop a system for keeping tabs on sales."
9. "We will advertise on TV, radio, and through newspapers."
10. "We must get our products into the public's eye."
11. "We will wage a low-pressure campaign."
12. "Our ultimate objective is to increase profits."
13. "Our primary emphasis will be on impressing our distributors."
14. "We will produce a different product."
15. "Our price to the channel (or final consumer) will be fair."
16. "We will seek a reasonable profit."
17. "Our detailed plans will be based on our market research."
18. "We must stimulate the consumer."
19. "We will establish intensive distribution."
20. "Our plan will increase sales."

Source: Edward W. Wheatley, "Generalities to Ruin a Marketing Plan." *Sales Management,* January 1, 1971, pp. 18-25.

jectives: "A marketing generalization is most often an exaggerated, hepped up description of a marketing objective. It is full of hyperactive verbs, catch phrases, and clichés. Missing, however, is a clear statement of the objective. It provides no way of evaluating whether the result can be achieved. And it doesn't even mention a method for insuring that progress toward an objective is being made."[3]

What does a marketing generalization look like? Figure 4-1 presents twenty generalizations gleaned from marketing plans in the consumer and industrial product and service arena.

Generalizations are a convenient shorthand and extremely useful in improving the efficiency of communication. However, the use of a generalization assumes that everyone understands completely what the generalization means. Professsionals inexperienced in marketing are particularly prone to the dangers of the marketing generalization. For example, you might agree to "aggressive promotion" as a desirable way to gain visibility among client prospects. On the other hand, you may feel that "soft sell" is a much better promotional strategy. Picture for just a moment a meeting of your professional staff in which an objective such as hard sell vs. soft sell was proposed. Depending on the philosophy and approach of your group, there may indeed be agreement on such an objective. The problem with the agreement is that selective perception takes place. That is, each professional defines for himself or herself what aggressive promotion vs. soft promotion might be. Your marketing staff or consultant or both go merrily on their way preparing client information brochures, trade brochures, events, and perhaps media advertising. When these materials are distributed or the advertising is run, your staff and even you may be shocked at the results. What happened? You stepped into the quicksand of marketing generalizations.

In addition to lack of communication, misunderstanding, and misdirection, the use of marketing generalizations has another deleterious side effect. That is, the professional may actually believe he or she understands what is meant by such generalized terms. Have you ever defined what "quality" means in your own practice? Does quality mean end results for the client? Does quality mean amount of personal time and attention given to the client? Does quality mean bringing the most qualified professional to work on the client's problems? Does quality mean you will have the most expensive, up-to-date physical facilities and equipment? Does quality mean you will charge only top fees? Does quality mean you will only recruit for your organization colleagues with the highest professional certification and training? Well, you can see what I mean by the difficulty in determining exactly what is meant by a generalization.

But generalizations are useful. As you make a first attempt at enunciating marketing objectives, don't be self-conscious about generalizing. Express your marketing goals in any way that is comfortable. Once you develop a draft marketing program, however, it is essential that you go back through the document and begin to clarify precisely what it is that is feasible, what it is that you would like to accomplish, and what means are available for carrying out these activities. Don't put yourself in the position of the professional portrayed in Figure 4-2. Such a situation is disastrous. Human and financial resources will be dedicated to the pursuit of a poorly conceived program. Not only will the results be disappointing, but it may be better to have had no program at all, since precious professional time was diverted from service delivery, resulting in double jeopardy. In today's competitive environment, clients have other alternatives.

HOW TO STRUCTURE YOUR MARKETING PLAN

As a professional, you are comfortable with structure. Accountants have a specific set of accounting standards and generally accepted principles. Attorneys have set and standard policies and procedures and forms that have been used for long periods of time. Financial consultants, engineers, and architects use certain basic analytical formats that were part of their training and apprenticeship. Medical professionals follow accepted diagnostic and treatment routines, and so on. This is not to imply that there is not a great deal of creativity, individual personal skill, and unique laying on of hands by professionals—indeed, this is what being a professional is all about. But please don't expect to find the same level of standardization and consensus in the development and execution of marketing programs. There simply is no one best way of structuring and implementing an MPS plan.

Although each marketing person may have his or her formula, generally we agree that if an approach is compatible with the professional or professional firm

FIGURE 4-2 A clear case of marketing generalizations

and produces results, then the specific pathway to those happy endings need not be similar across the board. You'll never offend me by saying, "Ed, I don't really like the planning structure you recommended." Each planning structure is merely a starting point, a way of organizing the developmental process for your marketing program. But no matter what format you eventually adopt, it will have several features in common with most approaches to marketing planning.

Each profession has its jargon; forgive me for infusing more of mine. From here on I will be referring to your marketing planning structure as your marketing planning *model*. A model is an abstract, miniaturized representation of some phenomenon. While we can't pretend to describe the full details of any marketing model in a book such as this, we can present alternative models for you to review and consider.

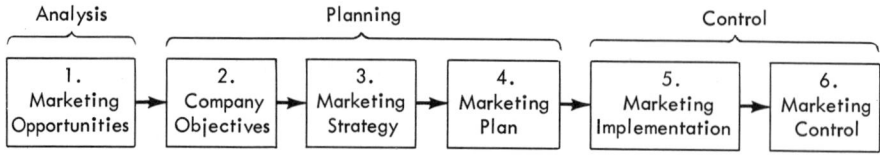

FIGURE 4-3 Steps in the strategic marketing process

Source: Philip Kotler, *Marketing Management: Analysis Planning and Control*, 3rd ed. (Englewood Cliffs, N.J.: Prentice-Hall, Inc., 1976), p. 46.

Figure 4-3 from Philip Kotler's *Marketing: Management, Analyis and Control*,[4] presents the steps common to the strategic marketing planning process. In Kotler's overall framework, we begin with an analysis of marketing opportunities. In light of these, we then develop objectives, the overall strategy to pursue these objectives, a plan to implement the strategy, a timetable and activity flow for the process, and finally a control and review step to see how we're doing and where modifications are needed. Mark Stern's marketing planning model, shown in Figure 4-4, is more detailed. You'll note, however, that it still fits in with Kotler's overall scheme.[5] Finally, Martin Bell's model of the marketing planning process is shown in Figure 4-5.

Take a moment, please, and examine these models. You'll notice that although different to some degree, they all have a considerable degree of similarity. For example, they all recommend analysis of the external as well as the internal environment. Each plan recommends early analysis to target client opportunities and the development of approaches to reach these targets. Next, most planners attempt to match the product and service mix, the service delivery or distribution system, promotional activities, and pricing to the specific market targets selected. Finally, the implementation step is given specific attention, as is the control and revision process.[6]

What model should you use? You've already been introduced to it. In Chapter 3 we took a preliminary look at your marketing and marketing-related activities. In the section called "How to Take Your MPS Audit," you may remember that we divided the audit into eight sections. This is the model we will use to develop your MPS plan. Figure 4-6 presents the recommended approach for structuring your MPS plan. Please note that in addition to the eight major sections, the model now includes several subsections.

MPS IMPLEMENTATION AND CONTROL

Having a structured implementation and control procedure is just as important as having a structured MPS plan. Implementation and control are part of the overall plan; they are vital steps necessary to ensure that action and progress occur and

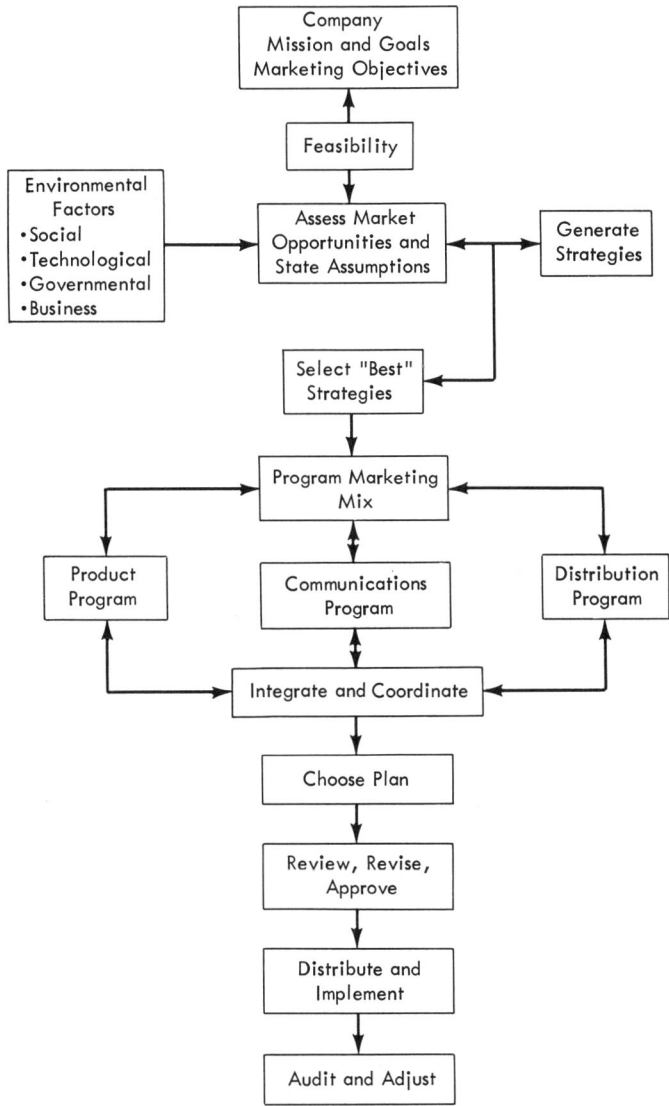

FIGURE 4-4 The marketing planning process

Source: Mark E. Stern, *Marketing Planning: A Systems Approach.* (New York: McGraw-Hill, 1966), p. 13.

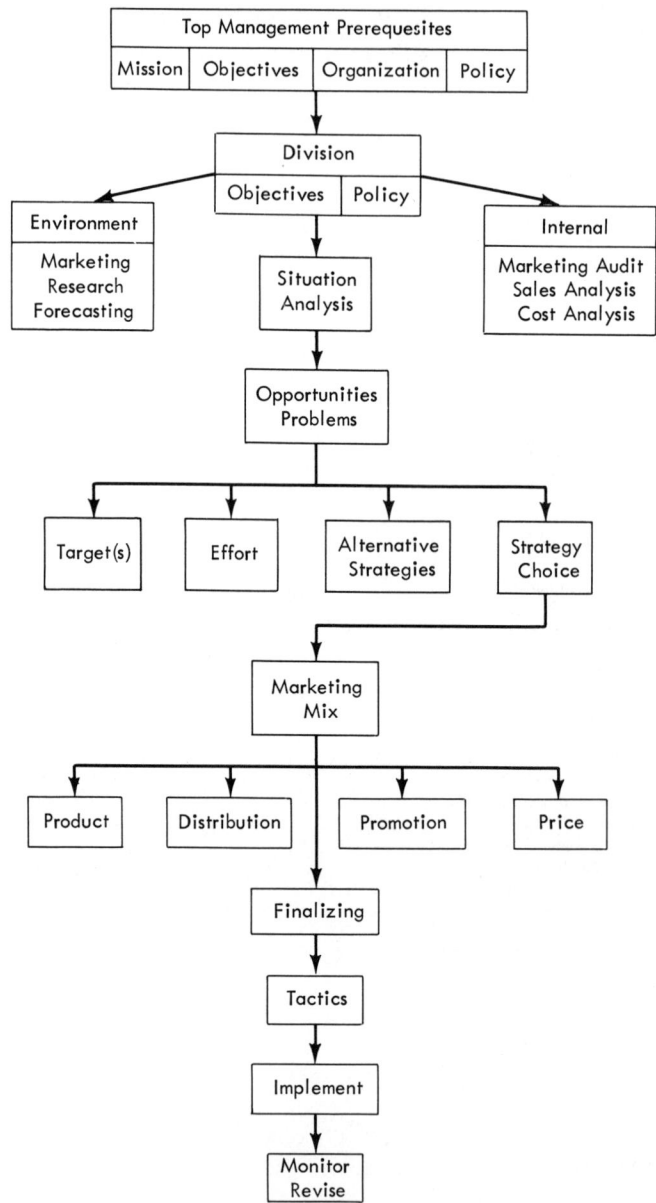

FIGURE 4-5　A model of the marketing planning process
Source: Martin L. Bell, *Marketing Concepts and Strategy,* 3rd ed. (Boston: Houghton Mifflin, 1979), p. 44.

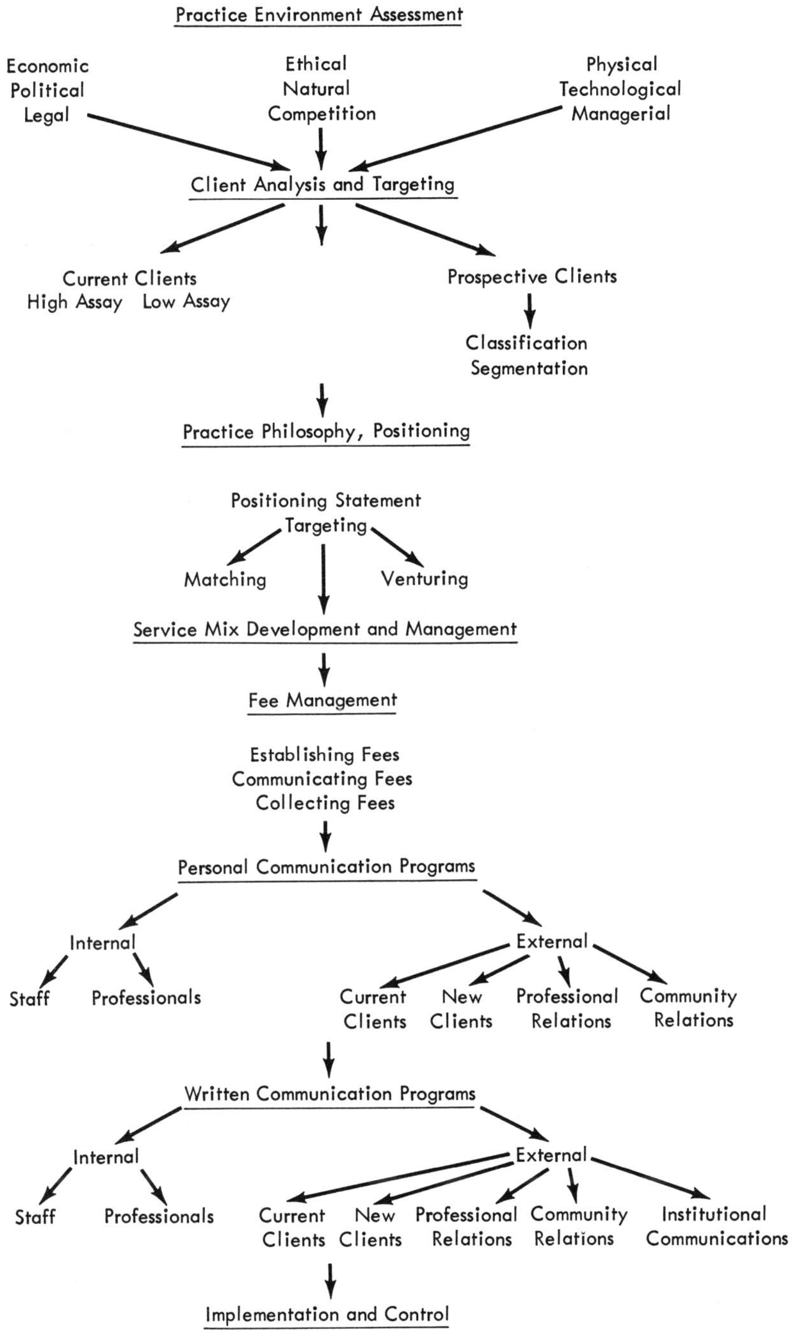

FIGURE 4-6 MPS planning model

that successes and failures are recorded and analyzed. The result will be the development of an effective MPS learning curve for your professional practice.

Please refer to Figure 4-6. There are three basic components to the MPS operation. The first we will label "analysis," the second "planning," and the third "implementation." Analysis refers to the MPS model steps of practice environment assessment and client analysis and targeting. These tasks involve gathering data and input. This information, combined with the professional's experience and personal and professional objectives, becomes the foundation on which the MPS plan is constructed. The planning step involves positioning, matching services to market needs, establishing fee policy, and the personal and written communication program. The implementation step involves the operations necessary to put your plan into action. Before I recommend a procedure for MPS plan implementation, let me address a broader issue—resistance.

Participation and Resistance

If you are a one-person office, no problem. You will decide if and how to use the marketing concepts presented in this book. If, however, you operate in an organization, an MPS plan may meet with various levels of acceptance and enthusiasm. There are two basic approaches to implementing a new MPS plan in the professional organization. These are the mandatory-formal approach and the voluntary-informal approach. The mandatory approach involves:

1. Development of written plans, activities, and scheduling.
2. Selection of personnel to carry out the program by the managing or senior professional.
3. Written assignment of specific responsibilities to each firm member.
4. Periodic and formal written progress reporting by each participant.
5. Regular and formal compliance and performance evaluation by the managing professional.
6. Reward adjustment (promotions, compensation or fringe benefits) based on compliance and performance levels.

The voluntary-informal approach involves:

1. Development of written plans, activities, and scheduling.
2. Communication of these opportunities for MPS involvement in a positive and enthusiastic manner.
3. Identification of those professionals and staff who are willing and able to participate.
4. Agreement by those choosing to participate and the managing professional as to what each person wishes to do.
5. Adjustment of the reward structure based on the performance of those who chose to be involved.

Which philosophy should you or your firm adopt? Personally, I favor an evolutionary rather than a revolutionary approach to professional service marketing.

Let's assume systematic marketing is new to your organization. The voluntary approach can result in interested and motivated staff successfully carrying out some new activities. These demonstrated successes, although initially limited, can have two desirable outcomes. First, participants will be positively reinforced and form a critical mass for your marketing effort. Second, reluctant firm members, who see program benefits may become supportive and in some cases involved. It would be naive to assume that the senior professional, managing partner, executive committee, or whomever could mandate immediate and complete adoption of the marketing concept for their oganization. I sincerely believe the marketing concept will work for you. But to give it a chance to root and grow, it must evolve. Does this mean that staff should have the choice of opting out? Not in my opinion. Everyone should be involved. However, that involvement should be appropriate. For example, while a senior professional might be comfortable making a speech at a conference of peers, a younger staff member might make a contribution by coaching a Little League team or joining a local service club. The key to the voluntary approach is identifying the activities and projects that are feasible for your staff. If, on the other hand, you have an experienced group of professionals and staff eager to move on a marketing plan, the formal approach may work for you.

What about nonparticipants? Consider these two statements from senior professionals in two different fields and firms:

> *Everyone* must participate in our new MPS program. If not, they can forget their bonus this year!
>
> If everyone decides to get heavily involved in this new marketing program, who will be left to do the work?

No, everyone does not have to be involved in the MPS program. Some professionals and staff make superior administrative or technical contributions to the firm. Each individual is different in ability, interest, and temperament. Persons otherwise making valuable contributions to the overall effort should not be unfairly penalized for lack of marketing motivation. However, everyone should be supportive.

All or Nothing At All

Frank Sinatra may have had a hit with that title, but it denotes something quite negative for the professional new to MPS programs. Seldom is it feasible for a new or small professional organization to implement a fully developed MPS plan. For example, I prepared an MPS plan for a medium size statewide firm. The plan recommended that several new activities be implemented in the areas of internal and external written and personal communications. Although the management group was pleased with the plan, they implemented it piecemeal over time. Why? First, professionals and staff were quite busy. Fitting marketing activities into their schedules was not always possible in the short term. Second, there were some major resource questions. Should the firm invest in advertising, and if so how much could it afford? Third, there were organizational and political questions. Which organizational alternative was best? Who should/would be able most effectively to implement and control the program? What about the few partners who were quite opposed to *any* MPS approach?

What finally happened? The firm implemented parts of the report almost immediately. Other actions were postponed to future periods. Some of the recommendations may never be implemented—but no matter. The important thing is that the firm investigated the MPS approach, developed an integrated structure from which to proceed, and implemented portions of the MPS plan that were appropriate and feasible. This is the approach I recommend. Develop a broad and energetic MPS plan. Don't let your creativity be constrained by current resource or personal problems. You don't have to, and probably won't, implement the entire plan. However, you'll have a blueprint for the future as well as some building blocks for the present. You'll have alternatives that can be given priorities and acted upon as future time, opportunities, and resources permit.

Implementation Steps

As a point of departure, we will assume that you have before you an MPS plan with a fully developed range of programs and recommendations. The following steps are recommended:

1. List activities that appear feasible within one year.
2. Set priorities for these items based on the anticipated benefit of each activity.
3. Identify the individual(s) to be involved in personally supervising and/or carrying out each activity.
4. Refine the list, based on their input.
5. Prepare an implementation schedule (see Figure 4-7).
6. Make written assignment of authority and responsibility for plan implementation.
7. Meet with all professionals and staff and brief them on the final version of the MPS plan and implementation schedule.
8. Implement, review, and modify as necessary.
9. Keep careful notes and file written reports from associates and staff.
10. Adjust current and future plans based on feedback.

The purpose of this chapter has been to acquaint you with the importance of careful development and planning of your MPS activities. We have taken a look at the various ways of organizing for MPS planning and implementation. And, we hope, it is clear that although there is no magic, single formula for developing the "best" MPS plan, all effective planning approaches have several basic characteristics in common. Finally, you have been introduced to the MPS planning model and process I recommend you use as a starting point for your own situation. The remaining chapters will take the planning steps and look at them in detail. By the time you have completed the book, you will have the information and the structured approach that will permit you to give full consideration to MPS for yourself or your organization. In addition, you'll have the guidelines necessary to assist you in the drafting of an MPS plan.

Winner, Champion and Humble P.A.
MPS Implementation 2001

Prepared by _____
_____ (Name)
_____ (Title)
Date _____

MPS Objectives and Activities	Responsible Professional Staff	Start Date	1st Qtr.	2nd Qtr.	3rd Qtr.	4th Qtr.	Comments
No.							
1.							
2.							
3.							
4.							
5.							

FIGURE 4-7 Sample MPS scheduling and implementation form

Chapter 5
Analyzing Your Practice Enviroment

Few of us ever stop to consider the environment in which we operate, and yet for the most part in the marketing of professional services, the environment is part of us and part of what we do. It affects how we operate and how our clients are served. In addition to affecting how we are perceived by clients, our practice environment affects our opportunities and constraints. Scholars, authors, and practitioners in the area of strategic planning tell us that really new ideas and approaches seldom come from inside an ongoing organization. The reason seems to be that individuals in organizations and the organizations themselves get caught up in the day-to-day short-run problems and performance. Seldom do we step back to consider the environment in which we perform our service and how that service might be modified to better fit the realities of the environment. This chapter will help you structure such an experience; it will provide you with a roadmap to follow and some specific destinations you are encouraged to visit along the way. I'll be surprised if you do not glean at least one idea for practice improvement in this process. Further, it is my recommendation that the assessment of your practice environment become a regular part of an annual practice management and marketing review.

The world of the professional is a complex and open-ended place. Unlike the world of the clerical worker, whose environment is carefully prescribed and constrained, the field on which the professional plays is often broad and undefined. Indeed, one of the key differentiators in being a professional is that you are expected, based on training and experience, to approach each situation creatively and to determine what would be best for your client's specific case. Before you can effectively position your practice and effectively market it, you should develop a thorough sense of the environment that forms the background to your marketing efforts. Management theorists have used a variety of ways to identify and describe the environments in which organizations and professionals exist. This is not an ironclad conceptualization. The world is, after all, different for each individual. However, the following classification is bound to stimulate some thought and some analysis and action on your part. Your practice environment consists of several discrete types of variables. Although these may not be mutually exclusive or collectively exhaustive, they'll provide a useful conceptual framework.

For the most part, the professional environment consists of two types of variables. First, there are the *uncontrollable* variables, which the professional has little opportunity to affect on an individual basis. These are the economic, political, technical, legal, ethical, natural, and competitive environment. Although you certainly can have input, the opportunity of the single professional or professional organization to significantly alter these environments in the near-term is limited. Rather, the task is to identify and understand each variable's influence on your practice and to adapt in the most efficient way to the real world. The second type of environmental variable is more amenable to direct input and change by the professional. These are the so-called *controllable* variables. They include the physical environment and atmosphere in which your professional service is rendered, the technology utilized to leverage your personal skills and time and in some cases to treat your clients, and finally, the managerial structure, organization, and operations that define the way in which your service is rendered. Let's take a few minutes and consider features of both the controllable and uncontrollable environments that may be important in analyzing and defining just who you are and where you fit in the spectrum of competitive marketing opportunity.

ECONOMIC VARIABLES

You would not be reading this book if you were not interested in the economic outcomes of your practice. The classic definition of economics is that the field is concerned with the way in which a society allocates scarce resources among competing needs and desires. This broad definition reminds us that current and potential users of our services have many conflicting and competing demands and desires which will directly affect their perceptions concerning the need for our services and our fees.

Economic variables are divided into two basic groups—macro and micro. Macroeconomic variables are usually those that affect the national economy. A general downturn in the rate of capital investment may not have a direct effect on your individual practice, but conservative or pessimistic macroeconomic news may have an impact on client attitudes. In periods of conservative or pessimistic economic circumstances, consumers of professional services may postpone or even forego everything from legal counsel and consulting services to medical treatment. Further, the procurement of specialized services, offered by a wide range of professionals from CPAs and architects to marriage counselors and estate planners, may go down drastically.

Microeconomic variables are those associated with a smaller segment of the economy. They are generally related to a specific industry or an individual firm. If you were a CPA in town of Millville, New Jersey, when the Millville Manufacturing Company closed its plant, you'd know what we're talking about. In that case, incomes were abruptly terminated for individuals from the janitor right up through and including top management. Not only were employees affected, but suppliers of all types and supporting businesses, ranging from dry cleaning establishments to food stores, felt the crunch. The textile industry was in a bad slump, and a large firm in a specific town had felt the results directly. Although the professional, in this case the CPA, was not an employee of the firm, his account client base included executives and a large number of business organizations whose primary source of income was the plant employees. The unfortunate thing in this case was that the failure of the company came as an almost complete surprise to everyone involved, both members of the business community and area professionals.

Is there some approach you might take to consider how macro- and microeconomic circumstances might affect your practice environment? Fortunately, the answer is "yes." It's impossible to be completely informed and correct concerning our economic future, but it is possible to stay tuned in to some of the variables that can have profound effects on your own well-being. The approach I recommend involves three steps: first, identification; second, tracking; and third, contingency planning.

Identification

What key macro- and microeconomic relationships can have significant effect on your practice environment? Your first task is to identify the economic scenarios that might have a positive or a negative impact on your service opportunities. For example, how would a period of forecasted high interest rates affect you and your client constituency? How many of your clients are tied into the need for long-term or intermediate term financing? Will interest rates postpone the expansion of business and governmental activities in your area? Professional service firms in Florida have been severely affected by the fluctuating and escalating interest rates of the late 1970s and early 1980s. Particularly hard hit are law firms, architects, consulting engineers, financial consultants, and others whose professional fees are derived substantially from residential and real-estate-related activities.

A physician I know was carefully tuned in to the microeconomic situation of his city in the Pacific Northwest. The city's economy was particularly dependent upon aerospace and defense-related government contract work. The majority of his patients were executives, professionals, and employees of companies specializing in that industry. Although the physician's practice was quite brisk, his contacts indicated that severe cutbacks in his clients' firms were in the offing. Rather than face the uncertainty of a peak and valley revenue situation due to the economics of the industry, he negotiated a retainer arrangement with several firms. His arrangement was based upon annual physicals and preventive medicine. This adaptation to the local economic environment helped smooth out and improve his longer-term practice income; maintain his organization, staff, and facilities; and, he believes, ensure a continued level of high-quality service.

Tracking

Once you have identified some of the key economic variables that affect your practice environment, it's important to tune in to and track information concerning the performance of these variables. There is no shortage of economic information. Your own professional association may provide economic analysis and forecasting in its publications and programs. Business publications, such as *The Wall Street Journal*, *Forbes*, *Fortune*, *Business Week*, and many others, carry regular articles concerning the macroeconomic situation and significant private and public sector news. State and local governments should be contacted concerning publications and reports they offer which are more specific to your own location. Local chambers of commerce frequently publish an "economic outlook" report. City, county, or state industrial development departments often wage specific campaigns to lure public and private sector organizations and jobs to their jurisdictions. Many cities have a daily or weekly business-oriented newspaper that carries specific information concerning the local scene. Planning departments in most municipalities utilize the services of staff and outside consultants to consider and develop five- to ten-year plans for community development. Colleges and universities frequently have faculty members and departments who are active in economic research in the local area.

I've only scratched the surface of available economic information. The problem will be information overload. You simply don't have the time, nor is it necessary, for you to read and consider every piece of economic data available. What is important and what only you can do is to identify specifically the type of information that is most helpful and relevant in your situation. In addition to the general macro information that can affect every practitioner in a community, particular attention should be given to micro information that can have a direct effect on your individual practice. Becoming economically aware may mean simply talking, reading, and listening as you have time, if you are an individual professional. For the larger organization, this responsibility can be delegated to someone with administrative or client development responsibility. In such a case, this individual would be required to brief staff and professionals concerning important potential changes in the economic environment.

Contingency Planning

Becoming aware of key economic relationships and tracking them over a period of time has a very specific purpose: the development of a contingency plan or approach before the good or bad economic news materializes. These so-called contingency plans or approaches to practice management usually take one of three forms. First, the professional can concentrate on increasing revenues. Second, the professional can concentrate on reducing costs. The third approach involves a combination of the first two. How would you cope if there were a significant downturn in your level of professional activity over a six-month period?

One professional service firm is coping very nicely under those exact circumstances. Just as the microeconomic situation in a southern state deteriorated, the firm called its staff together and developed a plan that would be implemented in the next fiscal year if the trend continued. The program was designed to minimize the bad effects of an economic slowdown, preserve the organization, and have it ready to grow and profit when the economic environment improved. The prospect of "bad times" and the frank communication of the founding professionals was enough to stimulate exceptional staff and professional cooperation. Extra effort was made to ensure that clients received the very finest of care and attention. Everyone from the reception office staff to the accounts receivable clerk did his or her best to preserve client loyalty and existing revenues. Some staff cut back their hours *and* compensation. Existing personnel accepted more responsibilities and duties. Individuals active in practice development made an extra effort to increase the visibility and awareness of the organization to potential clients.

Fortunately, this organization, weathered the storm and came out in a strong position. Its client base is growing again now that the economy is improving. Accounts that normally would have been bad debts are paying off their balances because of the excellent treatment they received during their own period of economic hardship. In the case of this firm, the "contingency plan" consisted of cooperatively developed policies set in anticipation of the event. We can't pretend that this was a totally happy situation; weathering difficult economic times never is. The point is that the organization was ready for it and did an excellent job of minimizing the negative impact on the organization and clients.

A less happy outcome, probably one of many, occurred in a law firm with which I am acquainted during the financial crunch of 1980-81. The firm had a healthy and growing practice specializing in all aspects of real estate. As financing and mortgage costs soared, the firm continued to ignore all signs. "Suddenly," a few major clients cut back drastically on the use of the firm's services. Rather than adapting to the situation, the firm reacted spastically. Staff was discharged, tensions mounted, rumors flew, and a severe cost-cutting and collection campaign ensued. In my judgment, it will take the firm a few years to recover from the bad image it created due to its failure to read the economic signs and develop a contingency plan. I don't know your professional environment and I don't pretend to have the answer to all of life's uncertainties. I do have faith, however, that most professionals can develop creative strategies to cope with economic slowdown or to take advantage of near-term opportunity.

THE POLITICAL ENVIRONMENT

Like all external variables, the importance of the political environment is related to the scope and type of your professional practice. A large national organization must be concerned with the national political setting, whereas the small sole practitioner has the option of political involvement ranging from zero to considerable. The political environment can affect you directly and indirectly. In a direct sense, elected and appointed political officials and the constituencies they represent can become your clients. With over one-third of our nation's gross national product the result of governmental and public sector activities, many professionals provide services to the public as well as private sectors. Understanding the political structure of an agency procuring services like yours is an important step for proposing and securing service contracts. Public officials and their staffs often have wide visibility in the community or market area. Their contacts can cut across functional and organizational lines. In some cases, they could be valuable referral sources for the professional service marketer.

Are you acquainted with the political structure in your community? Do any opportunities for growth exist through broadening your activities in the public sector? Professionals are frequently sought to serve on advisory boards, committees, commissions, and the like. Their ability, special training, and efficiency make them desirable committee members. Such points of visibility offer several advantages. First, professionals can become known to the political infrastructure. Second, working with other influential leaders in the community brings an opportunity to broaden visibility and contacts. Third, they may meet persons in the community constituency who could become eventual purchasers of professional services. This approach is not for everyone. However, it is an approach you should consider if a public sector route is open and productive for you.

The political environment and infrastructure of your market area can have many indirect effects on your practice environment. These include specific regulation of businesses—hours of operation, signing, zoning, handling of consumer and client complaints, fire and safety regulations, and so on. On the more positive side, your city, county, and/or state government might be actively involved in trying to attract public and private sector organizations to your market area.

Some professionals do more than attempt to understand and adapt to the existing political environment. They seek to have an impact by becoming directly involved. This involvement takes the form of actively supporting political candidates or in some cases running for elective office. Professionals with such inclinations often ask me, "Should I get involved in politics?" This is a very personal question and one which no one can answer for another individual. Active and visible political involvement runs the risk of alienating current and future clients who may not share your political views. If it is not necessary for you to be cognizant of the economic outcomes of your political activities, then this caveat is not applicable.

The best approach I have seen concerning active support of political activity is by a professional group that contributes equally to major party candidates in its area. The group lets both candidates know that it believes in being politically active. It believes in the analysis and airing of issues and the democratic process. Splitting support for both political groups helps, its members say, to get the issues before the public, where the electorate can make the best decision. This approach has put them in good standing with both parties and with the political infrastructure of the local communities.

Is this a political cop-out? To this question, my colleagues reply: "No—this is just the well-established business practice of spreading the risk." As in the economic environment, the most important step is to identify any relationships in the political area that could have a significant effect on your practice. Where significant relationships exist, public sector entities may actually become part of your client development target markets. On the other hand, an individual practitioner working with private clients may have little, if any, reason to become concerned about or involved with the political structure.

THE LEGAL ENVIRONMENT

Public Laws

Do any public laws or ordinances have a significant impact on the way your practice is conducted? How are clients treated under the law? Are there professional codes or regulations that affect you directly? What is your exposure and extent of potential liability to damaging legal action by dissatisfied clients, competitors, and the public at large? For the majority of individual professionals serving private clients, federal, state, county, and local laws deal with occupational licensing, taxation, unemployment and workmen's compensation, benefits for staff, occupational safety, and other general administrative areas. In addition, some communities may have ordinances dealing with hours of operation, architectural requirements, signing, parking, and other areas related more directly to the conduct of the individual organization. The larger the organization, the higher the overhead costs and administrative burdens imposed by these laws and regulations. While the professed philosophy of the federal government is to emphasize deregulation, it will probably be a long time until professionals feel any relief from the administrative costs and burden of the present. There is only one saving grace in this situation, if you can call it that. All competing professionals are bound by the same constraints, so that a competitive advantage resulting from these aspects of the legal environment is reduced.

Professional Regulations

Another set of written rules and procedures does have an important bearing on your practice. These are the rules and regulations of your professional association. Self-regulation of professionals is designed to provide a consistent level of quality service to clients. In addition, regulation is designed to ensure that certified professionals meet certain minimum standards in terms of education and experience. The promulgation and enforcement of self-imposed regulation has much to do with the public's image of the specific professional group. Unfortunately, investigation and enforcement by professionals are done on a spare-time, voluntary basis. Only the most flagrant, stupid, or unlucky violators seem to get caught. Frequently, it is media attention based on vociferous protest that causes professional boards to take action.

As you can see, I am concerned and perhaps beginning to sermonize concerning professional regulation. However, I wonder if you would not agree that a significant marketing advantage is lost when any professional group loses its standing in the eyes of its clients and the public? Ironically, the good guys far outnumber the bad guys, and yet most of us seem to behave like the silent majority—too busy or involved to play our part in the policing of our ranks. There is a marketing opportunity here, I believe, particularly for the firm that wishes to be known as "the professionals' professional." Being actively involved in professional regulation can create visibility for you and your organization that can lead to referral and consultation arrangements. In addition, clients who know of your activity may see you in a slightly different way than they see your competing professional colleagues.

Is it incongruous to talk about professional conduct and marketing in the same context? I certainly don't think so. Professional marketing is much different from marketing beer, tobacco products, and soap. Professionals have always marketed. The sharpening, focusing, and systematic implementation of marketing programs can be accomplished in concert with the professional image.

Malpractice

Today's legal environment carries an ominous and ever-present threat: malpractice. Believe it or not, the magazine *Academe*, a publication for members of the American Association of University Professors, now carries advertising for teacher liability insurance! That's right—you could finally "get your professor." For example, the Buckley amendment passed in the 1970s dealing with student rights prohibits the public posting of student grades. Attorneys at my university inform us that the only protection against being sued is to have written permission from every student in the class before any grades are posted by name. This legislation and the ominous atmosphere it created was based on student complaints that their privacy had been violated when their grades had been posted. I don't mean to imply that the legal exposure for the faculty member may be as severe as that for a neurosurgeon, but all professionals must realize that we live in an age of "sue-er" mentality. Frequently, professionals are viewed as having deep pockets, and any malcontent with the slightest complaint seems anxious to dig in and take a share.

As you assess your professional environment, I'd like you to consider what legal exposure you have. If you are an engineering consultant, what happens if a system or structure you design does not perform up to specification, or worse yet, fails or collapses? Legal exposure can take an even more ironic twist. One of the Southeast's largest local CPA firms is being sued by a client. The suit has been brought against each of the firm's partners. The basis of the suit is that the CPA firm failed to do exactly as the client had directed, resulting in the client's having to pay taxes and penalty. The problem is that what the client directed the CPA firm to do is allegedly illegal. Although it appears that the accounting organization will win this suit, the initial publicity in both the business and general media has created a negative effect.

Each time I work with an attorney, I ask her or him how I should advise other professionals concerning liability exposure. Their advice can be summed up in five principles.

First, be informed. This involves spending the time and money to identify and understand the content and scope of possible legal exposure. Your attorney and potential liability insurers can be helpful here. Second, be vigilant. Don't let fear of possible legal action paralyze your professional practice. At the same time, part of your assessment of each professional situation should involve potential legal consequences. Third, be prepared. Analyze, compare, and acquire appropriate liability insurance if you can afford it. In addition, establish a relationship with an attorney or law firm compatible with your own position or status. Having immediate legal counsel available can usually stop the majority of phony liability claims and threats. Fourth, act quickly to investigate and settle, if possible, any legal matters that might cloud your professional environment. The potential unfavorable publicity of a prolonged fight may not be worth it. And finally, fight when you're right. Naturally, litigating attorneys love this one! Yet if professionals knuckle under to every threat, they are guilty by implication in the minds of many people.

In the case of the CPA firm mentioned earlier, it is my opinion that the client will be soundly beaten in court. If my opinion is correct, the favorable outcome of the case will be publicized, and the firm and its partners will enjoy a considerable amount of favorable publicity. The community will be left with the impression that although the firm does everything possible to minimize clients' taxes, it always operates within the law.

There is another unfortunate, yet very practical aspect to controlling your own legal environment. Professionals cannot reform the world. There will always be a certain percentage of troublesome and dishonest clients. Presenting a well-informed and firm legal posture can help eliminate these clients from your environment and leave them for your competitors to deal with.

ETHICS

Ethics are criteria for conduct. They specify what should or ought to be. Ideally, professional ethical codes should be drafted, analyzed, and accepted based on input from the majority of the professional constituency. Further, these codes should be reviewed for relevance and updated as appropriate. No matter how relevant or eloquent a particular code might be, it has little or no meaning if it is not followed or enforced. Earlier in the book, we noted specific situations in law and medicine where ethical codes have undergone significant reexamination and modification, particularly in the area of marketing professional services. Ideally, each professional should be involved in and concerned about the ethical behavior of colleagues and competitors. But now let's look at the real world.

In many of the older and established professions, such as medicine, law, dentistry, and public accounting, we find strong national professional associations. In addition, state associations and local chapters of professionals come under these national umbrellas. The national associations have full-time staff, and both human and financial resources. Their responsibilities include not only public and governmental relations, professional education and communication, but also the maintenance of ethical codes and professional regulation. Individual practitioners at the local level are seldom involved with or concerned about the profession's ethics; they are more involved in operating their practice or organization. Usually, it takes a serious breach of professional behavior, accompanied by publicity, to mobilize local practitioners, and even then this attention to ethics may be episodic. Further, there may be conflict between the national pronouncements, state interpretations, and the feelings of area and individual professional chapter members and practitioners. This exacerbates the problem of self-regulation and enforcement.

Is there an answer to this dilemma of conflict and confusion concerning ethics and self-regulation? There is, and it's no mystery. It involves the development of professional association membership and active involvement by the numerical majority of professionals in every field. This means you; this means me. Each of us, individually and collectively, should be involved on an ongoing basis, as part of the fulfillment of our professional responsibility, in the development, monitoring, and enforcement of our own ethical codes. Will this occur? I doubt it. Our busy and fragmented professional and personal life styles don't seem to allow the time or energy for dealing with these aspects of our professional environment on more than an ad hoc or episodic basis.

As I mentioned earlier, this creates a marketing opportunity for some professionals to gain visibility by filling the vacuum of leadership in local, state, and national professional organizations. Please recognize that this is only one of many possible ways to gain visibility and do good work. Also, keep in mind that attorneys are clients for other attorneys only to a limited extent. Your professional association work is only a limited part of your marketing effort. But if we as professionals are unwilling to be involved in self-regulation, we can continue to expect an acceleration of what has happened since the 1960s—an increase in governmental regulation and consumer activism. It is clear that if we don't write and enforce the rules, someone else is bound to.

THE NATURAL AND CULTURAL ENVIRONMENT

You might wonder what trees and hills and climate have to do with your practice environment, or perhaps you have already guessed the point. The part of the country you are in, the topography, the weather, the physical layout, the cultural and ethnic composition of the population may hold clues for practice growth and development.

For example, I've spent a good deal of my personal and professional time in the widely diverse areas of the Northeast (New York-New Jersey metropolitan area and the New Jersey-Philadelphia metropolitan area.), the Sunbelt (southwest Texas and south Florida), and the mountain states (primarily Colorado). One of my biggest cultural shocks and most important professional lessons came when I moved from the Northeast to the Southwest. Even though I was on the consulting staff on one of the big eight accounting firms, my "Eastern ways" as a martini-drinking, fedora-wearing, umbrella-carrying Ivy Leaguer were a barrier rather than a benefit. It took a while to realize that I wasn't going to conquer Texas.

When I finally looked around, understood that I would have to adapt, and got down to the business of doing it, my career progressed remarkably. I began to gain acceptance by the leadership group in business and government. In addition to CPAs, attorneys, and members of the financial community, I had a chance to get to know another professional group. My wife ran a small clinic for five medical professionals, including a dentist. Through her job, we had the opportunity for some social contact with these individuals. Many of them were from other parts of the country, and it was interesting to see how they had adapted to their new environment. If a particular patient was a rancher, they were able to talk ranching; if another patient enjoyed deer hunting, they had their own hunting stories to tell. Since many of the patients were Mexican-Americans, there was also a special sensitivity and appreciation of Mexican food, culture, and music. They adapted to the southwestern life style and let people know that they enjoyed it. These physicians became part of the infrastructure of the community. Their practices thrived. I'm sure they were extremely competent technically. But I'm equally sure that they were extremely competent marketers.

If you're establishing a new area of professional service, look carefully at the natural environment. The key concepts are diagnosing and adapting. Try to determine how the natural environment affects opportunities for marketing your service. Has it meant that a certain type of industry has been attracted to the area? Has it resulted in a certain type of commercial structure? Does the climate or the ecology or recreational opportunities affect local economic activities? South Florida has very little manufacturing. It does have, however, a strong base of small and medium sized, and a few large sized, "clean industries." These firms are involved in everything from computers and electronics to retailing and international banking.

The marketing of consumer and industrial services probably accounts for the largest share of the local economy. Retailing, hospitality, transportation, private education, and entertainment are some examples. The climate is semitropical, with the emphasis on informal outdoor living. Abundant water provides unlimited recreational opportunities as well as unique settings for professional offices and locations. A professional seeking to establish a practice or organization in south Florida could not lose sight of the fact that over a third of the population of the

Greater Miami area is Latin. In addition, being the gateway to Latin America, a steady stream of Latin visitors flow through the market as tourists, investors, and entrepreneurs. They purchase a wide variety of professional services. The natural environment has a very direct effect on many factors, ranging from office location and decor to staff and labor resources.

If you are currently offering your professional services in an existing market, you may have made the necessary analyses and adaptations. If you merely hung out your shingle and waited to see who showed up, you may be missing some major and minor adaptations in your offering that could result in improved growth and/or profitability. Finally, if you are a new professional or are thinking of branching, you have a chance to give more complete and careful consideration to locating in a market where your own unique characteristics and those of your service are most appropriately matched to the environment and the opportunities it presents.

THE COMPETITIVE ENVIRONMENT

Every form of economic enterprise faces competition. The degree and intensity of the competition varies considerably. In addition, the scope of competition ranges from indirect to direct. As professionals, we face direct competition when another professional offering similar services seeks to win a client away from us or to woo a prospective client to that particular firm. Indirect competition comes from a wide variety of discretionary expenditures our potential clients can make. An example of such indirect competition is a case in which a computer and systems analysis consulting firm is proposing a computer feasibility study to an industrial client. The industrial client has about $20,000 budgeted in its uncommitted funds category. After considering the professional services expenditure, the management committee decides to refurbish the company's restrooms! The professional may wonder what went wrong and how the firm could have competed more effectively. However, in this case competition was not another consulting organization, but alternative uses for limited discretionary funds by the prospective client. In the case of direct competition, professionals should be in a position to know their opposition and to sell directly against the service mix being offered by the competitor. In the case of indirect competition, the primary strategy is to demonstrate to the prospect the advantage of making this expenditure now as opposed to postponing it to some future time.

Analyzing Competition

Many formats can be utilized to analyze competition. No one model will satisfy all needs. In *How to Market Your Law Practice,* Gilson, Cauley, and Schmidt[1] remind us:

> Because it's only realistic to assume that some other firms in your area may be conducting marketing analysis themselves these days, there is every reason

to keep well-informed about the nature and direction of their growth plans. You may even glean some information from your current clients in this regard as you audit your own performance. Other sources of competitive information abound in your community—advertising activity, speeches and seminars that other firms are conducting, news stories that their public relations staffs are getting into the local media, plus grapevine information that persons in your firm pick up through their own contacts.

These authors recommend that lawyers should assemble data in three categories, including the level of marketing activity observed in other firms. How high is their level of marketing consciousness, and which are most aggressive? What type of clients are the aggressive firms pursuing? Second, they recommend developing a client profile of competitor firms. The objective is to pinpoint opportunities for potential client satisfaction where competing firms might be lax in meeting changing needs. Finally, lawyers are encouraged to make service quality evaluations of their competition. Identifying strengths and weaknesses can help the individual practitioner or firm to best direct their own efforts to fill a market opportunity.

To help you structure your own review of the competitive environment, I've developed the material shown in Figure 5-1, "Your Professional Environment—A Competitive Review". The use of this form and approach will vary according to the individual practice or firm. As a minimum, you should be able to fill in a significant number of the blanks for your direct and major competitors. The ideal situation would be for you to have a complete competitive analysis, but even though it might be impossible to obtain every piece of data about every direct competitor, time spent analyzing competition can lead to inputs for developing competitive and client acquisition strategies. Let's briefly review some of the key components of Figure 5-1.

Personal Contact

It's a truism in professional marketing that the majority of new clients come from existing clients. The second major source seems to be referrals from other professionals who for one reason or another cannot or do not choose to handle the requirements of a particular client. It's important that you establish personal contacts within key competitive organizations. Make it a point to find out who the "shakers" and "movers" are, as well as the backup, key research, and operations people. In addition to discovering marketing opportunities, you'll be in a better position to build an inventory of key staff and professional candidates. Finally, merger and co-venture possibilities are enlarged. Gaining a picture of the multiple locations of competitors is an interesting way of tracking indirectly where the action is in the particular specialties they promote. Gaining an idea of the staff composition of competitors can be revealing. For example, a matter was referred to a local law firm by a national company. A competing firm was also contacted as a candidate to handle the matter. The "second choice" actually got the business. Why? Even though the first law firm had an excellent reputation, it simply did not have the full-time staff and backup organization to service the large action that

FIGURE 5-1 *YOUR PRACTICE ENVIRONMENT—A COMPETITIVE REVIEW*

1. Competitor I.D. and Address _____
   _____

2. Branch Location? a. _____
                     b. _____
                     c. _____

3. Key Executive—Names, titles, areas of expertise
   a. _____
   b. _____
   c. _____
   etc. _____

4. Other Key Personnel and Specialties
   a. _____
   b. _____
   c. _____
   etc. _____

5. Service Mix—Range of volume if possible. (e.g. major to minor service offerings.)
   a. _____
   b. _____
   c. _____
   etc. _____

6. Client Mix—List and/or discussion
   a. _____
   b. _____
   c. _____

7. Fee Structure (obtain schedules if possible)
   Type of work_____ , Fees as of 198X_____

8. Perceived Image and/or Positioning
   _____
   _____

9. Key Strengths
   _____
   _____

10. Key Weaknesses
    _____
    _____

11. Competitive Ranking and Competitive Strategy Statement
    _____
    _____

would be required to handle the matter successfully. The competing law firm pointed out to general counsel for the client corporation that although the first firm had an excellent reputation in litigation, it did not have the paralegal, research, clerical, word processing and other types of resources to handle the matter. The second-place firm found a weakness, recorded it, and later exploited it to advantage.

Service and Client Mix

Gaining some understanding of the service mix emphasis offered by competitors is fairly simple. Competitors will often share information concerning their areas of emphasis and expertise. They're hoping you will refer matters to them or include them as part of a team if a client requires complete service. Under client mix, try to identify clients by type—corporations, individuals, private sector, public sector. In addition, attempt to identify segments within the type of clientele your competition serves. For example, if a dental clinic services primarily private sector, lower-class individuals, that might signal an opportunity for presenting dental plans to public sector personnel such as school system employees, or perhaps to the industrial sector by means of mobile clinics offered on a company-by-company visitation schedule.

Fee Structure

If competitors have made proposals to public sector prospects, their proposals and fee structures could be a matter of public record; however, remember that fee structures and pricing policies change with time. My experience indicates that fee structures are relatively similar within market segments. For example, pharmacies providing prescription services to HMO members may be rather close in the dollar cost of annual prescription experience. In well-defined segments, nonprice competition, including numbers of locations, hours of operation, credit and payment plans, client education and information services, and so forth, typically become substitutes for competitive pricing. The exception is usually the new marketer on the scene. In such cases, penetration pricing may be used to obtain client trial. Pricing across market segments can vary, since the professional's experience in one or two segments may have created efficiencies, whereas a relatively new or unique type of engagement involves a certain learning curve that to some extent must be sponsored by the client.

Positioning

Based on the detailed information you are able to collect for items 1 through 7, attempt to position the firm in the competitive spectrum. (Later, in Chapter 7, We'll show you how to develop a positioning statement for your firm. You'll feel more comfortable with this convenient, conceptual tool.) For example, let's assume the competitor you are evaluating seems to be positioning its practice as that of the "professional's professional." This probably means that it is striving to be regarded as the most highly competent and up-to-date organization in the technical aspects of its operations. Once you have positioned this mythical major competitor, your information sources or own personal experience should be focused on identifying on the overall tactics the competitor is utilizing in marketing its skills.

Frequently, firms with this positioning are very active in professional associations, appear on panels and conference programs and serve as guest speakers, devote part of their time to research in their discipline that results in publication in scholarly and professional journals, and so on. If this is the case, your decision will be to determine whether you want to go head-to-head with this competitor or whether you will seek to find an unfulfilled market niche in areas of reduced competitive pressure.

Key Strengths and Weaknesses

These analysis items are useful in marketing strategy formulation and just as useful when you have to go head-to-head on a client opportunity against a particular competitor. I'm acquainted with three psychologists whose offices are within three miles of one another in a densely populated upper-middle and upper-class bedroom suburb. All three specialize in family counseling, particularly in situations involving marriage, divorce, separations, and child-parent relationships. When contemplating a lengthy period of counseling, more and more affluent and well-educated families are comparison shopping. They seek initial consultations with two or more counselors, and base their final decision on this exposure.

One of these professionals, in addition to being an eminently qualified psychologist, is a crackerjack marketer. He levels with clients during the initial consultation and tells them the type of person he is. He talks about his philosophy of counseling and his approaches. Why does he make a special point of doing this? Because he's aware that his local major competitors come across initially as being somewhat aloof. In addition, male family members seem to feel somewhat threatened initially by his competitors. Although it's often the wife who makes the initial contact, the final veto power is sometimes held by the husband. Women clients of the successful psychologist seem almost relieved that their men feel comfortable with this professional. This strategy has been consciously conceived and carefully developed to take advantage of the key weaknesses in the competitors' professional posture.

This professional's calendar is booked well in advance, and even canceled appointments are snapped up eagerly by clients and prospects who are placed on a waiting list. I'm not suggesting that a marketing gimmick can alter the basic personality of any professional; it's simply my position that effective marketing can enhance, accelerate, and perpetuate professional success.

Ranking and a Competitive Strategy Statement

This item has both a single and a collective function. If you are a new professional or entering a new area, theoretically the sum of all the competitive review statements would completely describe the current situation in your professional service environment. You could then look for unfulfilled needs, complementary relationships, or areas where you might wish to go head-to-head with existing practitioners. I'm in the process of developing such an analysis at the present time for a medical group. The results of the analysis will determine the specific recommendations we make on how to position and implement the service the medical group plans to offer.

On an individual basis, if you are ever placed in a direct selling situation against a competitor, your competitive strategy statement ought to describe your basic reaction. Although it would not be ethical or professional to downgrade a professional colleague being considered by a prospect, I can find no fault with letting the prospect know how you operate, carefully stressing the ways in which you are different from your unnamed competitor. Ultimately, the prospect will make the decision. That's what the marketplace is all about. This is precisely the strategy utilized by the successful psychologist in our previous example, and it will be the strategy followed by the medical group members as they open and promote their service facility.

Marketing professionals in the industrial and consumer goods and services areas don't have a one-track mind—they have a two-track mind! For example, Christopher Gibbs, founder and president of Car and Truck Leasing, Inc., has stated: "Each time I write a marketing plan for a new product, service or venture, I also sit down and write my competitor's marketing plan." What Mr. Gibbs means is that the competitive environment is such a factor in his business that he anticipates the competition's reaction to his marketing activities and prepares in writing his own reaction to their reactions. He knows that his competitors are behaving in precisely the same way. In my experience, most professionals are only beginning to pay sufficient attention to the competitive aspects of their environment. Indeed, it is often thought "unprofessional" to compete or to acknowledge that there is intraprofessional competition. Failing to consider the direct and indirect competition can be a serious professional services marketing mistake. Although the competitive environment may not have the direct impact it does in the consumer and industrial arenas, I believe it is growing in importance for professionals.

TECHNOLOGY

This is going to be a very short section. "Thank goodness," you say? You really shouldn't. The reason this section will be short is that it's impossible for me to be specific about the developing technologies in the various professions. First of all, no one individual could be that thoroughly informed. Second, it would take a whole volume to identify and go into all the applications. The simplest definition of technology I've ever heard is this: "the study of techniques we use to do things." Using this base, we can say that technological developments refer to changes, hopefully for the better, in the way we do things that make them more efficient and effective. Technology often involves processes and equipment. But just changing the financial recordkeeping system of your practice so that you have more up-to-date and accurate information concerning client profitability can be an important technological improvement.

What Using Technology Means

Technology takes two forms in professional service marketing. First, what's happening in the technology we use in the direct delivery of service to clients? Second, what's happening in the technology utilized to manage ourselves and our organizations? If you're thinking the line between these two is somewhat blurred, I agree. Earlier, we talked about one of the unique aspects of service marketing—the difficulty of separating the producer of the service from the service. Marketing theorists refer to this as the *producer/service unity*. How is technology related? Let's take some simple examples.

Suppose a client goes to a physical therapist in conjunction with a therapeutic accident recovery program. Therapist A studies the situation carefully, examines the patient, then prescribes a series of self-administered, at-home exercises. Therapist B, after doing the same analysis, sets up a series of sessions in a carefully appointed fitness room. This room utilizes the latest in ultrasonic, whirlpool, flex and stress, and heat therapy equipment. Let's assume that a patient utilizing the services of therapist A performs faithfully all the exercises prescribed. Another patient utilizes the services of therapist B's fitness room. If the results were identical in terms of patient benefits, it's my guess that therapist B would enjoy the stronger professional image and a sustained rate of client satisfaction feedback and referral. One therapist has used technology to advantage; another has not.

In another application, assume that a CPA firm had a well-developed computer-based system of client accounting. Work performed for clients was recorded weekly based on a predetermined numerical and personnel code. Client invoices were prepared accurately and completely with a description of the work performed, the professionals involved, and the fees and expenses due. Invoices were mailed promptly—immediately after the service was rendered. This use of technology would probably result in a higher collection rate and fewer fee writedowns. Clients would also be impressed in general by the professional way in which their own accountants managed their practice. These cases are based on two specific professional firms: the names have been omitted to protect the confidential relationship. However, in both cases, the firms track the technological developments related to the performance of their services which they feel could give them a competitive edge in the marketplace.

Does technology always mean expensive equipment, investment, or elaborate expert consultation? Not at all. A law firm client of mine invested heavily in a microcomputer practice administration system. The vendor justified this investment based on the gross billing size of the firm and said it was time for the firm to get into computers. The system was a disaster. In addition to mechanical problems, the firm's personnel were ill-suited to its use. The marketing result was negative. Clients became unhappy with inaccurate and late bills. Other technical matters in-house were botched. The senior partner wisely threw up his hands, scrapped the entire system, and went to a simple but efficient manual procedure. Fortunately, the equipment was leased. The installation of the manual procedure was, for this firm, a new form of technology. Even though the firm had a high gross billing figure, the manual system was suited to a small number of large, retainer-type and long-term clients.

Monitoring Technology

How does one monitor technology? I suspect the majority of professionals utilize a rather traditional approach. First, if they are members and if they are involved in their professional association, they may attend a session at the annual conference dealing with technological advances. Second, if they receive and review the professional journal related to their field, they may find articles and/or advertisements relating to technology. And finally, if they are able to give up 15 or 20 minutes of their time to a vendor of technological equipment and services, they may have an opportunity to learn directly. Ideally, the process should be reversed. Professionals should seek out and perhaps even be involved in developing technology that would improve the efficiency of their service in both the direct and the indirect sense. However, nothing succeeds like success. In a large and successful professional firm, there may be an individual responsible for monitoring, analyzing, and implementing the latest in technology. The individual professional may not have time or the funds to go much beyond the basics, at least during the beginning of the practice. Yet it is the firm that wishes to be a more effective marketer that is in greatest need of differentiating itself from competitors.

Technical and professional journals, as well as conference sessions, and workshop participation are one of the best ways to become familiar with technological changes. As a minimum, you and your staff should be involved in this type of monitoring. You should also identify the leading vendors of technology in your field. Make it a point to invite them to your office. Let them know that they are welcome as your schedule permits. Schedule time each month, or as appropriate, to see, chat with, and listen to these specialists. Don't close your door or your mind to the new marketer who wants 15 minutes of your time to acquaint you with a new or different way of operating.

Keep in mind the following suggestions: (1) If over time you're not changing the way you do things (not necessarily what you do), you're probably out of date. (2) Before you embrace a major change in technology, try it out on an experimental basis. Most vendors are willing to take this risk if they feel you are sincerely interested. (3) If you discover a technological change that will have a significant effect on clients or the way you practice—wait! Don't be stampeded or pressured by anyone or anything. As a minimum, take the following steps: (a) Invite other vendors of the equipment or service provided to analyze the application, to analyze the competitive proposal, and to prepare proposals of their own. (b) If the change involves a significant financial and operational commitment, such as an in-house computer system, consider calling in a consultant for an objective review. For example, the management services departments of CPA firms have developed a substantial practice in objectively analyzing the proposals of computer equipment manufacturers and vendors for clients who are considering such equipment. (c) If you are a corporation, partnership, or professional association, form a task force to evaluate the technological change and to recommend if, how, and when it should be implemented. (4) Please, *orient your existing clients and new clients concerning the ways in which the new technology benefits them.* (We'll talk more about this in Chapter 9.)

The only thing worse than becoming obsolete is generating continued and unnecessary change. Try to stay somewhere between these two extremes as you continue to evaluate and integrate emerging technology in your field.

THE MANAGERIAL ENVIRONMENT

The managerial environment refers to the system you or your organization have developed to allocate human, financial, and physical resources to the accomplishment of your objectives. This is probably the most highly variable and structurally unbound portion of a professional's environment. In a large engineering consulting firm, you might expect to find full-time administrative personnel. Their job descriptions and talents would range from data processing and accounting to personnel management and marketing. A new professional engineer joining the staff would be somewhat constrained by existing policies and procedures that have become institutionalized as a result of the management infrastructure. On the other hand, an individual professional engineer may be seeking her first consulting project. She might be operating out of her home or may have just signed a lease on a professional office. In such a case, the management structure is whatever that individual decides it should be. If you are a partner in a law firm, for example, your interest in stimulating professionalized marketing activities will have to be tailored to the existing infrastructure. This will include not only the managerial process by which decisions are made, but also the political process that may operate outside the formal managerial organization. Giving up part of your professional latitude to an organization is a decision each professional faces when he or she decides to become a member of a firm instead of operating a private practice. Realistically, even a two-person organization introduces some variance in the managerial environment. An attorney with a large and successful real-estate-based practice asked me to conduct a marketing audit of the practice and make recommendations concerning marketing professional services. The engagement never got off the ground. The attorney's partner refused to pay "his share" of the costs. This left the senior partner to pay 100 percent of the fee and resulted in the indefinite postponement of the review.

Specialization

I'm not an expert in managerial and administrative structures for professional organizations. It's a fascinating field, and one deserving of some of your time should your organization grow beyond the one- or two-person stage. There is one principle, however, that I believe that we as professionals can agree upon. I'm referring to the principle of specialization. If you're a member of a dental group, don't give the task of patient relations and development to the hottest oral surgeon on the team. In fact, it may not be cost effective at all to have a dentist or even a paradental person charged with that responsibility. If the clinic or dental group is growing, it may be time to hire an administrator. As the practice grows, an administrative staff, properly developed, can leverage professional time, effectiveness, and profitability, and more than pay for its own cost. The swing toward professional management in the medical fields, for example, has already taken place for that very reason. Public accounting firms often adopt a "managing partner" format and centralize the administrative duties in that office. In effect, the firm's partners give up certain authority to the managing partner and staff to perform the administrative functions of the practice on their behalf. Typically, management and administrative partners are appointed for specific period of time and reappointed based on a vote of the partnership.

Special Help

When should you as a professional move toward getting special help in the management area? My answer is—before you need to. Nothing is more frustrating or annoying to the consumer of professional services than to have the servicing professional preoccupied with minor administrative details. If this happens constantly, it is usually a sign that the practice is running the professional rather than vice versa. As you find yourself in that position, it is important to act quickly to get the administrative support and help you need. Failure to make these investments in monthly salaries for specialized personnel could result in limitation of services performed for existing clients or worse, the loss of existing clients. Finally, it is difficult to demonstrate the ability to serve more or larger clients unless the organizational infrastructure is in place, or at least the foundation stones have been laid. I am not suggesting that you rush out and hire ten people the moment you seem a little busier than usual. I am suggesting that when the level of activity seems to be picking up and sustaining itself, an additional investment in administrative and management expenses should be seriously considered.

The Large Organization

What if you find yourself in a large professional organization? How can you deal with the managerial environment? Basically, you can attempt to change it or accept it and work within the existing procedures to effect the changes you believe in. Whatever approach you select, you may wish to consider the advice of a CPA friend. This person is the head of a tax department in a large CPA firm. He has never liked the firm's managerial structure. He has sought over the years to change it and has had some success. However, his candidness and methodology have not necessarily endeared him to all the partners in the firm. One day I asked him, "Considering how critical you are of the organization's structure and managerial system, how did you ever get to be a partner, and how were you able to effect the changes you have?" "I'm good," he replied. "I know my taxes and I bring in more tax business than any other member of the firm." I have to admit he is right. He is good. And over the years the infrastructure had to recognize him and deal with his demands for more participatory decision making.

The Competition

In addition to looking for strengths and weaknesses, if there are any, in your own managerial environment, don't forget your competition. You may find weaknesses in the levels at which key decisions can be made and the speed with which final decisions can be reached. I'm aware of a consulting firm whose regional office had to approve any expenditures that exceeded a certain limit for proposal development and presentation. The managing partner of the office involved, against her better judgment, forwarded the request to the regional office. While the office was waiting for authorization, a major competitor landed the handsome $35,000 project. Is there something in your competition's management structure that might make it less sensitive, less responsive, less able to deal with a prospect's service needs?

Before we can hope to market professional services successfully, we must clearly understand just what it is we're marketing. Who are you? What is your organization? What is the environment in which you function? There are many ways to conceptualize the environment(s) of a manager. Whatever method is utilized, an environmental assessment holds two important promises. First, it makes us more realistic about what we can accomplish and what we might not be able to accomplish. Second, an important by-product of the analysis is usually the discovery or enhancement of marketing strategy or tactics that can be used to sharpen the effectiveness of the marketing planning process.

Chapter 6
Client Analysis and Targeting

This chapter has three major objectives. First, the materials presented will help you step back, exchange roles with your clients, and gain clearer insight into how they seek, evaluate, and select providers of professional services. The ultimate objective of these discussions will be to assist you in developing a client behavior map that will suggest the most appropriate ways to modify or influence client behavior in your favor. Second, a four-step approach will be presented to help you go from the general to the specific in identifying specific marketing targets for your MPS activities. Third, the topic of marketing research will be presented, with special emphasis on how traditional marketing research techniques can be adapted to the professional service environment.

YOU THE ANALYST

The foundation of any effective marketing program is as thorough an understanding as possible of what clients want, the reasons for their specific desires, and how they seek and purchase services. Theoretically at least, if a professional had a complete answer to all these questions and was both qualified and flexible, a marketing mix could be designed that would match client needs perfectly. Why does this happen only in theory? Because client needs are not precisely known or defined;

client behavior may be inconsistent; clients may not have sufficient knowledge or understanding to make a fully informed or intelligent search; and clients may not be able correctly to evaluate the qualifications of competing professionals.

In addition, many professionals are less than flexible in the practice of their craft. Professional training can result in an attitude of "I am the expert." If a professional truly believes this and disregards the unique needs, desires, and circumstances of each client, we are dealing with a production- or operations-oriented individual. Remember in Chapters 1 and 2 when we talked about the difference between a marketing orientation and a production orientation? A marketing orientation requires that professionals be tuned to and take the time to study and understand individual client needs and to respond to the unique differences in each client situation. This in no way implies that professionals must prostitute themselves, their ethics, their training, or their standards. It does mean, however, an important difference in orientation. Let's examine the what, the why, and the how of professional service client behavior.

What Do Clients Buy?

Clients buy S/S—security and service. Individuals seeking the advice and services of a professional usually have some sort of problem or opportunity that involves risk and uncertainty. They're not able to resolve this uncertainty or to define or minimize the risk themselves. They need help. This situation results in an unsettled emotional state on the part of most clients. They are insecure; they are unsure. This insecurity is reduced over time and through experience in the professional service marketplace.

An individual going through a divorce is much different (Heaven forbid!) the second or third time around. A bank board of directors that has decided to purchase or enter into a long-term lease for a computer is anxious about this decision. After two or three changes in their data-processing system, this anxiety and uncertainty may be reduced. However, it is essential that professionals focus on the emotional hookup with clients. This is particularly true of potential new clients, and even to a great extent of clients experienced in the professional service area. If a prospect or current client comes to you for consultation, your first task is to impress upon this person your sincere interest and understanding of his or her unique, individual situation. Your first personal selling job is to listen sincerely, to provide positive feedback through an attentive posture, nodding of the head, and brief reinforcing comments. This behavior reinforces the prospect's perception that he or she does indeed have a problem, that the problem is a significant one, and that you are sincerely interested in learning about the situation. Unfortunately, many professionals skip this step in marketing. They move too quickly to the second S in the equation—providing the service.

Many professionals are too quick to talk about and point up their technical, operational, and methodological expertise. Actually, most prospects are quite unqualified to evaluate and in some cases to even understand what the professional is talking about. The results of many professional services cannot be evaluated until some time after the service is performed. For example, if a management consulting firm proposes a complicated computer analysis to a bank's board of directors, it is only after the system is installed and operating that the bank can decide whether the recommendations of the consultants were valid. Yes, your clients need to know that you can reduce the risk, solve the problem, remove the uncertainty. Part of your marketing effort, including your personal and written communication, as well as the atmosphere of your professional environment, must convey that message. The greatest current weakness, though, seems to be making the emotional linkage that then smooths the way for reception of the service-related communication.

If clients are coming to you for security, for emotional relief, for removal of risk or risk reduction, how do you rate at conveying your understanding and empathy? Do yourself a favor and be honest. If you really don't care much about these aspects of the practice and don't like to spend time and energy on interpersonal relationships, you need to face that fact. Can you still compete effectively? Certainly. Professionals who are more competent and comfortable on the technical service side augment their deficiency through atmosphere, systems, and staff support.

I'm acquainted with a clinic of orthopedic specialists. One of the physicians is extremely gracious, enjoys people, and consciously seeks to make that emotional hookup with every new client and existing client he sees. This professional understands that part of what his clients are buying is security, reinforcement, and emotional support. Another surgeon in the group has the interpersonal skills of King Kong. He is rude, abrupt, and short with clients, yet he is probably one of the most effective surgeons and best diagnosticians in the area. This professional's practice is carefully orchestrated. His offices are given particular attention in terms of ability to make clients comfortable and relaxed. Extra staff are available to give personal attention and interact with the clients in every possible way short of professional diagnosis and treatment. A nurse, extremely skilled in interpersonal interaction, remains with the doctor through all examinations and treatment. In effect, this professional association understands the shortcomings of this physician and buffers them with facility, the systems, and staff. The approach works quite nicely, and I've seen it adapted in professional settings from medicine to law to management consulting to public accounting to pharmacy.

Why Do Clients Buy?

Individuals and institutions deal with professionals of all types for two basic reasons. The first reason is that they wish to. The second reason is that they are forced to. I'll provide a few examples. I'm sure your imagination will permit you to adapt them to your own situation. When was the last time you spent your spare time shopping and comparing dentists? If you're like me, you never have. You go to the dentist because you must—you hurt or you're having a problem. As a client, you assume that most dentists meet certain minimum standards or they would not be awarded a degree. Convenience is probably a prime factor in your selection of the professional. Once you've made your initial choice, your experience with that professional and the prices charged will probably determine whether you become a regular client or give another professional a try next time.

Naïve professionals may be quite pleased that a client chose them. However, our egos are quickly deflated when we find out the basis on which we were selected. Frequently, the clients have not done any comparative shopping, and know very little about the services we offer. Selection may be a matter of chance or convenience, rather than the result of our fantastic expertise or worldwide reputation. Clients are not particularly thrilled to be with us, to spend money to be represented before the IRS, or to analyze a complex business decision, a medical problem, a divorce, or building code requirements for architectural drawings. Considering this reality, it is doubly important that professionals focus on the emotional uniqueness and needs of the client.

In the case where clients come to us because they wish to, they are typically seeking a special or unique competence. Our job, after effecting that emotional linkage, is to demonstrate that we have the experience and knowledge to fulfill their specific requirement. For example, a husband and wife may decide to retain the services of an architect to design a retirement home to be located on a unique mountain site. The architect the couple selects will probably be one whom they like and who can inspire confidence in dealing with unusual lot sizes, shapes, and terrain.

What does this mean to you? Well, as you assume your role as "analyst," you need to make a quick approximation of the emotional state and needs of the prospect. You need to also assess why the individual is there. Is it a "must" or "wish to" situation? Finally, to the extent possible, you should adjust your receiving and dispensing of information to the specific client situation. Understanding and adjusting to client behavior is not a science. It can't be done by the numbers, although I know at least one architect who forces herself to spend the first ten minutes of each consultation getting to know the prospect. She does this because she knows she is probably more interested in the technical design challenges of the project than in the personalities of the clients. She recognizes that this is a weakness, so with her "ten-minute rule" she makes every attempt to be more relaxed, more personable, and more in touch with the human side of the professional assignment. In my view, it is extremely unfortunate that more professional schools and programs do not give greater emphasis to client relations. However, the emphasis on marketing professional services in the 1980s should have a positive impact on the situation.

How Do Clients Buy?

Many professionals serve both individual and institutional clients. An architect may have individual customers who seek consultation concerning the design of a personal residence. In addition, the architect may have institutional clients, such as a hospital group, municipal governments, and industry. There are significant differences in client behavior among these groups. Figure 6-1 highlights and contrasts those differences.

FIGURE 6-1. Contrasts in Client Behavior: Institutional and Individual Clients

INSTITUTIONAL	INDIVIDUAL
Purchases in quantity	Purchases fewer units
Group decisions	Individual decisions
Profit-oriented	Satisfaction- and security-oriented
Weighs alternatives	May buy on impulse
Specifications well-defined	Needs/desires often vaguely defined
Purchasing function carefully defined, organized, operated, and evaluated	Vacillation between orderly and random behavior
Experienced buyer	Inexperienced buyer

One of the objectives of every professional interested in marketing services should be to have a *client behavior map* for each client group. What is a client behavior map? It's exactly what the name implies: a graphic representation of how clients move through the purchase decision process from the time they become aware of a professional service need until the time they actually retain the professional. Figure 6-2, a model of consumer behavior, comes from the book Ed Fox and I did entitled *Modern Marketing*. As we advised readers: "Our general model of consumer behavior is only a starting point. In marketing literature, you'll find many approaches to consumer behavior modeling. The Howard-Seth model, for example,

FIGURE 6-2 Consumer behavior—A simplified model

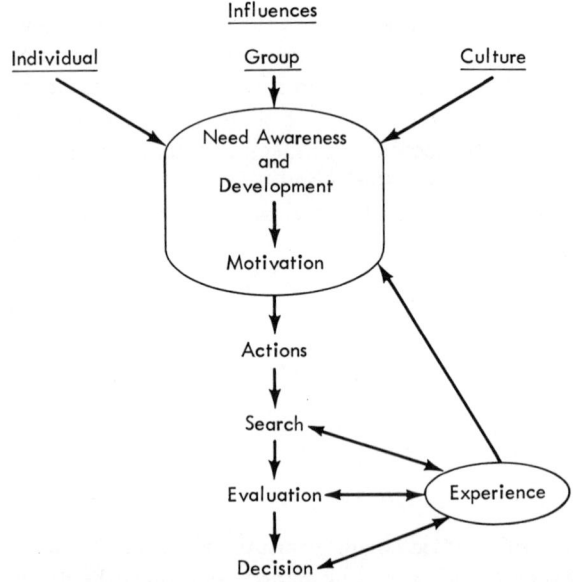

Source: E. J. Fox and E. W. Wheatley, *Modern Marketing: Principles and Practice*. (Glenview, Ill.: Scott, Foresman and Co., 1978), p. 97. Reprinted by permission.

traces the effects of several stimuli on repeat purchase attitudes, intentions, and action over time. The model developed by Engal, Kollat, and Blackwell traces the search and decision process through several "GO/NO GO" cycles. As you develop a model of the search and purchase decision process for your consumers, review some existing approaches, but don't try to re-invent the wheel. Adapt and modify what already exists. Take the bits and pieces that seem to fit your situation. Your objective should be a detailed description of the behavior of your target market(s)."[1]

The purpose of behavior modeling is to allow the marketer to develop as complete an understanding as possible of what consumers go through in their search and decision-making processes. With that knowledge in hand, the marketer can then adapt and intervene appropriately at the most promising points and with the highest probability of persuading the consumer to choose the marketer's product or service.

The preceding discussion may seem like marketing theory. It isn't. Let me show you how it can be used in your situation through an example in the professional services field. One of my clients is a chain of private schools for children with learning disabilities. This professional service organization operates in an environment of standards, accreditation, and ethical behavior. The psychologist who founded and owns the organization decided to evaluate the business side of the practice. I was called in to consult. One of the areas for review was marketing. The principals in the organization believed that student enrollments were generated primarily through attendance at national and regional conferences of educators. In addition, advertising announcements were placed in professional journals. The organization, not highly profitable to begin with, was spending tens of thousands of dollars in conference travel, exhibits, and advertising. In examining the what, why, and how of client purchasing behavior, we developed a client behavior map.

Our major source for mapping behavior was answers to referral questions asked at prospective client consultations and intake conferences. Most conferences were held with parents. We wanted to know how they heard about the schools, how they found the organization, who brought the services to their attention, and so on. This research led to the behavior map shown in Figure 6-3, but the process follows the simplified consumer behavior model in Figure 6-1. For example, we found that need awareness developed when a child began to have behavioral and/or academic problems in school. Motivation to take specific action to investigate what might be done came from teachers, from relatives, from friends, and from the parents themselves.

The actions taken normally included informal conversations with influential individuals and then visits to medical professionals, educational professionals, behavioral scientists, and in some cases all three. The specific types of professionals visited are shown in Figure 6-3. Let's take one example. Suppose a teacher felt that a child's school problems might be due to poor vision. Once a thorough eye examination was conducted by an optometrist or opthalmologist and vision was found to be normal, the medical professional might suggest that the child had a specific learning disability. The parents would then be advised to have some diag-

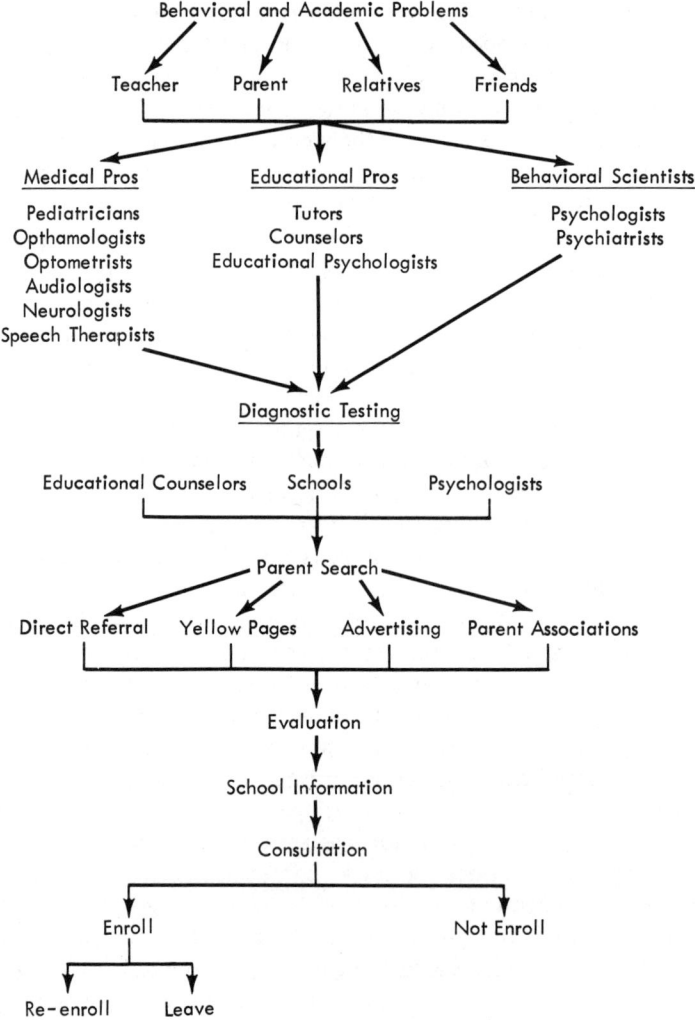

FIGURE 6-3 Client behavior map—Educational services

nostic testing performed by a counselor, a psychologist, or perhaps a learning disabilities specialist. This type of referral behavior sends the parents further along in their search process.

In some cases, parents were referred directly to the school chain in the example. In other cases, particularly for parents transferring into the area, the Yellow Pages were an important source of information concerning the location of these specialized schools. For parents who were considering what to do about a child's return to school in a specific year or dealing with grade frustration at the end of a term, local newspaper advertising had an important impact. Finally, there were parent associations, such as Better Opportunities for the Learning Disabled

(BOLD), the Association for Children with Learning Disabilities, (ACLD), and others. These associations hold frequent meetings, conduct workshops, prepare and disseminate flyers and brochures, and in some cases, publish newsletters. Finally, the parents went to individual schools. Sometimes they requested brochures or other detailed information concerning curriculum, services, schedules, and costs, or they made an in-person visit for consultation and obtained this information. Seldom did they make a final decision on the spot. Based on their evaluation and their review of the information, they often extended their discussions to include family members and friends and referring professionals. Finally, an enroll-no enroll decision was made.

What did we learn in this client behavior mapping project? First, we began to realize that the organization was not a national chain, but rather a group of eight independent local schools. Even though the group operated in four states, its clientele and environments were strictly local. Second, referrals did not come primarily from other individuals prominent on the national educational scene; they came from a multilayered set of educators, laypersons, and medical and behavioral scientists. In addition, we learned that many subsets of professions and specialties were included in these three major categories, ranging from the highly specialized field of neuropediatrics to the professional field of speech therapy. We also learned how important ongoing Yellow Pages and limited local newspaper advertising (properly scheduled) were in the marketing mix. Association membership and activity with the relevant local groups were also found to be important.

The preparation of brochures and information pamphlets was given special attention. And that all-important parent consultation and all the variables surrounding it were carefully studied and improved. The result? The marketing budget was trimmed considerably. The exhibits used at conferences are now gathering dust. The expensive travel budget is all but nonexistent. The schools interact with local medical, educational, and behavioral professionals. Workshops and seminars are held for parent groups. Community information materials are published and disseminated. New products and services are evaluated on an ongoing basis. For example, the schools are beginning to offer some business, secretarial, and computer training in an adjunct program for students who decide not to go on to college. Client behavior mapping worked for this professional service organization. It could work for you.

One word of caution is in order. Developing useful, detailed knowledge concerning client behavior is not an easy or overnight process. Client behavior maps can never be all-encompassing or totally accurate. They should always be developed in a tentative mode, for they will and do change. However, the opportunity to have clearer and well-documented understanding of client behavior makes the work worth the effort. As a minimum, you should try to develop a client behavior map for your primary client segment. Ideally, such information should also be available for all client groups and for prospective client targets. Time spent in the development of these data will be more than made up for in improving the effectiveness and reducing the unnecessary costs in your marketing program.

When you are dealing with institutional or group buyers of services, behavior mapping is even more critical. Where the decision-making unit (DMU) is more than one individual, it is important to try to assign weights and priorities to marketing activities directed toward this target. For example, if you are marketing a health care program to a teachers' union, it's extremely important to know the process and power mechanisms that will be used in soliciting, accumulating, evaluating, and deciding among service providers. The resources of the marketer can then be focused more clearly and effectively on the methods that will do the most good. In the large professional organization with many services clients and markets, client behavior maps may be numerous and complex. For the individual practitioner, an adaptation of the simplified model in Figure 6-2 may suffice.

CLIENT IDENTIFICATION, SEGMENTATION, AND TARGETING

Now that we've discussed the general area of consumer behavior and recommended an approach to document the search and evaluation process, it's time to become more specific. When a new professional looks out at the world and considers the "market," the picture is usually complex, confusing, and often overwhelming. This experience is not unique to professionals; it's something that happens to almost all inexperienced marketers. Why? Because there is no such thing as "the market." Markets are composed of subsets of business opportunities, and each subset possesses unique characteristics. When one discusses "the market," one is usually guilty of overgeneralizing.

To help you come to grips with the complexity of all existing and prospective market opportunities, a four-step process is recommended: market identification, market classification, market segmentation, and market targeting. If you are a new professional, this process will be applied to prospective clients; if you are a professional with an existing practice, you will apply this process to both prospective and existing clients.

Identification

The purpose of this step is to develop as complete a list as possible of any and all prospects who might utilize your service. For example, if you are a CPA specializing in audits, you would develop a list of all the organizations you can think of requiring the services of auditors. This is the time to be open-ended. When in doubt, include a prospect type rather than exclude it. Your object is to make the list as long as possible. Some organizations must be audited; some organizations wish to be audited. Include in this list any and all possible client types.

Classification

This step involves grouping the individual entries on your ID grocery list into client categories. For example, perhaps the CPA's ID list includes prep schools, universities, junior colleges, four-year colleges, federally or state-funded technical and vocational schools, and others. In the classification step, these types of organizations would all be classified under the general heading of educational institutions.

Segmentation

You have now classified scores of potential market opportunities into major groupings. The principle of segmentation involves further subdividing these groupings, based on certain common characteristics, into more clearly defined, homogeneous subgroups. In our CPA example, the educational classification might be broken down into private, public, college, university, academic, vocational, profit, nonprofit, individual, chain, local, national, traditional, nontraditional, residential, nonresidential, and so on.

With the background you now have in marketing, I'm sure you can see what we're up to. Few professionals can be all things to all people. We live in an era of specialization. Identification, classification, and segmentation are designed to help us clarify the differences among various types of client opportunities in what appears to be the same field. Let's say our CPA is particularly strong in municipal fund accounting. The public school market or special educational grants and programs funded through public monies might be a better opportunity than, say, the private university. The principle of segmentation is similar to the old combat advice of divide and conquer.

There are many ways to segment markets. The methods are limited only to the creativity of the analyst. Philip Kotler, in *Marketing for Nonprofit Organizations*, observes that the three major approaches to segmentation are geographic, demographic, and psychographic.[2] Figure 6-4 presents several segmentation variables within each group.

Another approach to segmentation involves identifying the major benefit sought by clients, and attempting to identify all prospects seeking that benefit. This form of segmentation cuts across many segments. For example, look at the newspaper as shown in Figure 6-5. Dr. Tannenbaum is appealing to any and all client prospects who fear pain. His approach is based on benefit segmentation. The benefit? Painless dental work.

Targeting

Remember earlier in the text when we talked about the principle of matching? The idea is to identify and analyze consumers in as much detail as possible and then to match the unique and particular skills of the marketer to the unique and particular needs of the consumer group. Let's examine market targeting for existing as well as prospective clients.

Existing clients are particularly important when we consider estimates that from 50 to 75 percent of professional practice growth comes from existing clients

FIGURE 6-4 Major Segmentation Variables and Their Typical Breakdowns

VARIABLE	TYPICAL BREAKDOWN
Geographic	
Region	Pacific; Mountain; West North Central; West South Central; East North Central; East South Central; South Atlantic; Middle Atlantic; New England
County size	A; B; C; D
City or SMSA size	Under 5,000-19,999; 20,000-49,999; 50,000-99,999; 100,000-249,999; 250,000-499,999; 500,000-999,999; 1,000,000-3,999,999; over 4,000,000
Density	Urban; suburban; rural
Climate	Northern; southern
Demographic	
Age	Under 6; 6-11; 12-17; 18-34; 35-49; 50-64; 65+
Sex	Male; female
Family size	1-2; 3-4; 5+
Family life cycle stage	Young, single; young, married, no children; young, married, youngest child under 6; older, married, with children; older, married, no children under 18; older, single; other
Income	Under $5,000; $5,000-7,999; $8,000-$9,999; $10,000-14,999; over $15,000
Occupation	Professional and technical; managers, officials, and proprietors; clerical, sales; craftsmen, foremen; operatives; farmers; retired; students, housewives; unemployed
Education	Grade school or less; some high school; graduated high school; some college; graduated college
Religion	Catholic, Protestant; Jewish; other
Race	White; Negro; Oriental
Nationality	American; British; French; German; Eastern European; Scandinavian; Italian; Spanish; Latin American; Middle Eastern; Japanese; other
Social class	Lower-lower; upper-lower; lower-middle; middle-middle; upper-middle; lower-upper; upper-upper
Psychographic	
Life style	Swinger; status seeker; plain Joe; other
Personality	Compulsive; gregarious; conservative; ambitious; other
Benefits sought	Economy; convenience; dependability; prestige; other
User status	Nonuser; potential user; first-time user; regular user; ex-user
Usage rate	Light user; medium user; heavy user
Loyalty status	None; medium; strong; absolute
Readiness stage	Unaware; aware; informed; interested; desirous; intending to buy

Source: Philip Kotler, *Marketing for Nonprofit Organizations,* (Englewood Cliffs, N.J.: Prentice-Hall, Inc., 1975), pp. 103-104.

or referrals of existing clients. Steps one through three can be followed for existing clients. However, once reasonably clear segments are identified, existing clients should be further subdivided into high-assay and low-assay categories. Clients making the high-assay list should be those who are providing current high income or profitability to your practice; those whose present position is not outstanding but who have high probability of growth and success and the possibility of expanding use of your services; and finally, those clients who do not fit either category, or perhaps both, but who have a high potential for referring clients to your organization. Low-assay clients meet none of these criteria. Where possible, they might be considered for termination, sell-off, or transfer of account servicing to a paraprofessional or lower-cost operational modes.

In consumer and industrial products and services marketing, product and service termination is a regular part of the marketing management process. Professionals will do well to make this approach part of their own management practices. I have worked with a law firm whose partners and staff are always "busy." However, much of their productive time is spent on minor, routine matters. Furthermore, the clients are high-contact-hour generators, but poor payers. Much of the practice with this type of client is on a loss, breakeven, or slight profit basis. While the firm is "busy" serving these clients, other firms are taking the time to invest their hours in high-assay client development and retention and in external marketing activities that will create new profitable business. It's been extremely difficult convincing the principals of this firm to deemphasize these clients and to refer them to law stores or law clinics.

A CPA firm with which I'm familiar has hundreds of small business bookkeeping accounts. Although these accounts keep everyone "busy," most of them are on a retainer fee basis, and do they abuse it! It's no one's fault that these small organizations can't afford to pay standard, regular fees for their services. I do blame the accounting firm, however, for continuing to apply its talents in a low payoff situation, rather than focusing on the high-assay side of its current business and future potential. A careful analysis of these accounts would result in the termination of a substantial number. This would free the professionals for bigger, better, and more profitable things, including more personal attention to their existing client base.

FIGURE 6-5 Benefit segmentation

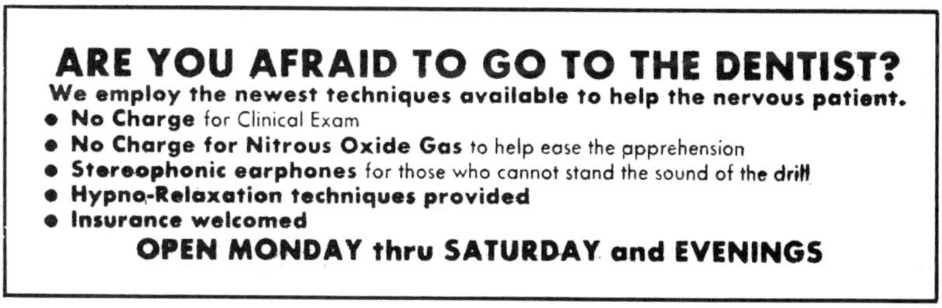

ARE YOU AFRAID TO GO TO THE DENTIST?
We employ the newest techniques available to help the nervous patient.
- **No Charge** for Clinical Exam
- **No Charge for Nitrous Oxide Gas** to help ease the apprehension
- **Stereophonic earphones** for those who cannot stand the sound of the drill
- **Hypno-Relaxation techniques** provided
- **Insurance welcomed**

OPEN MONDAY thru SATURDAY and EVENINGS

MARKETING RESEARCH AND THE PROFESSIONAL

While most professionals are tuned in to their clients' needs and to developing marketing opportunities, few appear to conduct systematic, ongoing, formal market research. This is one major differentiating factor between professional service marketing and the marketing of consumer and industrial goods and services. The presence of marketing research specialists and the conduct of ongoing, formal research studies is a normal phenomenon in consumer and industrial marketing. Marketers generally make a decision to conduct formal studies when the following criteria are met:

1. There is a clearly defined and agreed upon problem area that can be effectively delimited for research.
2. Information in this area cannot be satisfactorily obtained through existing secondary sources or internal information.
3. An effective and feasible methodology is available to apply in the situation.
4. A favorable cost-benefit potential for the research exists; for example, the cost of obtaining the new information will be more than offset by the reduction in risk supplied by the new intelligence.

Using a Specialist

Because market research is not part of the ongoing practice management operations of most professionals, it is best to turn to a specialist when such work is needed. Most firms begin utilizing market research through project assignments given to outside consulting firms. There are a few critical mistakes inexperienced individuals or organizations make as they begin to utilize market research. Try to guard against these situations.

First, a research study frequently involves contact with existing or potential clients and in some cases potential and existing referral sources. Be sure that the individual or organization you have retained operates in a manner that enhances the image you wish to develop. Experience and familiarity with the professional environment are unique prerequisites for your type of research. Second, beware of the panacea syndrome. Having a marketing research study in your hands and successfully implementing it are two very different things. Most good studies will suggest much more than an individual professional or a small group will be able to do. Study the actionable recommendations and the findings, set priorities, and get to work on a limited number of high-assay activities. Third, overexpectations about the scope and results of a study frequently lead to disappointment and sometimes dispute. Have a clear understanding of what the marketing research professional will do within the time and fee limits you specify.

Finally, good market research is not inexpensive. Most larger firms will not be interested in an engagement unless the fees exceed the $7,000 to $10,000 minimum. If your budget necessitates the delimitation of a research engagement, go for depth and quality within the limited area as opposed to attempting to learn everything all at once with only one project. Please listen to the recommendations of your consultant. A large national client of mine insisted on utilizing a survey questionnaire that contained 101 questions! After considerable debate, we were able to reduce that to 51 questions, still far too long to yield accurate and reliable data. The problem? The client had done no recent research and was attempting to learn everything at once within the constraints of a limited budget. The quantity and quality of the research returns would have been considerably enhanced had the client been willing to go narrow and deep for the same research expenditure. Although the study did produce some useful information, its value was needlessly compromised by the expectations of the client.

The Research Process

How might you use market research in your own professional situation? Aubrey Wilson defines six basic areas where professional service marketers can use marketing research. In addition, he gives specific examples of useful information in each area (see Figure 6-6).

Once you have decided a formal research project is needed, defined the area or areas of inquiry, and satisfied the criteria mentioned previously, what happens next? Figure 6-7 provides an answer to that question. Please take a moment to consider the following comments concerning the process. First, note that the researcher utilizes in-company analysis and available secondary sources *prior* to external activities. This step helps the researcher identify any further problem areas, clarify existing research needs and requirements, and in some cases find full or partial answers to some of the questions to be investigated. You'll note that the researcher takes an additional intermediate step, the informal investigation outside the firm prior to the conduct of a formal study. The reasons for this step are the same as those for the internal analysis. Researchers who are anxious to "get into the field" without proper internal analysis or familiarization with your professional external environment, are not, in my opinion, exercising their own professional responsibility to do a thorough and responsive job of market research.

If a formal study is done, you'll note there are four basic methods: the market test or experiment, the survey, observation, and focused group activities. Let's briefly define and discuss each of these options.

1. Market tests and experiments. Tests and experiments attempt to simulate real-world market situations. The experiment is closely monitored under controlled conditions. An independent variable, such as advertising is modified to note its effect upon some experimental dependent variable such as sales. Almost all experimenters and market testers are seeking to establish causal relationships between the marketing mix and marketing outcomes. The key disadvantage is the difficulty in replicating the real-world situation and the artificiality that must be introduced to provide the necessary experimental controls.

FIGURE 6-6 *RESEARCH OBJECTIVES*

1. Identification and measurement of the markets
    Total markets
    Significant segments of individual markets
    Market coverage—new markets for existing services, new services for existing markets, new services for new markets
2. Analysis of the characteristics of the markets
    Customer needs for services, function of services
    Desirable service features
    Customer practices in seeking services
    Customer attitudes and activities
    Competitive conditions, share of market, marketing service costs, and related practices
    Required commercial conditions
    Market, facilities, and competitive trends
3. Projection of the markets (5- or 10-year period)
    Basic growth or decline forces
    Identification of "top out" conditions
    Trends or changes in customers, type of new competing services
    Environmental changes—social, economic, technical, political
    Projection of total market value
4. Critical factors for successful operations in individual markets
    Nature of service market (industry-merchandised, selected account development)
    Range of services to be offered
    Key functions necessary to operate service
    Costs, systems, and related factors
5. Projection of available share of the market
    Projection of market share based on market trend
    Degree to which competitive strengths and weaknesses may affect position
    Extent to which improved operations can contribute to higher market share
    Development of market share for 5-and 10-year period
6. Market development program
    Statement of objectives
    Functional requirements to implement program
    Organization for implementation
    Action program related to organization facilities, business development, advertising, promotion, and so on

Source: Aubrey Wilson, *The Marketing of Professional Services*, (New York: McGraw-Hill, 1979), p. 74, Fig. 8-1.

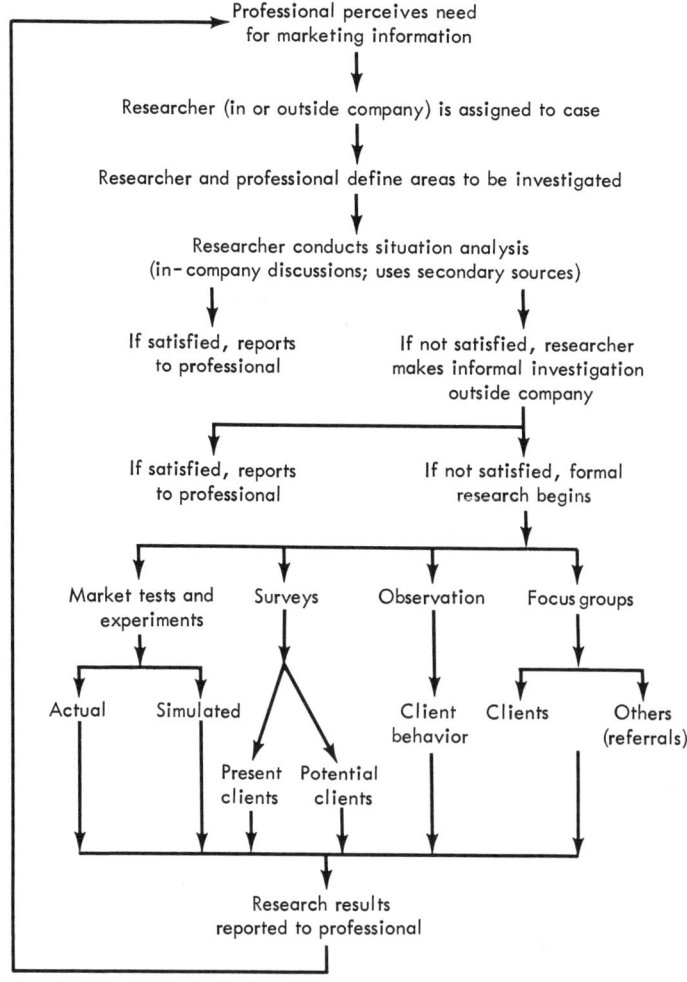

FIGURE 6-7 Professional service marketing research process

A few years ago we were working with some developers and architects on a condominium project. The firm was interested in learning more about condominium buyer behavior. It wanted to apply the marketing concept by designing a planned 10-building project to more carefully meet the needs and desires of prospective buyers. A research experiment was developed as part of the overall marketing research investigation. Couples were invited to dinner. After dinner they played a game; the game was "building your own condominium." Couples were given modular building blocks and some play money. They were told they could design their own condominium. After their units were finished, they were given some good news and some bad news. The good news was that their daughter had been accepted to medical school; the bad news was that we were going to relieve them of a substantial portion of their condominium dollars. They were then asked to redesign the condominium based on a new, lower level of funding available for the unit. We were, of course, attempting to see how their ideal unit differed from the unit they would settle for based on certain financial constraints. We were carefully observing the priorities their needs seemed to dictate. Some excellent ideas came out of this approach, but causality is one of the most frustrating and intriguing questions of all time. For this reason, marketing research experiments and tests must be carefully interpreted. The results are only part of the input for the total decision.

A market test is broader in scope. It usually introduces a new service in an actual market area with a specific marketing mix. Results are carefully charted, and the marketing process and the service itself introduced more broadly, terminated, or taken back to the drawing board for further refinement. Let's say you are a member of a dental group. Your practice has been conducted pretty much along the standard model. However, group members suggest the introduction of a prepaid dental plan with unlimited emergency service. Let's further assume that your group operates in a four-state area of the Southeast. A market test would involve introducing the service in one, or possibly two, limited markets. One market might stress heavy media advertising and price competition. In the other market, there might be modifications in the service mix and in marketing appeals. The purpose of the test would be not only test to the idea of a prepaid dental program, but various approaches to the presentation of the service.

Consumer and industrial goods marketers utilize this technique frequently in market testing new products or service concepts. One of the advantages of the market test approach is that in addition to the new service mix ingredient, you can also test various marketing mix combinations. But there are several problems. First, is the area in which the test being conducted truly representative of the market in general? Second, there is considerable complexity and expense in organizing and implementing any market test. And finally, the use of an actual market test may tip your hand to existing or potential competition. If you are not efficient in refining and implementing the service, you may find that it is copied and promoted even though you were the originator.

2. Surveys. A key advantage to surveys is that they can involve a larger number of people, and if conducted in accordance with sound statistical sampling procedure, may produce results generalizable to markets at large. In addition, if the survey is a personal one, the interviewer may probe and have a higher probability of uncovering answers to "why" questions dealing with consumer behavior and motivation. Problems with surveys include developing a research instrument, for example a questionnaire, that is free from ambiguity, confusing connotations, and leading questions. In addition, bias is always introduced by the interviewer-respondent interaction. Poorly planned and executed surveys predictably yield poor results. Response rates may be low; and even when response rates are adequate, the data received may be misleading or meaningless.

3. Observation. In the classic sense, observation is characterized by the absence of respondent-researcher interaction. In market tests, experiments, and surveys, respondent and researcher come together either in person or through some intermediary such as the research questionnaire or interviewer. In an observation situation, this does not occur. For example, in the condominium case mentioned earlier, the respondents could be videotaped and audiotaped and left to their own devices to play the game. Tapes could later be analyzed and inferences developed. The beauty of observation is that it does not interfere with natural behavior. A drawback is that researchers must draw conclusions based on their own interpretations of what the respondents are doing. Observation techniques have limited applications. For example, it would be useful to be able to observe the meeting of a municipal committee charged with selecting the city auditor, although it is doubtful that such an observation could be arranged. In the professional service area, the use of focus groups is a more feasible approach to observational data collection.

4. Focus groups. A focus group is a small, market representative, eight- to ten-person, group assembled and operated on an informal basis under the guidance of a skilled moderator. The purpose of the focus group is to provide a relaxed and seemingly unstructured environment where respondents can share their opinions, experiences, and attitudes concerning a topic of interest to the researcher. For example, last year I was involved in the conduct of focus groups for a marketer considering bringing an imported super-premium beer into this country to compete with Heineken. Focus groups were used to attempt to identify consumer motivation and perceptions concerning the purchase of super-premium imported beers.

Several groups were conducted. A skilled interviewer was used to lead a seemingly unplanned freewheeling discussion of beer consumption and specifically, imported beer consumption. The groups were video- and audiotaped, and a great many useful perceptions and ideas concerning the product were revealed. To supplement these activities, taste tests were conducted and also taped.

The focus group might be used in a professional environment to gain preliminary reactions to new service mix entries, fee policies, the use of media advertising, and so on. The focus group selected should be representative of the ultimate market. In addition, a skilled moderator who can structure and lead a productive discussion is a must. Finally, focus groups are used in the preliminary stages of the research process. They are not a substitute for the formal investigation: focus groups do provide useful and interesting information, but these data need to be confirmed by more extensive and statistically valid research activities.

The field of market research is a complex subspecialty within the field of marketing. Research that yields inaccurate or unreliable information which is then used in the decision-making process can be more dangerous than no research at all. The brief comments I have made serve only as an introduction to the use of market research professionals. You are encouraged to utilize outside specialists until your firm becomes proficient in the conduct of market research.

Remember that the basis of modern marketing is discovery, understanding,

FIGURE 6-8 *ANALYZING THE MARKET*

1. *Market Identification*—Develop complete list of possible users
2. *Market Classification*—Group entries into client categories
3. *Market Segmentation*—Group categories into homogeneous subgroups
   Three Approaches
   a. Geographic—region, state, county, city, density, etc.
   b. Demographic—age, sex, family size, income, education, religion, etc.
   c. Psychographic—life style, personality, benefits sought, user status, loyalty, readiness stage, etc.
4. *Marketing Targeting*—Match your unique skills
   a. To unique and particular needs of consumer group.
   b. Identify new markets for service mix development

and tracking of client needs and desires. In today's increasingly competitive environment, professionals who excel in understanding and satisfying clients will be the survivors and winners. In the broader sense, the practice of individual professionals in a fee-for-service, free-market economy is being challenged. The professions are under attack by individuals seeking increased regulation and, in some cases, socialization of professional practice. The best guarantee that professionals in all fields will continue to operate in the free market setting is a satisfied and loyal client constituency. In this sense, the use of marketing by professionals takes on an even greater importance.

Regardless of your research approach or your skill and success in developing a behavior map you can use the four-step approach recommended earlier in the chapter. Figure 6-8 summarizes this process.

Chapter 7
How to Position Your Services

A professional can't go anywhere these days without hearing or reading or being exposed to the term *positioning*. Every professional service seminar around the country spends considerable time discussing the positioning of the professional service practice. The purpose of this chapter is to make you familiar and comfortable with the concept. In addition, we will provide real examples so that you can see the concept in action in both the product and service categories. We'll illustrate how this unifying concept has application not only for developing individual service mix items, but in promotion, competitive strategy, pricing, and just about any area in which you might wish to use it. Finally, we will discuss the application of positioning to the professional service environment in detail. One of the most useful aspects of this section will be the presentation of several alternative professional positioning statements. These statements may not mirror your exact conditions or professional opportunities, but I'm sure you will be able to utilize one or more of the samples as a basis for developing your own positioning statement.

WHAT IS POSITIONING?

To begin, let's look at several alternative definitions of positioning. My own definition is this: positioning is the management practice of focusing competitive strategy and activity within a specified space (position) in the total competitive spectrum.

Let's take a simple example from a field familiar to most of us. The entire competitive spectrum for the sports car market might be classified as follows. At the upper level, we find the custom, handmade, limited production cars of Ferrari and Maserati. At the lower end of the spectrum, we find the mass-produced sport models of MG, Fiat, and a whole range of lower-priced Japanese and Italian imports. The first step for a marketer seeking to develop an advantageous competitive position is carefully to define and specify each individual unit within the total competitive spectrum. In doing so, there will usually be certain positions that are not "taken" or which, in the marketer's estimation, are not represented adequately. This gap may give the marketer an opportunity to develop a product to fill that position and give it a unique, market nich with sales potential.

The Datsun Z-car is an excellent case in point. Above the Z-car in terms of price and performance is the Chevrolet Corvette. Below the Z-car we find models like the Mazda RX7 and below that, of course, the MGB, Fiat Spider, and so on. Although the 280-Z is not the muscle car represented by the Corvette, it is certainly a step above the MGB and the Fiat Spider in terms of price, performance, handling, and comfort. In bringing out the Z-car line, Nissan Motors carefully evaluated the existing competitive spectrum. It believed there was a gap in the space between the American Corvette and a group of imports that were being marketed at the lower price levels. The Z-car was positioned to fill that gap and did so very successfully. In fact, its market position in the United States today is so dominant that American manufacturers have not brought out a true sports car to compete with the Z. The new model Porsche, while somewhat competitive, is positioned slighty above the Z-car, and of course the addition of higher performance and higher price takes it out of direct competition with the successful Z.

James L. Heskett, professor of marketing at the Harvard School of Business, presents still another definition:

> The process of relating a product to present potential markets has been termed product positioning. It can be used in the design and introduction of products with significantly different characteristics than competitors, such as freeze-dried coffee, to largely uninformed market segments. The term has also been picked up by advertising managers to denote the means by which products, often of essentially the same composition and capabilities, can be given a character that will appeal primarily to certain segments of a market. It is thought to be particularly effective in aiding a company in gaining a share of a market dominated by a competing product, or in aiding a company with a dominant share in fending off competition by adding new products, each of which captures a dominant share of a particular market segment.[1]

Christopher Gilson and Harold Berkman credit a series of articles in *Advertising Age* as the source of the positioning concept. They identify the period 1970 to 1980 as "the positioning era." In their view, positioning was developed as marketers sought effective ways to compete in markets dominated by many competitive entries and deteriorating economic conditions.[2]

The *Advertising Age* article, "The Positioning Era Cometh," offered the following discussion:

> Positioning has its roots in the packaged goods field where the concept was called package positioning. It literally meant the product's form, package size and price as compared to competition . . . today, we are entering an era that recognizes both the importance of the product and the importance of the company image, but more than anything else, stresses the need to create a position in the prospect's mind.[3]

The Trout and Rise utilization of the positioning concept stressed the space within a consumer's mind reserved for identification of competing products and services. They likened the mind to a memory bank that has slots or positions for information. Unlike a computer, however, the mind rejects much information that is presented to it. They stressed that in the first place a mind can recall only a limited amount of information, and second that information has to square with experience if later stimuli are to be effective. They analyzed as an example the National Cash Register Company's campaign, which was based on a series of television ads. The theme was "NCR Means Computers." In the opinion of Trout and Rise, the computer position was already well established by IBM. The authors believed that this positioning strategy for advertising purposes was ill-advised. Their hypothesis was that for most people IBM means computers, while NCR means cash registers.

POSITIONING:
SOME FAMILIAR EXAMPLES

In a *Wall Street Journal* article, Jonathan Kwitney discussed the repositioning of Schaefer beer through a successful consumer advertising campaign:

> Jim Jordan, vice-president of the Batten Barton, Dursten and Osborne Agency, gives an explicit account of why he switched Schaefer's advertising campaign from the former, pointless theme of "What do you hear in the best of circles? Schaefer, all around!" to the current, "Schaefer is the beer to have when you're having more than one!"
> "Beer commercials used to be the same as soft-drink commercials," Mr. Jordan says. "There were guys and girls on beaches, swirling around, presenting pilsner glasses to each other." He adds: "We went out and talked to a lot of beer drinkers." And it turned out that "fifteen percent of the people of this country drink about 85% of the beer." These 25-49-year-old, middle-income men routinely down three or four bottles an evening, but they complained that "the flavor seemed to fade a little" as they sloshed further through a six-pack.
> "We thought, Gee, we ought to address ourselves to the problem they're talking about." Although Schaefer didn't change its beer formula, the ad-men found a couple of quirks in the brewing process that they felt would justify a new claim: Schaefer was uniquely designed to taste the same after you were "tight" as it did when you were stone sober. The result: lowly Schaefer

quickly passed Ballantine, then Rheingold, and now—Mr. Jordan says—it is neck-and-neck with Budweiser as the largest selling beer in the East.[4]

A familiar example of positioning in the service industry was Avis's claim, "We're #2, we try harder!" Avis knew that Hertz dominated the automobile rental market. Its dominance was so complete that there was little Avis could hope to do in the short run to overtake Hertz. Rather than fight the car rental giant, Avis elected to use an extremely creative admission of its market position as the major promotional strategy. Consumers could readily accept the positioning of Avis as #2 and it seemed to make sense that if you haven't become #1, you might surely try harder to beat the leader.

7-Up found itself in much the same position as Avis. Coca-Cola dominated the soft-drink industry and, of course, still does. Furthermore, the cola form of drink in general dominated the soft-drink market. Recognizing this, 7-Up adopted the positioning statement of the "un-cola." If you wanted a cola drink, then 7-Up couldn't help you. However, 7-Up positioned itself as the un-cola of the industry. This positioning strategy led to an entire series of advertising campaigns and is believed to have assisted 7-Up in expanding its market share significantly.

POSITIONING: EXPANDING THE CONCEPT

With this general conceptual background and examples of the use of positioning in the consumer product and services market as a basis, let's begin to focus on the marketing professional services situation. Positioning is an extremely useful concept. It is a unifying or umbrella abstraction that can be utilized in many contexts. Positioning could be utilized in placing a product or service or a product or service mix within the existing competitive spectrum. Positioning could also be used to take an undifferentiated and existing service and establish a specific identification in the consumer's mind based on the so-called memory ladder concept of Trout and Rise. Positioning could also be utilized to describe management's efforts to establish and reinforce an entire organizational image. And finally, positioning could be used in ways that combine the preceding application.

Before we prescribe ways in which you might develop you own professional services positioning statement, it's important to consider several questions. The answers to these questions will determine not only advantageous positioning alternatives and approaches, but also suggest background work that should be done prior to implementing your positioning strategy. Trout and Rise ask six questions that should be considered by anyone utilizing positioning:

1. What position, if any, do you already have in the minds of your clients?
2. If this position is nonexistent or different, what position do you wish to have?
3. What competitive organization must be outgunned if you are to establish this position?

4. Do you have enough money and other resources to take, occupy, and hold that position?
5. Does the organization have the termperament to establish and stay with one consistent positioning concept?
6. Does the creative approach to communication with clients and prospective clients match your positioning strategy?

In addition to these questions, I'd like to introduce a few more. First, is the positioning statement true? That is, can it be verified? Does it rest on fact? For example, if you were to take the position of being Chicago's largest law firm, can that be demonstrated in a significant way? Is your firm the biggest based on annual billings, amount of office space, number of clients, number of staff, number of attorneys on staff, or some other criterion? The use of positioning strategies involving puffery and exaggeration are ill-advised in the professional service market environment. The professional may get some intial mileage from the position, but if it is found to based on flimsy foundations, it will often discredit rather than enhance that professional's long-term position. Consumers are used to hearing car dealers profess that they are the largest Ford dealer in the West. They expect this kind of puffery and do not generally take it as the literal truth. However, the statements of professionals are generally regarded with a good deal more seriousness.

Second, is the positioning believable? For example, it might literally be true that a particular architect is extremely efficient and therefore the fees related to any particular job typically end up being much lower than those of competitors. But before adopting the position of the lowest-cost architects in town, the firm would be wise to determine if this is a believable position in the minds of prospective clients. For example, if the offices are modern and well appointed, it may be difficult for consumers to translate low cost into high efficiency. Rather, they may believe the low-cost strategy is merely a come-on. In cases where the position is literally true but may not be believable, the professional's written and personal communications must be strategically developed to explain why and how the position promoted is indeed possible. A dental clinic stressing painless dentistry will have to go to great pains (no pun intended) to explain specifically how it can accomplish this when in the minds of the majority of consumers, dental work is almost always associated in some way with pain.

Third, is the position what the professional wants it to be? That is, is it congruent with the individual and/or the organization? It may be possible for a marketing consultant or advertising or public relations professional to develop a positioning strategy for you, but a strategy that does not square with your own approach to the profession is likely to be misleading to clients, uncomfortable for you, and short-lived in its durability.

Is the position enduring? Does it have staying power and long-term potential? This fourth criterion is related to the others. Positioning is a strategic-managerial tool. It implies an overall approach to providing your professional service. It is a long-run rather than a short-run phenomenon. Positioning a CPA firm as local, regional, or national experts on some particular piece of tax legislation could be dangerous if the tax laws in question change frequently. In addition, such positioning locks the firm into a subsection of tax practice as its primary point of identification with the market.

Is the position expandable in a useful way, or is it limited or self-canceling? The preceding example of the CPA firm attempting to establish itself in a very narrow and deep area of tax practice is a case in point. While for the short run the firm might be happy to service additional clients as it gained recognition in this limited area of tax practice, undoubtedly it will wish to expand the practice in the future. Such expansion might include, other tax as well as audit and management service work. These may not be related to its specialized tax practice position. It may be difficult for a client to believe that the same accounting organization that has been providing service in a specialized tax area can be equally expert in the areas of audit, computer systems, and management service work in general. More likely, a client would seek additional outside help from other organizations in these areas.

YOUR MPS POSITIONING STATEMENT

A positioning statement is the written record of the competitive positioning strategy adopted by the firm. It's a policy statement that provides some long-term guidelines designed to keep the professional practice on course toward some predetermined objectives. The statement provides guidelines that prescribe what the professional or organization will and will not do and the way in which the practice will be conducted in the pursuit of its objectives. The positioning statement is a very important document for internal development. It serves as the basis for orientation and direction for new as well as existing and potential associates. Since many professionals expand their practices today through mergers and acquisitions, merger candidates can also use the statement to understand the type of professional or organization with whom they might be affiliated.

The positioning statement should be fiercely your own. I will present several alternative statements, and these can serve as guidelines for the development of your own statement. Effectiveness and usefulness of the positioning concept are directly related to the diligence and specificity exercised in the previous activities recommended in the book, particularly those dealing with client analysis and targeting and the analysis of your uncontrollable competitive professional environment. Ideally, your positioning statement should square with the real competitive spectrum you face and be responsive to the opportunities for market growth your research has indicated are realistic.

The following statements are meant to present contrasting approaches for positioning, and any one might be appropriate for an individual professional or professional organization. The approaches taken include the professionals' professional, the everyone's professional, the price competitor, technical tops, narrow and deep, and the "we're exclusive" approach.

The Professionals' Professional

Let's assume you are the senior partner in a small law firm, Smith, Gomez, and Smith. Your positioning statement might read this way:

1. Smith, Gomez, and Smith's goal is to become known as a firm of exceptionally skilled negotiators and litigation specialists.
2. Our area of emphasis is commercial practice, concentrating on corporate clients. Within that area of practice, we are deeply skilled in negotiation and litigation arising from major real estate transactions.
3. Within the area of real estate, our primary area of expertise and experience lies in representing real estate developers and development corporations.
4. We are an extremely professional firm. We seek to be respected by other nonlitigating and litigating attorneys in the field of real estate as well as related real estate referral sources.
5. Our acceptance of new clients will be on a selective basis. Partner emphasis will be on the pursuit of the practice development objective of specialization. We do not seek to become all things to all people or a general legal practice.
6. Our fees are to be established and maintained at the level of other high-quality litigating law firms. In accepting any engagement, fee level must be carefully assessed in order to permit us to provide the degree of personalized service and partner involvement congruent with our highly professional image.
7. At Smith, Gomez, and Smith, a partner will always have significant direct involvement in any major matter. Partner presence is a key variable in our service mix.
8. We do not seek to become a large law firm. Our size will be controlled in order to maximize our flexibility, responsiveness, and partner presence in client matters.
9. We are aggressive and systematic in the development of our specialized practice. In seeking to become recognized by other professionals and referral sources, partners and associates will be active in professional and trade associations. They will speak and publish in their respective areas.
10. When a matter outside our direct professional expertise comes to our attention, we will refer the matter to another professional who meets our high standards rather than attempt to stretch our time and expertise to matters we cannot service as satisfactorily as we would like to.

You'll notice that this positioning statement says as much about what the firm will not do as what it will do. The statement provides focus, specificity, limitation, and philosophy. It touches on many areas of the marketing mix, including services, market analysis and targeting, the role of MPS in the organization, and pricing.

The Everyone's Professional

The following positioning statement might be developed for a growing CPA firm seeking to penetrate the small business market and nonusers or light users of accounting services in the middle and lower classes. We'll call this firm Elwood and Everything.

1. Elwood and Everything is the complete accountant for the small organization or individual. Our practice development plan is based on securing a high volume of smaller accounts and providing these individuals and organizations with fairly routine and repetitive accounting and tax services.
2. Our services are clearly specified in our client information brochure. We do not provide exotic financial or tax services such as corporate mergers and acquisitions, complex estate tax planning, elaborate systems analysis, and computer feasibility studies. Rather, our emphasis will be on preparing individual and small business income tax returns, providing basic bookkeeping and compilation services, and conducting annual year-end closings and audits.
3. The use of standardized, completely documented routines, as well as the preparation of simplified tax returns by paraprofessionals and by minicomputer, will permit us to be price-competitive with local, regional, and national CPA firms.
4. Our pricing structure and competitive position will be between those of franchised tax preparers and bookkeeping services such as H&R Block and local regional and national CPA organizations.
5. All work will be performed under the supervision of a CPA; however, whenever possible, work will be performed by paraprofessionals.
6. We are aggressive marketers and price competitors. Our use of mass media, particularly newspapers, direct mail, and radio, is congruent with the market targets we have selected.
7. Since we are striving to become known as your "neighborhood accountant," it is not essential that partners and associates be highly visible in state and national associations. Partners and associates are expected to be extremely active in local civic, service, and social clubs and organizations.
8. Our future growth strategy will be based on replication of existing small offices through branching rather than the development of a large, centralized service complex.

The Price Competitor

This example is based on an optometrist seeking to compete in an established market area. We'll call this professional Dr. Foresight.

1. The Foresight Eye Clinic seeks to provide low-cost eye examination, prescription lenses, and frames to the greater urban market.
2. Foresight's policy will be to meet all competitive, advertised prices for its products and services.
3. Our strategy is to bring individuals who feel they might need eye examination or a prescription change, but cannot afford it, back into the market.
4. Since we seek to be a high-volume, low-margin practice, our fees will be prominently displayed and no extended credit plans will be available. Cash, bank credit cards, and local personal checks will be accepted.
5. We do not seek to be a provider of customized products or services. We will cheerfully refer individuals requiring such products and services to appropriate area professionals.
6. To reinforce our price-competitive image, monthly specials on basic examination, prescription, frames, or contacts will be featured in our regular newspaper promotions.

7. The low-price strategy is designed to build traffic. Revenue expansion will be actively pursued through suggestive selling of related items such as sunglasses, clip-ons, and cleaning equipment.

The People's HMO

This positioning statement is an example of a strategy that involves the delivery of services similar to those of competitors, but emphasizing one major strategic difference that runs throughout the fiber of the entire organization. In all other respects, this health maintenance organization is essentially similar to its competitors; however, it seeks to establish its position in the market based on personalized attention and service.

1. Family Physicians Practice Group will offer a full range of prepaid medical and health care services. While our services are similar to those of competitors, our client base and delivery approach is not.
2. We serve the unaffiliated, individual, private family. Our primary area of focus is the individual community in which our practice clinics are located. We do not pursue, nor do we accept, large client groups such as public and private employers.
3. Our practice will combine the best of both the prepaid medical plan approach and the fee for private service approach.
4. Medical professionals, associates, and staff will be selected and retained on the basis of their interpersonal skills and interest in the humanistic side of practice, in addition to their technical competence.
5. Each family will be assigned a physician or have the choice of selecting a primary physician. That health care manager will develop a personal relationship with family members, and even though referrals may be necessary from time to time, retain a role as the central figure in the delivery of health care services.
6. This "personal" concept and practice group client loyalty will be developed through semi-annual health reviews and complete physical examinations. Client relations will be differentiated by a purposeful but slow and deliberate approach to consultation, examination, diagnosis, and prescribed treatment. Each patient will receive a minimum of a full fifteen-minute, one-to-one appointment with the physician. Our goal is to overcome the bureaucratic, mechanistic, and depersonalized image of HMOs while enjoying the benefits of this mode of operation.
7. Our prices will be generally slightly above those of large-group HMO plans, but below the private fee for service practice schedules.
8. Our promotion will be professional in nature, stressing the opportunity to get to know the physician on a long-term basis as an individual. Our strategy will be to minimize turnover of associates and staff so that continuity and personal attention is maintained at all levels.
9. Our physician staff will be recruited with the idea of making them truly partners in our operation. They will benefit from our growth and profits over time and have major policy input into the medical and administrative operations of the group.
10. Rather than grow by building a monolithic, centralized structure, we will grow through branching, controlling clinic size in order to deliver the personal service characteristic of our approach.

Urban Laboratories, Inc.

In this example, a medical lab group has decided to do a variation on the professionals' professional and to position itself as the crème de la crème of a group of competitive laboratories in a large urban market. The positioning statement might look something like this:

1. Urban Labs, Inc., is the top technical organization in its field in this region. Our technical skills and qualifications represent the latest state of the art.
2. While we do accept and promote work from normal laboratory users, our primary emphasis is on doing difficult procedures or validation tests for other laboratories or institutions and organizations that have their own internal labs but want outside confirmation.
3. Our technical personnel are the most qualified we can obtain. Their skills are enhanced by continuous training.
4. In addition to the impeccable performance of important laboratory tests, a research and development staff is dedicated to refining, developing, and even inventing new approaches to testing procedures and new tests and methods.
5. Our marketing is subtle and indirect. We do no media advertising. Staff members are active in local professional associations. They are expected to publish frequently in the learned journals in their field. They are also expected to conduct training seminars for other laboratories on a consultant basis. Our professionals are considered experts and are available as such for court cases involving expert testimony.
6. We are not interested in price competition. Our fees for regular services are at the top of the scale. This is necessary to guarantee the latest and best in both equipment and staff. Our fees for custom and consulting work are proposed on an individual engagement basis.
7. In addition to numerical test results, we provide clients with a descriptive evaluation that is helpful in their interpretation of the quantitative data.
8. The addition of new items to our service mix will be carefully controlled and restricted. We are not interested in growth for growth's sake. The addition of new services or the servicing of a new market will be authorized only after careful screening and a consensus decision by both our administrative and our technical executive committees.
9. Our objective is to have a client mix of individuals and organizations that come to us through referral as well as individuals and organizations that deal with us directly. Our goal for 1990 is to have 75 percent referral business and 25 percent direct business.
10. Although our technical and scientific staff are not expected to engage in direct client development, they are expected to establish and maintain positive working relationships with their peers and other related professionals in referral source organizations.

These sample positioning statements cover a wide variety of topics. This is typical, since any statement for a specific professional or professional organization will be unique. Some positioning statements may be more strategic in nature and deal with future expectations for the practice. This is particularly true when a professional seeks to establish a specific direction at the beginning of a practice.

This is also true when a professional or small professional firm seeks to grow by carving out a special place in the market and sets to work to create management and development programs that will achieve that objective. In drafting your own statement, try to cover as many points as possible without getting too specific about details.

You may wish to make some minor changes in time, but generally practice positioning should be a long-term strategic activity. Statements typically include reference to the longer-term objectives of the organization or individual, service mix ingredients and expansion, growth policies and strategies, fees and pricing, promotional strategy and practices, and the types of personnel and staff who would be most congruent with the organization. Like any overall policy statement positioning should be reducible to some manageable dimension. Most professionals should be able to fit their positioning statement on one or two pages. When you go much beyond that, you begin talking about ways of implementing the positioning strategy. These considerations are more appropriately left to the detailed marketing professional services plan.

Chapter 8
Your Written Communication Program

Do you have a client services information brochure? How does it look? What does it say to clients about who you are and what you are? How can you integrate your stationery, business cards, and other general written materials to convey the professional image you want? Should you advertise? What are the advantages and disadvantages? How does advertising really work? Do your engagement proposals or reports convey the proper image? Do you use a new-client letter? How can invoices, purchase orders, checks, and other materials help convey the proper printed image? What do your internal materials, such as manuals, working papers, memos, and preprinted forms, tell the staff about you?

The service field is one in which we perform for each other. Our performance is characterized by the heavy use of written and printed materials. The thoughtful development and use of printed materials is an important component of any marketing professional services program. Unfortunately, many professionals do not see written communication as an important professional service marketing system. The result is often negative or at best confusing messages to internal staff and to external clients and prospects. This chapter will help you improve your performance in this critical marketing area. We'll look at three types of written communication: institutional, competitive, and administrative. The questions raised above will be addressed and answered. In addition, we will examine other topics that relate to this area of professional practice.

YOUR IMAGE

Recently I had the pleasure of appearing on the program of the Florida Institute of Certified Public Accountants Annual Accounting Conference. Appearing with me was Norman Rachlin, founding partner of a large CPA firm, Rachlin & Cohen. Norman's presentation was entitled "Using a Printed Image to Expand Your Practice." Norman Rachlin's marketing professional services philosophy can be summarized in his own words: "If you have pride in your profession, confidence in your ability, and are convinced that you can render valuable services in today's economy, don't be secretive about it!" Norman recommends that professionals "be ethically aggressive." I've adapted his introductory remarks to his colleagues and passed them along to you. I think they capture concisely this successful professional's approach to written communication.

> One of the critical factors in practice development is the reputation of the professional firm. Many elements contribute to the evolution of a firm's reputation—the quality of its service, its expertise in certain areas, community service—but it is primarily what others see and hear about the firm. The marketplace of practice development is becoming increasingly competitive. The specter of advertising is upon us. It is therefore important that the professional firm consider the allocation of time and resources to create a printed image which will be reflective of its practice and serve to enhance its reputation.
>
> The subject of printed image covers all communication to clients—correspondence, annual reports, management letters, tax form transmittals, and newsletters. It covers printed matter of general use such as firm brochures and seminar material. And it also covers internal communication—from agendas to checklists, from forms to house organs, from memos to manuals.
> I once had a client tell me that I would be getting a call from an attorney who was preparing an estate plan for him. After I recovered from the shock I said, "But—but—we are very experienced in estate planning matters." He replied with the saddest words I ever heard, "I didn't know that you did that kind of work."[1]

Norman Rachlin's words were directed toward CPAs, but the concepts are directly applicable to anyone marketing professional services.

In today's world of depersonalized communication we hear a lot about "image." What is image? Marketing professionals define image as the way in which the marketer is perceived in the consumer's mind relative to functional and emotional attributes. As professionals, it is important that you take a minute and consider this definition. It has three important parts. The first is consumer perception: It doesn't matter what we think we are or how we think we come across in the consumer's eye. What counts is what our clients think of us. One of the most interesting studies any firm can undertake is an image assessment. It involves discussions with the firm's publics to try to determine how the firm is perceived.

Frequently clients have a different image of us than we do of ourselves. Since they are the buyers of our services, what they think is of critical importance.

I remember the case of a professional who characterized himself as a hard-driving, well-organized, efficient and effective decision maker. Discussions with clients revealed that they felt he was disorganized, and they also felt uneasy about his professional thoroughness even though they liked him personally. The reason? His office was a shambles. The reception room, secretary's office, and administrative offices were neat, clean, well appointed, and cheerful. The professional's personal office was crammed with papers, knicknacks, and furniture. His desk looked like it would spew forth an avalanche of papers at any moment. The furniture did not match. The office exuded an air of disorganization and uncompleted work. The professional had grown used to his office and never saw it through the client's eye. We suggested that if the professional couldn't clean up his act, he should have an anteroom that he could use as his "Fibber Magee" closet. Thank goodness his wife took a hand in reorganizing his office; it now is congruent with the impression created by the rest of the facility.

The second important factor is functional versus emotional impressions. As we've mentioned earlier, clients do make judgments about our professional capabilities. However, they are not as qualified to make discriminating judgments as are other professionals. Although clients do rate us on our functional attributes, they generally assume that if we are professionals, we have the ability to do the job. Clients therefore tend to rate us more carefully on the emotional component of our practice. How do we make them feel? How are they treated? How do we behave? As we stressed in Chapter 6, professionals seeking to convert prospects into clients and maintain client loyalty should minister to these emotional image dimensions as well as to the technical and functional aspects of their practices.

The third important part of our image definition is conscious versus subconscious cues. Feelings and attitudes frequently develop at the subconscious level. Clients respond subconsciously to cues in the environment and in personal interactions. We'll talk more about personal communication in the next chapter, but it's important here to note that the cues provided by your written material should evoke the type of image identification that matches your own professional marketing objectives. All professionals have an image! If you don't think about image development, you will permit an image to be formulated by default. The result may or may not be what you would desire. It is therefore important that the image cues you present to clients be appropriately developed. Your printed image is one of the most important parts of the image-building process.

Well, we've defined image. So what? And why all this concern with your printed image? Consumer behavior specialists have found that people tend to do business with individuals and firms whose image reinforces their own self-concept. This image congruence makes consumers feel at ease, makes them feel they are in the right place. The right image can result in a growing customer base and increased client loyalty. This assumes, of course, that customers' functional needs are being met.

Image congruence is particularly important when you are segmenting your professional market through specialization. I'm familiar with an accounting firm that specializes in small service industry clients. These clients are typically entrepreneurs or operate family-owned businesses. The sales of these firms range from $1 to $5 million per year. The accounting firm is constantly oversubscribed for clients and is extremely successful in terms of compensation and net profits. In addition to being expert technicians, firm members carefully manage the firm's image. Since its clients are long-hour, shirt-sleeve, hard-working, no-frills operators, the accounting firm also works in this mode. Few firm members drive a Cadillac. The mode is Fords and Chevrolets. The firm's facilities, while not spartan, are certainly not elegant. Written communications are functional but do not convey a feeling of high prestige. Clients of this firm not only recommend them to other businesses, but even to other competitors. In addition to its professional expertise, the firm has adroitly managed its image development for the segment it serves.

The first step is to recognize that all written communication, both external and internal, represents an opportunity to convey a development-enhancing image. To organize this broad area so that you can identify it, develop it, and manage it effectively, I recommend you classify written communications into the three basic components illustrated in Figure 8-1. While this taxonomy is not totally discrete and overlaps do occur, it serves the purpose. Institutional communication is concerned with creating a general favorable image for the professional or firm as a whole. Its primary purpose is informational, not persuasive. Institutional communications do not have a direct and immediate sales objective. They therefore seem less threatening to prospects, and in my judgment present no ethical problems for the professional. Competitive communications are primarily persuasive in nature. They have a specific sales objective and almost always fall under the category of advertising. Administrative communication refers to those written materials that are necessary to the conduct of a professional practice—invoices, purchase orders, checks, routine correspondence, manuals, forms, memos, and so on. In many cases these materials are never seen by prospects or clients. They exist in the restricted world of the professional's staff. Other administrative communication is seen by clients. Nonclient external third parties such as suppliers and service reps represent yet another audience for administrative written communication.

FIGURE 8-1 The components of a written communications program

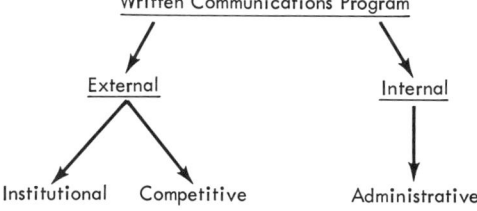

In the following pages we will treat institutional, competitive, and administrative written communications separately and indicate opportunities for improving your MPS effectiveness in each of these areas. But first let's look at logos.

HAVE YOU SEEN OUR LOGO?

I'd like you to consider the use of a logo as a vehicle to integrate your written communication pieces. A *logo* is an identifying symbol or distinctive mode of expression used to identify a product or organization. There are many logos that you recognize. Why are logos so widely used? Each marketer is hoping to reserve a spot in the consumer's memory in which the logo will be filed. Upon seeing the logo, the consumer will remember the organization and its products and services. This is a convenient form of communication shorthand. The logo is to institutional marketing what the brand is to product marketing. Building logo recognition is a long-term proposition. That's why it is essential that the logo be imprinted on every piece of written communication utilized by the professional.

Effective Logos

Selecting a logo is one of the key written communication program decisions. Of course, you want your logo to say what you want it to say and convey an impression that is congruent with your own image objective. The logo should be consistent with the positioning of your professional practice and the market segment you seek to serve. Here are a few other desirable characteristics of an effective logo:

1. Meaning. Logos that are far out on the spectrum of modern art might win awards; however, they cause difficulty for clients. Highly abstract logos may find eventual recognition, but the costs of establishing identity and the time taken to achieve this objective should make this approach inappropriate for the professional.

2. Descriptive of the firm. This is a tough one. The Bell System logo is extremely descriptive and calls to mind the well-known communications firm. Figure 8-2 illustrates a logo we developed for a chain of private schools for children with learning disabilities. This logo features the head of a young child with a rainbow of knowledge lighting up and radiating from within the illustration. This award-winning logo is extremely effective in color. More important, it relates to the professional service—turning on the young learner and developing capabilities for academic success. Frequently, logos have a slogan, saying, creed, or philosophical statement that appears with the emblem or symbol. In this case, the child's head logo is usually accompanied by the statement, "every child can succeed."

3. Endurance. Selecting a logo based on some current fad or area of professional emphasis may be effective in the short run but in the long run can be the kiss

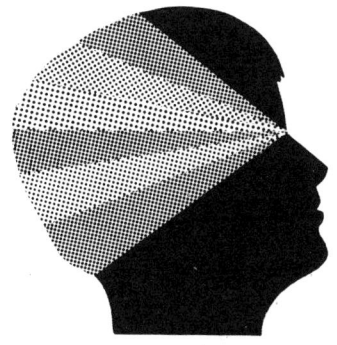

FIGURE 8-2 A descriptive MPS logo
Source: Gables Academies Inc., general information brochure.

of death. An engineering consulting firm utilizing some variation of the space shuttle imagery might find that such a logo dates it or conveys the impression that its professional skills are limited to one specific form of technology. It is better to look for a symbol that is broader in application and that will have meaning over the indefinite future.

4. Distinctiveness. Easy to recommend, difficult to achieve. Figure 8-3 illustrates a logo for Tom Collins Yacht Charter Services, Inc. As a matter of fact, the owner's name actually is Tom Collins. You can see the logo capitalizes on that well-known tropical drink while utilizing the straw in the cocktail as the main-mast for the sailboat image. This type of logo design opportunity is the commercial artist's dream. While your own professional specialty might not be as nifty as that of "Tom Collins," you may be able to use symbolism regarding the service you per-

FIGURE 8-3 A distinctive service logo
Source: Tom Collins Yacht Charter Services, Inc. brochure.

form or feature the well-known "tools of your trade" in your logo. The trick, of course, is to do this in a distinctive manner that is unique to your own professional practice.

5. Universality. Will your logo travel well? For most professional individuals and organizations, this is not a major consideration. However, if you anticipate providing services across regions or national borders, you may be concerned. I'm involved with a firm founded to do research and marketing work for clients who develop and market planned communities. Since it was anticipated that the clientele would include not only North American but Central and South American firms, the acronym CASA was chosen. The CASA logo actually stands for Corporate Advisory Services Associates, Inc. The word *CASA* means "house" or "home" in Spanish and in several other Latin-based languages. The name is distinctive, does identify one aspect of what we do, and travels very well.

6. Availability. Before you settle on a particular logo, have your attorney check the Federal Register to be sure that this symbol, name, or distinctive mode of expression has not already been registered by someone else. Take a look at that soda can, pack of cigarettes, or bag of potato chips you have in your office. You'll note the small initials "tm" or "®" next to the brand or brand name. This means that this particular brand is registered. Registration does not necessarily mean that no one else will use your symbol. It is, however, the first step in successfully defending yourself against use of your logo by others. I was recently involved in the development of a logo for a client in the marine manufacturing industry. We developed twenty-three logos. The client liked three, but the legal department found that two of the three were already in use and registered. Fortunately, the third was not and it was the logo selected for the new product line. The recommendation is obvious. Develop some alternative logos and check with your attorney to see which are available before making your final decision.

Who Should Do the Job?

Should you develop your own logo? I wouldn't recommend it. For something as important as your logo, I suggest you go to a specialist. Check your Yellow Pages under Art and Design firms. In addition, the art departments of advertising agencies may accept the assignment if they think you could be a future client. At least they will usually recommend a freelance artist whose specialty is creative design. The cost? It can vary quite a bit. It pays to shop. I paid a freelance artist $150 for five sketches, one of which later became the logo for a corporate client. On the other hand, working with top professionals and developing alternative logos can easily run from several hundred to several thousand dollars. I suspect you'd be able to get several renditions of a logo for under a thousand dollars, however. Please remember that a logo for a dental clinic specializing in orthodontia will be a great deal more difficult to develop than a logo representing a firm that manufactures children's toys. It's up to you to provide design input to help the creative specialist satisfy as many criteria for successful logo development as possible.

INSTITUTIONAL COMMUNICATION: THE VIP APPROACH

The VIP approach to communication is one many professionals have found helpful. I utilize the VIP approach as a way of conceptualizing the communications jobs to be done and the proper sequence for these tasks. V stands for visibility, I stands for information, and P represents persuasion. One way of looking at the role of communication is that the basic effort is aimed first toward establishing visibility for the professional; second, toward providing useful and needed information to clients; third, toward persuading prospective clients to become clients and continually persuading existing clients to remain. In addition to being easy to remember, the VIP approach presents the communications objectives for the professional in a logical and sequential form. In reality, visibility and information are tied together. Being on a community board might provide visibility for an area professional. However, it is not likely that a wide number of people will be aware of important information the professional would like to communicate. Institutional communication is information-based. It is not persuasive in nature, at least not nearly so as advertising or other forms of persuasive communication. It is usually nonthreatening to the receiver and in many cases may be welcomed and beneficial. It is my opinion that even the most conservative professional would find little objection to the development and dissemination of institutional communication. Perhaps you're taking a shopping trip through the new area of marketing professional services. You're still trying to determine whether developing a marketing program is for you. It would be my guess that no matter how you feel about marketing you may find that you want to carry out some of the recommendations in the institutional communications area. Institutional communication is the area of greatest common agreement concerning "acceptable" marketing practices.

Functions

In addition to providing information, institutional communications serve two very specific marketing functions: preselling and alleviating postpurchase doubt.

While you would expect no one to sign an order for services or retain you or your organization based on a review of a piece of institutional communication, you have every right to expect that that prospective client would be more favorably predisposed to purchasing your services. Each piece of institutional communication should be designed with the preselling objective in mind. A "special topics brochure" dealing with critical design problems in municipal structures would not directly solicit clients for an architect, but this institutional piece should convey the message that the professional firm is aware of public sector management problems and is capable of dealing with and solving them. Unlike persuasive communication, however, the emphasis should always be on providing useful information. But a city manager who has read the architectural firm's brochure should be more favorably disposed toward that firm than he or she was prior to reading it. The development of effective institutional communication will greatly enhance the probability of acceptance of the professional individual or firm. The decision to retain will then be focused upon details such as schedules, fees, and other special requirements pertaining to a single engagement.

Earlier in the book, we discussed the phenomenon of cognitive dissonance, the feelings of doubt and uncertainty we frequently experience after we have made a significant purchase decision. The retention of a high-priced professional or professional firm to assist us with our problems usually triggers postpurchase doubt. Such doubts on the part of consumers of professional services run the gamut from small individual purchases to large organizational contracts. For example, an individual who has just spent $400 for a complete annual physical may wonder whether or not the physician and staff utilized were the best for the money. Similarly, officials of the National Aeronautics and Space Administration may have serious doubts concerning the engineering consulting firm chosen to work on the guidance system for the modified Space Shuttle.

What do these professional service consumers have in common? They are all wondering, "Did we do the right thing?" The presence of well-developed institutional communications will do a lot to alleviate these postpurchase doubts. If, for example, the medical patient and the NASA purchasing group could read an institutional brochure about the professional or professional firm they are utilizing, the reasons for selecting that firm or individual would be clear again, and postpurchase doubt reduced.

Your Institutional Communications Arsenal

My approach to institutional communications involves a number of the following tools: the client services brochure, the partners brochure, special topics brochures, newsletters, updates, publications, directory listings.

1. The client services brochure. Most professionals are qualified to perform a wide range of related services. Often new clients utilize only one or two. How are consumers to know of your specialties if you don't tell them? It would be unprofessional to give a sales talk to every prospect or client. Let your client services brochure do the talking for you.

The client services brochure is informational. In addition to cataloguing and briefly describing the services offered, it should be written from the client's point of view. That is, it should describe the typical types of problems clients have and how the organization is equipped to deal with them. This brochure should face the issues many professionals seem to leave as mysteries to be solved by clients— appointment systems, fees, billing systems, credit availability, and any other administrative procedures that affect the client-professional interface. The basic philosophy is to reflect upon your professional environment and then attempt to identify with potential and existing clients who may be seeking your service. What are their concerns? What negative and positive experiences might they have had with other professionals? What would *you* wish to know about a professional or organization you were evaluating? Placing your client first in the consideration of any marketing question will provide you with the probability of developing the satisfactory answer.

Professionals frequently ask, "Should we put pictures of ourselves and our staff in the general brochure?" The answer is a qualified "yes." Pictures are not necessary, but they do provide clients with a sense of a more personal identification with the organization. Some communications specialists argue that pictures may be damaging; that is, individuals may make judgments based on certain prejudices they have relative to appearance. These prejudices may operate at the subconscious level, but nonetheless be powerful. Whether or not photos are used, there should be a section describing the background and qualifications of the individual professional staff. Since professionals and staff members do change in organizations over time, it is not advisable to have a photograph of the whole group or information concerning all professionals and staff. The brochure should feature senior personnel who have a high probability of remaining with the group at least for the life of the brochure!

This brochure may be placed in waiting rooms; inserted in the response to every inquiry for services whether the inquiry came via phone or in writing; handed out at seminars, meetings, or any other occasion when the professional is involved in some formal program. The professional should never travel without a supply. The client services brochure is the basic institutional communications document.

2. The partners, associates, or principals brochure. This brochure is recommended for any professional service firm in which there may be two or more members in the top management group. This group may be called partners, the executive committee, principals, or something else, depending on the profession. Two is not a magic number; the decision to issue a separate partners brochure is strictly up to you. In the smaller organization, the "meet the partners" communication task can be handled as part of the client service information brochure. In larger organizations, you may wish to consider a separate publication.

The objective of this brochure is twofold. First, the specific and impressive qualifications of individual partners and of the top people in the organization create confidence and an acceptance of the firm's capabilities. Second is what I call the "one-stop shopping" objective. In scanning the brochure, prospective clients will be aware that the firm has technical expertise in a wide range of areas relating to the profession. Remember Norman Rachlin's lament when a client utilized another CPA firm for estate tax planning? The reason was that the client did not know Rachlin & Cohen did estate planning work. There would be slight chance of that happening today. In addition to the firm's general brochure, the Rachlin & Cohen "Meet the Partners" brochure clearly makes the point that there are several partners who specialize in tax and estate matters as well as a wide range of professional accounting and management consulting services.

Finally, this brochure has a nice way of personalizing the organization. Both brochures may be circulated among staff in a prospective client's organization. The preselling and personalizing these two pieces accomplish can improve the chances for client acquisition and retention.

But beware! There are a few kisses of death for "Meet the Partners" brochures. Be sure not to have partners provide photographs that have been taken by amateurs. Have all photographs taken by the same photographer to maintain technical and esthetic consistency. Let people be themselves. A partner who is always smiling and has a cheerful twinkle in his or her eye should not be made to adopt a Supreme Court Justice pose. Conversely, a serious and reserved individual should not be asked to look like Hermione Gingold or Chevy Chase. If your partners are really a team, show them as a team. Supplement the brochure with photos of group meetings, partners working together, and partners working with staff and clients. This will help emphasize the point that all the expertise and personal service of the firm are available to each client.

3. Special topics brochures. The objective of these supplementary pieces is to provide specific and useful information to prospective and existing clients. Special topics brochures generally address one of two types of topics. The first is a topic of general interest to all types of prospective and existing clients. For example, a consulting engineering firm might publish a special topics brochure entitled "The Revised Clean Air Act—Implications for the Small Manufacturer." This brochure would be of interest to all small manufacturers regardless of specific industry or product category. If the brochure is problem or solution oriented, it would probably be well received and carefully read by a majority of recipients. The second type of brochure is much more specific and is usually targeted to one market segment—for example, "Maximizing Scrubber Efficiency for the Coal-Fired Public Utility." This brochure deals with one aspect of pollution control in the public utility industry. It has a highly specific subject matter and audience. While this brochure might be more difficult to develop, it gives the consulting engineering firm an opportunity to demonstrate excellence in this highly specific design and consulting area.

Ideally, professional organizations should have both types of brochures. One orthopedic clinic, for example, has a brochure entitled "Health and Aging." This brochure cuts across many segments and is of wide general interest. Another brochure entitled "Recovering from Back Surgery" is highly specific. Both are extremely helpful to patients, create an excellent professional image, and provide useful information.

In some cases, professional associations or suppliers to the profession provide brochures. These brochures address both general and specific topics of interest to professional clients. In addition to providing information, they usually make the point that seeking professional assistance is advisable. You may wish to utilize such brochures to augment your own creations. But before you order a year's supply, be sure to review these brochures carefully. Sometimes they are designed to be all things to all people, and while generally well done may not necessarily fit the image or specific target market you are seeking to pursue. Please remember special topics brochures are soft-sell. Like all institutional communication, they seek to establish you as a knowledgeable individual with the appropriate professional image.

4. Newsletters. The decision to publish a newsletter is a major one that should involve a great deal of analysis and discussion. A well-prepared and distributed newsletter received by an interested and appropriate audience accomplishes three goals. First, image enhancement can take place on a regular basis. Second, the reduction of dissonance and maintenance of existing client loyalty is enhanced. And finally, there is a probability that the expansion of services to existing and potential clients can be affected, since the newsletter provides an excellent vehicle for demonstrating service needs and your own capabilities.

Newsletter disadvantages are numerous. First, producing and distributing several hundred or several thousand quality pieces could cost anywhere from $1000 to $3000 and more. This figure assumes a good deal of internal involvement in preparation. Second is what I call the "burnout rate." This involves several phenomena. First, your own enthusiasm associated with newsletter production will dim as time and operational problems connected with your primary practice intervene. Second, the hot news items aren't always there when you're ready to prepare a newsletter. A certain amount of filler seems always to be necessary. Third, clients, who find initial newsletters a novelty, may soon get used to them. When was the last time you anxiously awaited and read a newsletter from some outside source?

Finally, mailing lists need to be constantly updated if waste circulation is to be kept to a minimum. I was involved in writing and supervising the preparation of a newsletter for a client. This national newsletter went to a mailing list of over 8000 professional individuals and organizations. I was alarmed to learn that the mailing list had not been updated for five years. On doing a positive purge—sending a card with the newsletter indicating that it needed to be returned if the individual was to continue being on the mailing list—we received only 450 returns indicating desire to continue the newsletter.

Here are some additional tips: (1) Putting together a bimonthly or monthly newsletter is almost a full-time job in itself. The burnout rate will get you. Consider the alternative of quarterly or semi-annual newsletters. Or publish a newsletter when you really have something important to communicate. (2) Do it right or don't do it at all. A newsletter says much more about your organization than your partners brochure. It may have pass-along value and long life. It also indicates what you think is important and demonstrates your graphic as well as your written image. (3) Each newsletter must be sold—that is, the recipient must be told why he or she should take the time to read it. (4) The use of diagnostic checklists or self-help questionnaires can enhance readability. The Rachlin & Cohen newsletter contains a full-page calendar of essential tax dates. This calendar can be removed from the letter and taped to the desk of financial and accounting personnel. (5) I receive a newsletter from a large national professional firm. It basically tells what's going on in the various major offices and is a newsy who's who. I could care less! This firm has the newsletter confused with an internal house organ. Internal house organs have the staff as their primary audience. Their communications task is much different from that of an external newsletter. Don't confuse the two. By the way, this newsletter costs the firm over $50,000 per year. It is largely an internal ego trip. (6) Beware of newsletter inertia. I recall one instance in which it took us about two years to gradually strangle a newsletter out of existence. Why? Well, because of newsletter inertia. It had always been there, so why shouldn't it continue to exist? And second, because the "President's Page" was dearly regarded by the fine chief executive in that professional firm, he was reluctant to let his forum go. However, this particular newsletter finally got a quiet yet decent burial.

5. Updates. A variation on the newsletter is the development and dissemination of periodic updates. This form of communication might be nothing more than a one-page letter on special stationery. Your update could also take the form of a one-fold four-page newsletter. The update format has a lot to recommend it, particularly for the smaller and growing professional organization. A psychologist friend recently enlarged and refurbished his office facilities, took in a partner, and began to offer special group sessions dealing with divorce, death, parenting, and other family-related matters. The update format used assumed everyone knew about the professional practice and proceeded to "update" them concerning the new services, personnel, and offices.

Professionals have an excellent opportunity to use the update mode to disseminate new knowledge, legislation, court decisions, methodologies, or changes in local area conditions. If you've done your homework concerning target market identification and segmentation, you're in a position to begin developing a mailing list for your update. An inventory of update materials should be maintained in each update. Let your readers know that they may receive, at no charge, prior update information of interest to them.

6. Publications. This broad label covers articles in professional journals, general magazines, and newspapers. If you want to position yourself or your firm as the professional's professional, then one requirement would be that you establish and maintain a presence in the appropriate professional journals. If you have a dearth of creative writing skills, don't let that bother you. You do have the technical expertise necessary to generate useful insights and information. Professional articles can be co-authored or ghostwritten. I've co-authored articles with bankers and psychologists. In addition, I've done a good deal of ghostwriting. Ghostwriting may involve no more than giving a detailed outline and background material to a freelancer and having him or her prepare a rough draft for your final polishing. If you utilize a collaborator, it's best to develop a working relationship with one individual over time. That person will become familiar with your field and with your own personal style and image objectives.

Please remember you are writing for the reader and not for yourself! If you are a dentist writing in a professional dental journal, then the conventions, language, format, scientific support, and conservative approach might be utilized. However, the same dentist writing an article on reducing dental costs in the large family for a popular magazine will have to convert to lay language, simple illustrative stories based on actual cases, and firm, prescriptive suggestions presented in a light and readable manner.

I've recently finished reviewing an article by an attorney client. The article is fantastic, one of the best I've ever read—if it were intended for other attorneys! However, it's meant for executives in a particular commercial field who utilize legal services. The article is intended for an industry magazine. It needs some surgery before it will have a chance of being accepted for publication. The attorney recognized this and welcomed constructive critique and revisions.

Our approach will be to develop a list of relevant publications read by industry leaders. We will then secure copies of the magazines, review them, and select primary and secondary targets. In addition to complying with the technical and mechanical requirements for manuscript submission, we will also point out to the editors that this particular article is targeted specifically to decision makers and their readership group. We will indicate that we welcome their critique and would be pleased to make the revisions necessary to make this article acceptable for publication and useful to their audience.

7. Directory listings. There are literally hundreds of professional directories of one type or another. Some, like the Martindale-Hubbel for attorneys, provide miniature resumés for each individual listed. In addition, the Martindale-Hubbel system provides a summary ranking. Other directories are based on membership in certain professional organizations. Although it is doubtful that directories are the basis of consumer decision making in the selection of professionals, they do serve as a starting point in some cases. In others, they are a confirmation that the professional is one who should be considered or possibly retained. Directories are important, and the following steps should be observed concerning their role in your written communications program: (1) Identify the directory or directories basic to your professional field. (2) Study the requirements for listing and the existing listings of professionals with whom you are familiar and who operate in your market area. (3) Rank available directories in priority order where more than one major candidate exists. (4) Comply with listing requirements and submit your listing or request to be included. (5) Enhance and update your listing on a regular basis. Such enhancement might involve additional certifications in your field, honors and awards received, or the publication of a professional article.

A final word on directories. Sometimes opportunistic entrepreneurs develop "directories for no one." The beneficiaries are the entrepreneurs who develop them and enjoy the fees collected from gullible subscribers. Before you try to get into every directory available, make a careful attempt to determine that prospective and existing clients also receive and use such directories. In my judgment, the several professional associations would be well advised to develop, publish, and control their own directories. Being active in your own professional organization is one way to see that this goal is reached.

COMPETITIVE COMMUNICATION

The objective of competitive communication is to persuade perspective and existing clients to try, to continue, or to broaden their use of your services. For the 1980s, advertising is the hottest topic area in competitive communication. In addition to considering advertising, however, in this section we will also look at proposals, reports, and seminar materials.

Before we launch into our discussion of advertising, it's important to note that advertising can be institutional as well as competitive. Would you object to having your name or the name of your firm and your specialty appear in a two-by-four-inch space in the conference program of a professional association? This type of announcement merely lets people know that you or your firm assisted in the financing that made possible the publication of the conference proceedings. Yet, this activity does fit the definition of advertising. *Advertising* is the paid communication of a message over a mass medium by an identified sponsor. There is a gray area along the border of the continuum between institutional and competitive advertising. Let's say, for example, that you are a consumer psychologist. You place an ad in the *Journal of Marketing* which simply says: "Johanna Winston, Ph.D., specializing in focused group research and interpretation." Is this an institutional or a competitive ad? While the ad is primarily informative, its placement in the *Journal of Marketing* is designed to stimulate inquiries by clients who might be interested in conducting small group research. Because of my acknowledged marketing orientation, I would find an announcement such as this extremely inoffensive and highly institutional. What would your reaction be?

ADVERTISING

How It Works: Short-term and Long-term Objectives

No one is precisely sure how advertising works. Researchers have long attempted—futilely—to trace a linear, causal link between advertising and sales. Savvy marketing professionals recognize that advertising is merely one ingredient in a marketing program, albeit an important one. And yet you may argue that your household treks to the supermarket in response to Thursday's newspaper advertising for food and beverage specials. Is that not a cause and effect relationship? Let's briefly examine and differentiate between the short-term and long-term effects of advertising.

Effective short-term advertising seeks to stimulate awareness, interest, and action *now*. To be successful, it requires an interested potential consumer. The reason you are so responsive to the Thursday supermarket ads is that you need to replace food and beverage items in your household inventory. You're going to do the shopping anyway; it's a habitual pattern. Food marketers are attempting to lure you away from your normal purveyor through the use of small price differentials, heavily promoted in the bastion of retail advertising—the newspaper. Did that one newspaper ad cause you to behave? cause sales? I doubt it. It was part of an overall marketing and buying behavior pattern. You were already an interested and experienced consumer.

How does this relate to the professional environment? There may be specific situations or patterns of seasonality common to your profession. An optometrist friend noted that his local practice exploded shortly after public school system vision examinations were administered. This might represent a perfect opportunity for the placement of short-term competitive advertising. Parents whose children need help will be actively considering and seeking professional assistance. A two- or three-week series of ads in local newspapers and on spot radio might be just the ticket.

Long-term advertising should pursue three basic objectives. First, the professional should seek to develop and maintain consumer awareness. The content of this advertising is primarily informative and somewhat institutional in nature. Once it is verified or believed that the desired level of client awareness has been achieved, advertising should be modified to contain more persuasive appeals. These appeals are aimed at getting prospective clients to take action now and to promote expansion of consumption by existing clients. Finally, if and when the professional or professional firm achieves dominance in the marketplace, advertising objectives should shift toward reinforcing client loyalty and maintaining professional image.

Before a professional decides to adopt long-run advertising objectives, including information, persuasion, and reinforcement, it's important to consider how advertising works. Like all fields in marketing, advertising is a highly specialized and complete career field in its own right. With due apology to my own professional colleagues, I've attempted to simplify this approach for the beginning professional reader. Before you as a professional decide to engage in advertising over the long term, you should be willing to accept and carry out the activities and costs involved in achieving *matching* and *momentum*.

The process of matching involves what we have already discussed in terms of market identification and segmentation. You must be the expert or get professional assistance in determining specific objectives for client acquisition. Based on this knowledge, it will be possible to match existing communication vehicles and creative strategy to the targets you have specified. Momentum refers to setting an activity in motion and leaving it in motion over time. I liken long-range or campaign advertising to packing a small snowball at the peak of a very high mountain. As the snowball slowly begins to roll down the mountainside, it gathers both mass and velocity. If properly packed, aimed, directed, and permitted to run its full course, it has the greatest likelihood of reaching the conclusion of its journey with the potential of high impact. Engaging in long-run advertising, then, involves making a significant commitment over time. Please consider this carefully.

As professionals began to engage in advertising during the 1970s, my suspicions that we would see a lot of the "spastic syndrome" were confirmed. If the following discussion describes you, don't be embarrassed. It also describes a majority of business firms who are just beginning to utilize advertising in their marketing mix. The spastic syndrome goes something like this: First, the prospective advertiser begins considering the should-I-advertise question. Second, a highly persuasive media salesperson, marketing consultant, or ad agency representative convinces the prospect to advertise. Third, the prospect agrees with trepidation, putting a toe in the water and limiting the budget and scope of the advertising on an experimental basis. Fourth, because of the limited budget, scope, and exposure of the advertising, the advertiser is extremely disappointed. Thinking that advertising means marketing and expecting an overnight bonanza, the advertiser concludes: "Advertising doesn't work for me." Fifth, the advertiser vows never to advertise again. Sixth, as time passes, enter another persuasive media salesperson, another short-term and impotent campaign, and another failure. And there you have the spastic syndrome.

Other than short-term advertising discussed earlier, I strongly recommend that you engage in no advertising at all if you are not prepared to accept the campaign approach.

The Campaign Approach

An advertising campaign consists of the development, placement, running, and evaluation of objective-directed advertising over time. A campaign typically covers a period of months and involves repeated media insertions during that period. In this case, time is your mountain and the snowball is the combined cumulative effect of carefully placed and appropriately developed advertisements. Developing an advertising campaign involves the following steps:

1. Market research and analysis. You will have already accomplished some or most of this as part of your marketing program development.

2. Objective formulation. Keep your objectives limited in scope. For example, a professional client wanted to utilize advertising to develop sales. We suggested that the advertising be directed toward creating inquiries and requests for professional publications. Our campaign was nonthreatening to prospects, resulted in the distribution of informative, institutional publications, and stimulated a number of inquiries, some of which were turned into engagements. Remember, the more precise and limited your objective, the better opportunity for measurement in the development of a learning curve.

3. Budgeting. We usually do it backwards. The first question is often "How much do we have to spend?" This should be the last question raised. Forget your constraints—it's called creativity! Rather, develop a list of desirable objectives. Once your list is completed, make priorities from most to least important. Next, enumerate the tasks necessary to pursue and achieve these objectives. Finally, figure the cost of accomplishing each task. Sometimes, this results in a rearrangement of objectives. You'll get to cost constraints soon enough; it's self-defeating to begin with them. Advertising costs money. Major regional and national campaigns are frightfully expensive. Procter & Gamble's annual media advertising expenditure is rapidly moving toward three-quarters of a billion dollars. Don't panic, you're not Procter & Gamble. For many professionals, the market is highly localized and reachable at a reasonable figure.

4. Media selection. Which media are most often listened to, viewed, or read by your target market? What are the advantages and disadvantages of each medium? Campaign planning requires careful analysis, selection, scheduling, implementation, and follow-up on promotional media.

5. Creative development. Once you've determined to whom you wish to speak, the basic campaign objectives, how much time or space you are going to be able to afford, and the vehicles to be utilized, the next major decision is what do you say and in what form. You must gain attention, but that attention should be focused in a professional manner, and the information and appeals conveyed congruent with the positioning of your practice.

6. Approval. If your advertising is prepared by an agency, a consultant, a public relations counsel, or some other outsider, it is *essential* that you be comfortable with the creative approach taken by the specialist. I like to talk in terms of "comfort zones." For example, it is doubtful that professionals would agree with every aspect of the creative approaches recommended to represent them to their markets. This does not mean that you as an individual might not approve the recommendations of an outside specialist concerning your campaign. As long as the approach is in line with your service positioning, is appropriately geared to your target market, and is in good taste, you may decide to give approval even though you don't agree with every aspect of the plan. The basic question is this: "Are you fundamentally comfortable with the overall approach being taken?"

7. Scheduling and implementation. You should be involved in discussions concerning the timing and release of campaign materials. Presumably you know your market as well as anyone. When you are seeking to penetrate a new market, your client analysis and targeting work should place you in an excellent position to assist in scheduling the campaign. Implementation is usually the job of your outside specialist or media representative.

8. Evaluation. This step is often missing in a formal campaign plan. It is difficult to pinpoint precisely and quantify the effects of advertising. However, if your objectives are limited and clearly stated, there may be a way to measure results. In professional service marketing, what you're really looking for are inquiries or consultations. It's doubtful that people decide to become clients based on what they see in a particular ad or in a campaign. What they may decide to do, however, is request further information so that they can study your materials and make a decision as to whether or not to contact you by phone or in person. Requests for information—client services brochure, partners brochure, special topic brochures, updates—can be measured. Phone inquiries, appointment bookings, and requests for consultations can also be quantified.

A useful way of tracking specific media response is to key inquiries so that the inquiry identifies where the consumer heard or read your advertisement. For example, a return address specifying that the reader include "Department L" might be keyed as the *Los Angeles Times*. Written requests for literature can then be compiled and the advertising results from the *Los Angeles Times* compared to inquiries based on radio spots or some other medium. The field of advertising research is a complex specialty. Major regional and national advertisers should consult specialists in advertising agencies or market research firms to develop appropriate measurement methods. As important as attempting to measure the effect of one ad campaign is the development of comparative measures over several campaigns. Careful measurement permits the development of an efficient learning curve as to what type of media, message, timing, and insertion rate are best for you. With the campaign approach, you will become more and more efficient with your advertising investment. There will be mistakes, but with careful tracking and comparative analysis, you'll begin to see what works and what does not.

How To Get the Job Accomplished

In their book *How To Market Your Law Practice*, Gilson, Cawley, and Schmidt observe that an attorney who is his own advertising agency has a fool for a client![2] This statement answers one question and raises another. I agree with these authors that professionals should seek outside input concerning how best to communicate their messages to prospective clients. But there is still a good deal of debate as to how to get the job accomplished. Let's examine a few of the alternatives, including your own department, a public relations firm, media representatives, independent consultants, and the retention of an advertising agency.

If your practice size and staff are developed sufficiently to warrant a full-time person in charge of marketing, that individual should be responsible for the development of the total written communications program. There's a significant advantage in this approach. The staff person knows the organization, its services, its personnel, the competitive environment, and the profession in general. In some cases, that individual might also be a professional. It's probably not unusual in the larger professional service organizations to have an executive in charge of client development who is also a member of the profession in question, such as an architect, a consulting engineer, or a CPA. The major disadvantage of this approach is that the internal person may suffer from organizational constraints, biases, politics, and a limited perspective. In cases where this individual is subordinate to top management, there may be a reluctance to present bold and innovative programs or to advocate techniques that experience has shown will not receive general approval from key partners or principals. This danger is not as great in consumer and industrial products organizations, where the majority of individuals operate under the marketing concept and where tradition is something to be challenged, not necessarily preserved.

Outside sources include media reps, the PR firm, consultants, and ad agencies. For the small professional advertiser, the sales staff of the media being evaluated can be very helpful in the suggestion and development of creative ideas. I always recommend that professionals invite a wide range of media reps in for discussions concerning their potential advertising program. Reps are then given an assignment to develop some ideas for the prospective client. These ideas are presented and discussed. While this is a speculative mode, this is the way the game is played. The reps know it. Frequently they will outdo themselves to develop and even produce good commercial materials at no cost for prospective clients. They're hoping to earn commissions on the sale of time or space and sell their prospective client as a repeat advertiser. The major danger here is that few media reps have experience in or sensitivity to professional service marketing. Dependency on media reps is best backed by your own internal marketing specialist as a campaign development and placement strategy. No matter how creative or sensitive a media rep might be, there may be a tendency to overstate the case for the particular medium.

Hiring a public relations firm has been a popular way for professional firms to stick their toe in the water of professional service marketing. Public relations firms specialize in maintaining positive communication flows to the "publics" of an organization. In a corporation, these "publics" include labor, consumers, the government, unions, investors, and the community. The basic objective of public relations activities is to develop and maintain a favorable image with the publics in question. Public relations specialists are skilled communicators, have good contacts with the media, and are aware of major community affairs that might be utilized to showcase their clients. Public relations, in my opinion, is one part of an effective marketing program. However, it is only a part of marketing. Retaining a PR firm can be expensive for the smaller professional practice. There are useful marketing activities that can be carried out without retaining PR counsel. Professionals considering retaining a PR firm should look for a full-service organization, one that is capable of doing client research and analysis, market segmentation and targeting, practice positioning, and the development and writing of facilitating communications and advertising programs. I'm not anti-PR; in fact, every professional should probably contact PR firms and evaluate the services they can perform.

Consultants are typically called in on a one-time basis to deal with specific problems or develop specific programs. Marketing consultants may be found as part of the professional staffs of management consulting firms, in the management services department of some large CPA firms, on the staffs of marketing research firms, on the staffs of some of the larger advertising agencies, or as independent professionals. Like the PR counsel, they can bring valuable outside insight and creativity without all the preconditioned biases and political constraints of the internal marketing specialist. Many university faculty members maintain an active consulting practice in their field of specialization.

The media rep works at no charge; earnings are based on commissions on media time or space sold. Most public relations firms like to work on a retainer agreement. Within the retainer, they perform certain agreed-upon services. Consultants are usually paid on a project basis. Project fees are based on the number of hours anticipated for the completion of the project, multiplied by their hourly or daily rates and rates of staff plus expenses. In some cases, consultants work out well enough to be offered retainers and to become long-term members of the professional service management team in their area of expertise. Hiring a consultant, a PR firm, or an ad agency is a professional service buying situation in reverse. These marketing and communications specialists run the gamut in every important criteria from cost to quality of service. Be cautious in your selection. Shop comparatively. Talk personally with the individuals or organizations you are considering. Outside marketing assistance is a professional service of the most personal nature. These individuals will work closely with you and your staff. They will be privy to the most proprietary details concerning your practice. Their reputations and qualifications should be beyond reproach, and the personal chemistry should be positive.

Advertising agencies are middlemen in the channel of distribution for communications. They buy media at a discount, bill you for the retail price of the media, and for the difference prepare and place your advertising. Although most agencies are not geared to handle the individual practitioner or small account, agencies do have some distinct advantages. First, they may have experience with the market you are trying to reach. Second, they are highly specialized, with individual departments for media, copy, production, art, research, and other tasks associated with campaign development and implementation. A powerful argument for hiring an agency is that since the advertiser has to pay the retail rate for media anyway, why not place the advertising through an agency and enjoy the services of a specialized, professional firm? But please remember that services beyond the preparation of advertising ideas and programs are typically billed on a fee basis. If you were to want an expensive TV commercial, production costs would be billed on top of creative costs. Please don't get the impression that advertising agency services are free. For the larger user of mass media, media commissions can cover a large portion of agency expense; however, additional work such as special production, research, and marketing work are usually billed at cost plus about 17.5 percent for agency overhead and profit. Before you make the ad agency decision, be sure to consult the many excellent books and articles concerning agency selection.

Classic Advertising Mistakes

There are scores of books and hundreds of articles that treat the topic of developing effective advertising. If advertising is a major part of your professional service marketing program, presumably you will be getting expert assistance. There are, however, some special dangers I want to bring to your attention. These situations can lead to significant errors for inexperienced advertisers in the professional service field.

FIGURE 8-4 Advertising—A poor example
Source: "The Flyer" a community shopping guide.

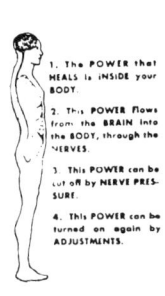
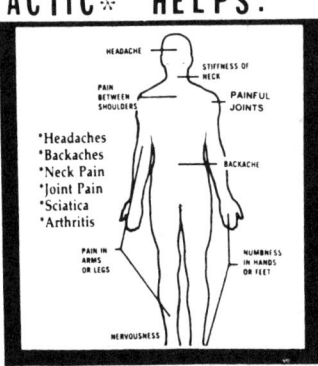

1. Underinvestment. Don't "try" advertising in little sample bites. For an ad to be seen or heard, it must have either dominance or sufficient repetition. The American Advertising Federation has estimated that the average family of four is exposed to from 1000 to 1500 promotional impressions daily. What makes us think that our one column inch ad in today's newspaper will even be perceived as existing? Ask yourself, What chance does my message have of being seen or heard? It may be better to place your dollars somewhere else in the marketing program than to fund a series of small, sporadic ads which are predestined for failure.

2. The spastic syndrome. We alluded to this problem earlier. Now that you have had an opportunity to consider the campaign approach to advertising, you should utilize this strategy. The only exceptions would be for seasonal or special happenings ads run in concert with natural patterns of consumer demand.

3. Tell them everything. Most inexperienced advertisers literally cram their ads full of every conceivable piece of information. An advertisement is not an encyclopedia. Define a simple objective, and put together an ad around one theme designed to achieve that objective. Figure 8-4 is an ad for a professional service clinic and an excellent case in point. This ad is so full of data, different typefaces and sizes, and details, that it's doubtful any consumer would remember very much

FIGURE 8-5 Advertising—A positive example
Source: "The Flyer" Kendale Lakes, July 29, 1961, Page 17.

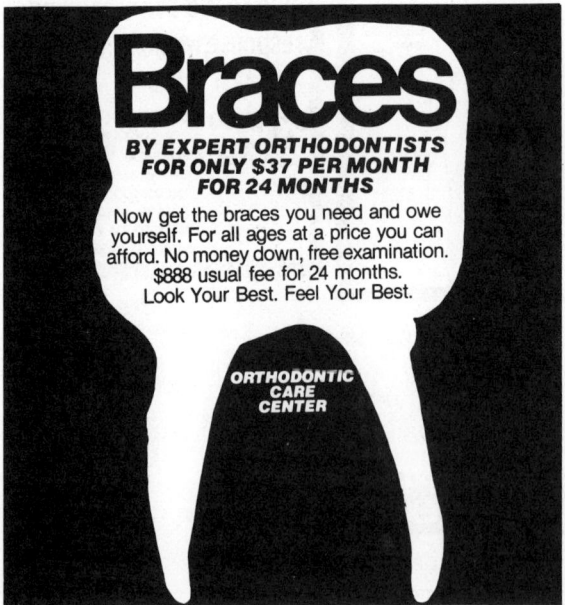

> **ARE YOU AFRAID TO GO TO THE DENTIST?**
> We employ the newest techniques available to help the nervous patient.
> - **No Charge** for Clinical Exam
> - **No Charge for Nitrous Oxide Gas** to help ease the apprehension
> - **Stereophonic earphones** for those who cannot stand the sound of the drill
> - **Hypno-Relaxation techniques provided**
> - **Insurance welcomed**
>
> **OPEN MONDAY thru SATURDAY and EVENINGS**

FIGURE 8-6 A headline of interest to the reader

about it. It actually looks like several ads. Contrast this ad with that of the orthodontic care center, Figure 8-5. If you or your family need braces, there is a high possibility that you'll notice and possibly read this carefully integrated advertisement. Your tendency will be to want prospects to know everything about your practice, but a skilled marketing professional would counsel you, justifiably, to "keep it simple."

4. We're the greatest. No doubt, you're good. After all, you're a professional. However, consumers don't really care very much about you; they care about their own problems. Professionals usually want to tell the world about their qualifications and expertise. This is only natural. Prospective clients want to know that their problems will disappear. Make the attention-getter or headline in your commercial an idea of interest to the prospective client. Figure 8-6, taken from an ad for a dental surgeon, represents the preferred approach. "Are you afraid to go to the dentist?" This is an idea of interest to the prospective patient. Sure, we're all afraid, or at least we don't enjoy it. This professional focused in on a consumer motivation and turned it into an ad for his practice. Figure 8-7, an ad by one of the Big 8 accounting firms, skillfully utilizes this approach. We all wonder whether we're paying too much in personal income taxes. Note that the ad has a limited objective—to generate phone calls or written inquiries concerning the service. Note too the firm logo and its motto, "Beyond the bottom line." This ad was inexpensive to produce, but it does a good job of piquing consumer interest during income tax season.

5. Prolingo. The jargon and language of each professional specialty is a privileged, precise, and meaningful form of communication—assuming you're communicating with other professionals! Remember to speak the language of your prospect in your written communications program and especially in your advertising. Sensitive and experienced professionals soon learn to relate to clients in their own language. Sometimes new professionals—and, unfortunately, some with long tenure—insist on regaling prospects with thirteen-letter words and highly technical descriptions.

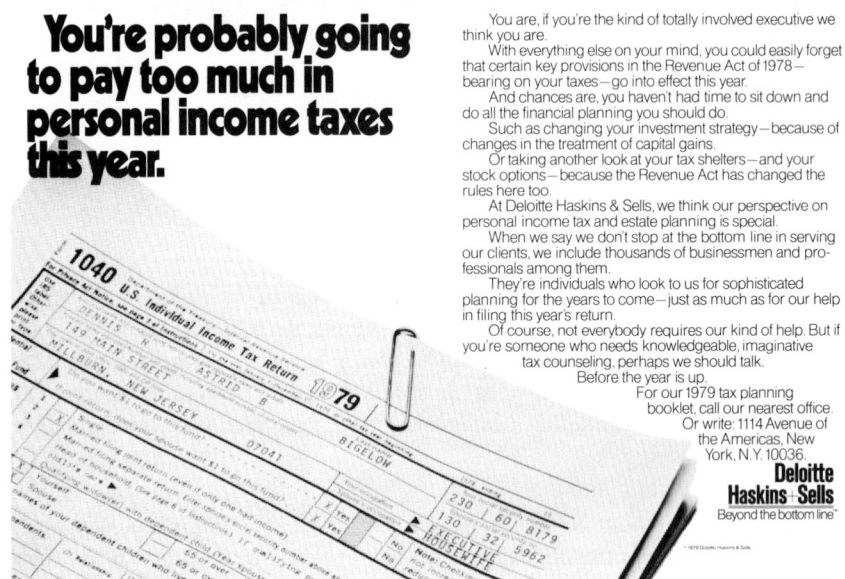

FIGURE 8-7 A headline of interest to the reader

Source: Used courtesy of Deloitte Haskin & Sells. © 1979 Deloitte Haskin & Sells. Reprinted by permission.

6. Coordinate, coordinate, coordinate. When you run advertising or disperse institutional communications, be sure to have your act together. There will probably be responses. Everyone in the organization should be informed that the campaign is under way. Clerical people must be ready to process requests for information promptly and accurately. Receptionists must know how to answer and respond to phone requests as well as handle requests for appointments and consultations in a positive manner. The ultimate in self-inflicted marketing wounds is to generate inquiries from potential clients through effective written communications and then drop the ball at the response level. One of the greatest problems in service marketing is inability to forecast client demand. Before you implement your advertising program, be sure you are in a position to respond to inquiries and to handle any projected increase in client demand. Once a communication has been released, every individual with whom an inquiring prospect has contact becomes a member of your personal sales team. Everyone from the receptionist to staff professionals should be briefed concerning the appropriate response modes.

OTHER COMPETITIVE COMMUNICATION

Proposals

Each professional field is different. One morning a client may walk in off the street with her tax folder, requesting that the CPA do this year's tax work. That same afternoon, the CPA may be requested to deliver a proposal for the performance of services to a prospective corporate client. As a professional, you work very hard to develop a reputation that warrants your getting to the proposal preparation and presentation stage for an engagement. And yet I'm constantly amazed to see the production line, cookie cutter, and sometimes casual approach given to proposal development and presentation. The role of the proposal in the purchase decision-making process varies considerably. At one extreme are situations where the engagement is sold prior to proposal submission. In such cases, the proposal is the icing on the cake and is utilized to close the deal. At the other end of the scale are proposals submitted in a truly open and competitive process. Often these proposals receive extra attention and are regarded as a key persuasive communication in the competitive battle.

All proposals are equally important. Each proposal, no matter how small the engagement or how after the fact, is a tangible representation of your professional positioning and image. In addition, it shows regard for the importance of the client and your own professional self-concept. Proposals have a long shelf life. They may be reviewed often. They may pass through several hands now and in the future. Does that written document say all you want it to say? Does it convey a professional impression that makes you proud?

Some professionals find proposal development a bother. As professionals, we are interested in performing our services. We get our kicks out of doing, and we are often weak in presenting what we propose to do in a creative, enthusiastic, and unique way. Let's consider several recommendations concerning proposal format, preparation, control, and delivery.

Typical professional proposals contain long opening sections discussing the virtues of the professional or the professional organization. Such material is useful and interesting *after* a prospective client is seriously interested in the firm. However, the letter of transmittal and the opening of the proposal should be designed to achieve certain objectives in a specific and sequential way:

1. First, you must demonstrate that you as a professional have complete and sympathetic understanding of the unique needs and problems facing a particular client. The language used must convey the fact that your prospective client is unique in some way and that you understand and have experience with these unique situations.

2. The transmittal letter and the opening section of the proposal should seek to resolve uncertainties by assuring the client that the professional understands and is in a position to solve the problem. For example, a city manager, mayor, or city council seeking to retain a consultant to study, recommend, and implement a computer-based data-processing system is concerned that the municipal records will be maintained in compliance with applicable laws and regulations. This is a primary area of sensitivity and insecurity. The client wants to be certain that its specific legal requirements and responsiveness to constituencies will be preserved and enhanced by the new data system. This is an extremely strong buying motive and must be addressed in the letter of transmittal and reemphasized in the proposal.

3. Once you have demonstrated understanding of the client's uniqueness and responded positively to insecurities and uncertainties, you should discuss the specifics of the engagement. Particular emphasis should be given to the way in which you will approach the work, project management techniques, scheduling, planned completion date, and so on.

4. At this point, the professional and/or team handling the engagement should be introduced and their qualifications presented in an image-enhancing manner. Biographical sketches should be customized for each proposal. A careful updating routine should be maintained. Finally, the proposal can end with the typical opening remarks of most proposals—a discussion of your experience and expertise in the field, an enumeration of past engagements or past specific work in the area. Institutional communication can be appended for the prospect's information. These materials give prospects the feeling they are dealing with a stable, well-established organization. In addition, they pinpoint services provided by the professional not covered in the proposal.

Proposal quality and the differential advantage sought depend primarily on intelligence gathered at the preproposal stage. Ideas for customizing proposals should be carefully noted during all formal and informal prospect contacts. Too often, professionals court prospects, get to know them, are invited to propose, and then prepare or submit a canned, cut-and-paste proposal. Proposals do contain similar materials that can be replicated, saving some preparation time. However, the ability to prepare apparently unique and individualized proposals can give you an important competitive edge. Differentiate your proposal physically. The use of colored paper and padded, bound, and embossed proposal covers is recommended. High-quality paper is a must. The proposal envelope should be specially designed. Every avenue of creative differentiation should be carefully explored and tested with your marketing staff and oustide suppliers to provide a uniquely differentiated appearance.

Be sure to implement centralized proposal control. Ideally, each proposal should be drafted by the professional working with the prospect and a marketing specialist. The proposal would then be technically and professionally correct and also have the proper persuasive component. As a minimum, proposals should be reviewed in draft by the managing partner or executive committee prior to entering the final preparation stage. If a total top management review is not possible, then some fee-based cutoff could be adopted. For example, all proposals for work over $5000 are subject to marketing review. Many national professional firms have a full-time communications specialist to assist in proposal development.

You should seek to present proposals formally where possible. You should suggest that prospects and any related executives participate in the presentation. Where applicable, color slides can be used to amplify proposal content (more about slide presentations in the next chapter). A formal proposal presentation, skillfully handled, will give you a distinct competitive advantage. Even if your proposal is not accepted, the prospect will know who you are and that you sincerely want his or her business. You'll have an important opportunity to convey a highly professional image. While you may not be retained as a result of your presentation, your probabilities for having an additional chance at future work are greatly enhanced. In addition, institutional messages will be communicated, letting the prospect know more about the firm in general.

Reports

If your professional specialty involves the delivery of a written report, the following comments are directed to you. Proposal format, style, preparation, and presentation are extremely important. However, a report for a completed engagement has an infinitely longer shelf life and a higher probability of becoming a hands-on working tool for your client. In some cases, clients will show your report to other individuals who themselves might be prospective clients. For example, a professionally prepared estate plan developed by a CPA, an attorney, or an insurance specialist might be shown to a close friend or relative who is considering having some additional tax work done. A computer feasibility project report done by a consulting firm for a bank might be shown to a bank customer, a colleague or even a competitor. Finally, the report is your best long-term client loyalty builder. In addition, of course, to its technical components, a complete and thorough report, attractively presented, can go a long way toward relieving postpurchase dissonance and increasing the probability of additional work.

I'm not suggesting that every client receive a bound tome as a result of utilizing your professional services. For small engagements and clients with low budgets, you may have to tailor report preparation and presentation to realistic fee limitations. In some fields, particularly health care, reports are seldom seen by the client. For example, if a referring physician receives a report from a colleague specialist concerning the referring physician's patient, the results of that report may be communicated verbally in consultation with the client. The tendency in this type of reporting situation is for professionals to neglect the importance of the nontechnical components of their report. What they fail to recognize is that all written communication says something about you, your professional self-image, and the image you wish to convey to others. If reports fit at all into your professional practice, please compare your reporting methods to the following checklist:

1. Letter of transmittal. In addition to any cover letter you might wish to forward with a report, a letter of transmittal should be part of the report document. It should be bound with the report contents and remain as part of the report if this does not violate customary practice. Where multiple reports are issued, the special report intended for the client should contain this transmittal letter. There may be users of the report in addition to the client. In such cases, extra copies of the report will be provided for distribution outside the client organization. Financial statements are a good case in point. A financial audit and management review report intended for the client should contain the letter of transmittal. Extra copies for use by regulatory agencies, investors, or the general public need not contain this document. The letter of transmittal is a selling tool. It should restate the objectives of the engagement based on what was agreed to in the proposal. It should briefly summarize the work performed. It should acknowledge that the professional will be available to serve in the future and should thank the client for the opportunity to be of service. The transmittal letter should not exceed one page. It should typically be signed by the highest-ranking professional dealing with the particular client on the engagement or the senior or managing professional in the firm.

2. Report format. A detailed table of contents should be provided. If the report is lengthy, the reader should be able to scan the annotated contents and know that the report will contain the topics agreed to in the proposal. In addition to developing a positive mental set toward the remainder of the report, a detailed contents assists the reader in jumping to sections of the report he or she might be most concerned with at the moment. The basic format includes topic title and a list of the key words reflecting the subtopics treated in each section. For example, the contents of a report by a dental group proposing to be the sole supplier of an organizational dental plan might have a section on plan participants. Immediately under the "Plan Participants" listing should be the subtopics contained in that section. In this case, they might include executives, administrative and clerical staff, factory employees, immediate family, and other dependents. In essence, the annotated contents should present a snapshot of the entire report. The table of contents for this book is an example of an appropriate format.

No one likes to read long paragraphs or uninterrupted pages of narrative. Once you have annotated the contents, provide report subtitles that exactly match the model you have established. This method breaks longer reports up into bite-sized chunks, and sections can be separated and given to various functional area personnel. Begin a new topic on a new page. This will facilitate separation, duplication, and distribution. If there are a limited number of charts, graphs, statistical data, financial data, or whatever, you may include them in the body of the text. If these materials get to be quite lengthy or numerous, the report could be separated into a narrative section and an exhibits section. Exhibits should be identified by letter and marked with a finger-tab. This will facilitate the client turning to the exhibit you are discussing as the report is read. Minor mechanical problems in format and illustrations can cause disproportionate aggravation for your client. These minor distractions can get in the way of a positive response to your total effort.

3. Graphics. Where appropriate, reports should be bound in more or less a permanent way. Padded and embossed covers are impressive. One creative professional I know submits reports in attractive covers and features the embossed logo of his firm along with the logo for the client organization side-by-side on the report cover. This is, after all, a report for the client. His message comes across, and his clients often comment on the creative format. When they are used, graphics should be impeccable. Space, layout, the use of color, and the normal eye motion of the reader must be considered. Report paper should be heavy stock, high quality, and of a special color and style utilized by the firm. Some professionals have their logo on every page or at least embossed into the paper so that it is always present.

4. Report control. If you are in a professional firm large enough to have a marketing or communication department, you are indeed fortunate. Whatever its title, one important job would be to review draft reports for their image development, communicative skill, and consumer satisfaction quotient. This aspect of communication is quite different from the technical correctness of the report contents and recommendations. It's probably not realistic to expect technically oriented professionals also to be experts at format, layout, graphics, and creative writing. And yet I think all professionals will agree that any written representation of their work is a critical component of their professional image. If you are a sole practitioner, have someone else read and critique your report before the client sees it. If you're part of a small firm, assign the report control and approval function to a single individual.

Seminar Materials

Seminars, conferences, workshops, and speeches will be covered in detail in the personal communications chapter (Chapter 9). Equally as important as the personal communication, however, are the materials professionals utilize to supplement their personal input and leverage their presence. During the last six months I participated in two seminars staged by professional firms. These were primarily marketing ventures. In the first case, a high-quality program, complete with photographs, was printed and distributed in advance. In addition, each speaker had printed copies of presentations, along with several checklists and analyses that would be useful to prospective and current clients in the future. An ample supply of the firm's general brochure, partner's brochure, and relevant special topic materials was available. The registration packet contained one copy of all materials and was nicely packaged in a folder with notepad and ballpoint pen included.

The seminar attracted over one hundred existing and potential clients. At the opening plenary session, the senior professional and co-host went over the registration packet to be sure each attendee understood what it contained and the potential use and value of each piece. Participants were also introduced to a staff person who would be available to provide extra copies of material. In addition, each packet contained a checklist and mailing request should participants wish to have materials sent to their offices or to friends or colleagues. Naturally, the materials were all printed on high-quality paper in the color and type style consistently utilized by the firm, and with the logo prominently displayed. I had been retained as a silent observer and critic for this seminar by the principals of the professional firm. While there was some room for improvement in certain of the topic area workshops, their "printed image" performance was perfect.

Contrast this to the second seminar, which I attended as a participant. Materials were poorly organized and presented. Low-quality paper was used for materials in the workshop sessions. There were typos and proofing errors in many of the materials. Participants received only the handouts for the sessions they attended. Much important material was missed. Each workshop leader, apparently, prepared his or her own materials. There seemed to be no centralized control, no consistency, and no thematic approach to the formats, and graphics utilized in the materials. This organization wasted a golden opportunity to create a valuable professional impression. Furthermore, these makeshift materials were carried away by some participants and may increase that negative effect with other individuals and organizations who could have become prospective clients.

ADMINISTRATIVE COMMUNICATION

Administrative communications are those routine printed materials common to the operations of almost all professional organizations. They include letters, invoices, forms, purchase orders, checks, manuals, working papers, memos, business cards, envelopes, and so on. Administrative communication takes two forms: external and internal. Please remember that your printed image is the cumulative result not only of institutional and competitive communications, but also of the several building blocks represented by both external and internal administrative communication. Let's examine and comment on a few of these building blocks.

Stationery, envelopes, and professional cards should be selected with the guidance of a graphics specialist. This is no place to economize. My own professional stationery, envelopes, and cards are quite expensive. They utilize a high-quality paper stock, a slightly off-white ivory-beige color combination, and a subdued, brown ink. A friend of mine who is a partner in a behavioral science clinic and a clinical psychologist uses an ivory paper stock with a deep blue ink. This gives a very professional impression, yet stands out as being quite distinctive in the flood of communication we all receive. Your logo should, of course, be embossed on stationery, envelopes, and cards. A similar thematic treatment should be given to invoices, purchase orders, checks, and any other external materials.

The individual professional will be dealing directly with clients both in person and through correspondence. It is important that each new client be made to feel a client of the entire organization. In addition to meeting other members of the firm, the "new client letter" is a recommended method for achieving this objective. Don't make this a form letter! New clients may know one another, and some may resent the "cookie-cutter" treatment. The professional handling the account can draft the letter welcoming the client, making it personal to some degree and offering the assistance of the entire firm. Regardless of who drafts it, the letter should be signed by the senior professional so that contact is established at the highest level. Brief mention can be made of other services available to the client, and the senior professional can indicate that the client may contact him or her if there are any emergencies or problems.

Internal communication is the most often overlooked area in professional communications programs. Developing and maintaining a group of professional staff and colleagues is a critical part of the growth requirement for any organization. From the staff employment letter through operations manuals, working paper forms, memorandums, and house organs, professionals should utilize the same design and quality approaches recommended for external communications. Let staff and other professionals know they are members of a prestigious firm that has a high degree of healthy self-respect. Charity begins at home. Proper design and quality control of internal forms and materials is just as important as any other part of your written communications program.

Chapter 9
Promoting Your Practice: Personal Communication

This chapter is not designed to make you a super salesperson, nor is it intended to help you win the Nobel Prize in interpersonal communication. Its purpose is to improve the probability of success for your personal communications efforts and those of your staff. We will do this by recommending a structured program approach targeted toward current clients, referral sources, prospective clients, group presentations, and general community relations. But before we begin, it's essential that we consider your professional image. We'll look at your office atmosphere—the environment in which you communicate—your personal image, which is affected by clothing and grooming, and your interpersonal communications skills. When you complete the chapter, you'll have some how-to recommendations on initiating a structured personal communications program. If you or your organization are already moving in this direction, you'll have an opportunity to compare your program to some of the recommendations. Finally, and equally important, you'll have an increased sensitivity to yourself and your professional environment and the potential impact these stimuli have on your marketing success.

One of the prevalent misconceptions about professional service marketing concerns the area of personal communication. I overheard an architect in a consulting firm remark, "Well, one advantage to having a marketing person onboard is that we're not going to have to worry about this marketing stuff anymore." The implication of this comment was that "someone else" can market his professional services.

As we stated earlier, the addition of marketing staff to a professional organization and the development and adoption of formal marketing planning and programming can enhance the probability for success and profits. However, in the final analysis, professionals market professional services. The July 1981 issue of *The Practical Accountant* was devoted to building a larger practice through professional marketing. The lead article for the issue was written by Robert W. Denney. Bob is president of his own consulting firm, which provides management and marketing assistance to professional organizations and other companies. He spoke directly to the point of personal marketing:

> One of the fundamental misconceptions many accountants have about marketing is that all of this activity should generate new business without any personal effort on their part. They think that someone else can bring in new clients and then they can take over and do the work. Unfortunately, they are wrong.
>
> A well conceived marketing plan merely identifies growth opportunities and presents an organized approach to maximize these opportunities. While some aspects of a marketing plan (such as advertising, a firm brochure or contributions to a worthwhile cause) do not require much personal contact, the successful marketing of accounting services really becomes, basically, a personal marketing activity.
>
> *It takes an accountant to sell accounting services.* The public relations firm, the ad agency, the graphics artist and the marketing consultant can't do the final selling. *You* have to make the plan work. You have to do the personal marketing.
>
> Most accountants need help in this regard. Few people are "natural salespeople." Most of the good accounting marketers have had to *learn* how to market their firm. The best-conceived marketing plan will not be successful unless the members of the firm receive some training in how to make the plan work. They must learn: (1) how to "sell prospects," (2) how to turn contacts into business opportunities, (3) how to obtain more business through clients.
>
> If some of the professional staff are reluctant to do their share of the marketing effort, it is usually because they don't know how to get started. Work with them, train them, or get some practical training for them. Include marketing training in the CPE program. Educate them in what marketing is and how they can be most effective. This training is inexpensive in comparison with the results your plan can achieve.
>
> The point is this: a marketing *plan* only becomes a marketing *program* when people implement it![1]

These remarks, directed toward accountants, hold true for the entire range of professional service marketing activities. Is personal communications truly an onerous task for the professional? I'm reminded of the systems consultant who was considering the establishment of a marketing plan for his firm. He said to me, "Ed, I really hate selling—I'm really bad at it." I asked him if he had enjoyed our last thirty minutes together. With a quizzical expression on his face, he said, "Why— of course!" I reminded him that he had just spent thirty minutes telling me about himself and his organization, what its capabilities are, what special talents it has, and what interesting work it has done during the last year. He had done an excellent job of personal selling!

Professional personal communication basically involves understanding the prospect's needs and telling him or her how you or your organization can fulfill those needs. That's not so difficult, is it? The systems analyst had never thought of personal selling from that perspective. He was being too hard on himself and his staff because they were not golden-tongued orators whose very presence mesmerized every contact or audience they faced. Unfortunately, the myth of the "born, natural salesperson" hinders personal communication. Admittedly there are different levels of skill and personal inclination concerning the sales function. However, I'm in total agreement with Bob Denney that the majority of professionals can do an effective job of personal communication and promotion given the required support.

IMAGE: THE MIRROR THAT DOESN'T REFLECT

I call image "the mirror that doesn't reflect." Why? As you stand before a mirror, you see yourself in a certain way. What you see is based on your self-concept, selective perception, and a long historical process involving many stimuli resulting in who you are and where you are at the moment. Another individual standing next to you and looking at your reflection may see something totally different. Other people bring to that mirror their own experiences, perceptions, and motives, which shape and color what they see. Even those closest to you—your family, your friends—will probably define certain attributes of what you are differently than you would. In this context, *image* is the way in which the professional is defined in the mind of the client. As we indicated in our discussion of your printed image, image attributes are both functional and emotional. In addition, all professionals will have an image, whether they seek to cultivate one or not. That image will exist at both conscious and unconscious levels for all individuals who are in contact with the professional.

The phenomenom of image exists. A positive image enhances the effectiveness of the professional at all levels. A negative image of an otherwise qualified professional detracts from all aspects of the professional practice. Therefore, image is one of the greatest potential enhancers of personal communication; correspondingly, it is one of its most dangerous potential detractors.

COMPONENTS OF YOUR PROFESSIONAL IMAGE

The components of image you can most directly program and manage include your written communications program, institutional contacts between prospects and your organization, personal visits to your place of business, consultation between you and prospects, and finally, the way in which you perform on the job. We've already discussed your printed image, and I'm counting on you for effective delivery of your professional service once it has been sold. I'd like to focus here on institutional contact, visits and consultation. I'm going to put myself in the prospective client's shoes for these discussions.

Institutional Contact

Before you ever have an opportunity to develop your own professional image, other forces have already begun to shape it for you. Your professional referral sources, the comments of existing clients, the message conveyed through your printed image all have an impact on shaping what the prospective client will perceive when you finally come face to face. At the very minimum, your prospect will make telephone or written contact to request an appointment or set up a meeting. Personal selling and image building begin anew at this point. If you are a one-person operation with an answering service, it is essential that the answering service be selected based on the warmth, friendliness, professional demeanor, and helpfulness of its staff.

This sensitivity to all individuals who make contact with the professional organization or the individual professional is a critical ingredient at the switchboard and reception desk. This is no place to economize. I've had personal experience with horrible examples of ineffective institutional contact by health care professionals, Big 8 accounting firms, and Wall Street law firms. In each of these cases, I've placed calls to key executives in these organizations, only to find that I could not understand the name of the firm as pronounced by the contact person. The problem is not fluency in English, but rather the speedy and mechanical way in which the professional firm's name was recited by a gum-chewing switchboard operator. Of course, we could all recite a litany of horrors, which include being disconnected, being put on terminal hold, being connected to the wrong extension, and having messages garbled in a number of insidious ways.

In a small professional practice or one-person show, recruiting, developing, and retaining an effective switchboard operator/receptionist/secretary must be a top professional priority. Instead of improving, the situation seems to be getting worse. Instead of putting a band-aid on the problem through the use of temporaries and the constant flow of revolving-door people who stay for a few months or years, professionals need to understand the objectives of the contact persons they've hired, meet those objectives to the extent possible, and be flexible as the circumstances and objectives of contact people change.

There is help available. It ranges in scope and cost from the free brochures of the phone company on telephone etiquette to customized personnel training programs conducted by experienced consulting organizations. Evaluation of the institutional contact function should be part of any marketing audit you undertake. At the very least, you should call your own office from time to time, posing as a prospective client. Make note of how quickly your phone is answered, how clearly the operator speaks, and to what extent the warmth and interest you wish to display toward each client-prospect is communicated during that first institutional contact.

I received a call one day from the president of an electronics firm. He asked if I was available to assist his company in the development of a marketing evaluation for an innovative new product. It was an interesting and challenging assignment. I asked the client how he became aware of my services. His answer surprised me. He said, "I called your office by mistake. I had been given the name of the chairperson of the marketing department in another school of business administration." He told me that rather than saying simply "wrong number," my secretary was extremely helpful. "During the conversation, she inquired what company I was with." He said one word led to another, and when she found out he was seeking a marketing consultant, she said: "I don't know whether you are aware that Dr. Wheatley is very much in demand and experienced as a marketing consultant to private firms." My new client stated: "You know, your office staff was so helpful, pleasant, and interested in my needs that I decided I'd talk to you prior to contacting the gentleman to whom I had been referred."

Well, thanks to Deborah Jones, my former staff coordinator and secretary, this "prospect" was already presold. By the way, Deborah is no longer with us. She is now the assistant to the president of an industrial firm. Her earnings in the first year of her new position were 50 percent higher than what we were able to pay. However, we helped her develop her skills and encouraged her professional growth. During the two years she was with us, she won many friends and solidified existing relationships for our organization. We do miss her, but we're already developing another top-quality, front-line person to help convey the proper professional image.

One basic principle ought to be followed in the organization and management of the customer contact function: wherever and whenever possible, separate the reception and operations functions. For example, a pediatric medical group with which I'm familiar has a serious front-office problem. The receptionist handles the switchboard, the appointment book, insurance forms, typing, and some light bookkeeping. No, she doesn't do windows! This individual is so harried and continually frustrated that patients almost feel guilty trying to let her know they've arrived. Her telephone style is almost hostile. Why not? She resents the phone, and her cumulative hatred of that diabolical instrument increases each time it rings.

Why have the professionals permitted this condition to exist? Two reasons. First, they were honestly unaware of the negative image being conveyed. And second, believe it or not, they were quite proud of themselves for their efficiency as managers in "getting so much work" out of one employee. In a nearby suburb, a competing group of three pediatricians has a full-time receptionist who handles phones and appointments. She spends time chatting with each parent, visits a bit with the children, and has become almost an extension of the physicians' caring and warm personal attitude. Patients bring her gifts and remember her on holidays, and many of the kids hold a special place in their hearts for her.

It's difficult not to digress into a discussion of front-office management, but the topic is not within the scope or purpose of this book. By now, I hope you're in agreement that the personality, appearance, dress, and efficiency of customer contact people must be an established part of your personal communications program. How does your practice rate on this critical dimension?

Atmospherics

In his text *Marketing Management, Analysis, Planning, and Control*, Philip Kotler uses "atmospherics" as an umbrella concept for all the signs communicated by an organization through its physical facilities, printed materials, product packaging, executive and sales staff appearance, and so on. We've treated parts of the atmospheric component in other parts of the text. Now let's focus for a moment on the messages conveyed in the staging area—your outer offices or reception/waiting room. We're still talking about ways to enhance your effectiveness as a personal communicator through developing a favorable image for your organization prior to direct contact between you and the prospect.

There are several topics to be considered when programming the atmospherics for your facility. When you have the opportunity and funds to attack this practice development component, I recommend you seek professional assistance. In the meantime, let me highlight some of the critical areas for your consideration. These include office location, layout, decor, sound and light level, and the professional's individual office.

In the retailing of consumer goods and services, there's one well-known law: "There are only three things that count in retailing—location, location, and location." One of Newton's Laws explains this phenomenon. Two objects cannot occupy the same space at the same time. This means that if one object, such as your practice or office, is in the "right location," then by definition your competitor's location will not be right. Irving Steele is a professional colleague of mine. Irv is the director of research for one of Federated Department Stores most profitable divisions. He and his staff spend considerable time carefully analyzing alternative sites for each new store opening. The work involves extensive demographic analysis, consumer and area profiles and trending, and economic analysis. One of the most interesting aspects of Irv's procedure involves driving-time analysis. Members of his staff actually drive outward in all possible directions from a proposed location. Their movements are carefully plotted on a map, and exact time notations made by stopwatch.

How did you select your firm's location? Over the years, many professionals have candidly told me about the "wrong reasons" for selecting locations. They include convenience to the professional rather than to clients, personal identification with the style of the building, cost, reserved parking, being in the same building with friends, and so on. There is certainly nothing wrong with professionals setting and pursuing their own objectives. My assumption in this book, however, is that one of your objectives, or at least one to be considered, is how you can use modern marketing techniques to improve client development and retention. If you're considering branching or relocating, remember the basic principle of marketing—matching. Match your location selection as closely as possible to the highest concentration and least competitively saturated market area.

For the "atmospherics" component of location, the message given by your address should be congruent with the self-concept of your prospective clients. If your market consists primarily of urban sophisticates from the upper managerial and professional ranks, they are going to be right at home with the downtown skyscraper view of the city office. The reverse holds true if your client base consists of suburban, lower-middle-class, blue-collar families. I liken the selection of a practice location to marriage. Before making the final decision, you should consider several alternatives. You should develop, list, rank, and evaluate all aspects of the location decision. Remember that once the decision is made, like marriage, it's one you'll have to live with. It also typically has long-term legal and financial ramifications. And making a change can be very expensive!

The details of layout and decor are topics better left to architects, designers, and interior decorators. But it doesn't take a degree in design to know that the physical arrangement of a room and the style, quality, texture and arrangement of furnishings convey subtle but important image cues to clients. Sound and light levels must also be controlled. A professional consultation is an extremely personal activity. It is also usually expensive. There should be no glare or "interrogation effect." Panoramic views should be temporarily shut out by drapes, and external noises ranging from street traffic to the typewriter in the next office rendered nonexistent through appropriate insulation and accoustical treatments. I'm not advocating that every reception and general office area be a Taj Mahal. If you're running a law store in an urban setting, the atmosphere should be congruent with the self-concept of your target clients.

During the same week recently, I had an opportunity to visit with the partners of a highly respected law firm and later with the managing partner of a regional CPA firm. These professional firms were located in the same city. Each occupied expensive urban locations, and there was a good deal of similarity concerning the types of individual and organizational clients they served. I had an associate with me who has a good deal of organization experience and who is extremely perceptive. She later volunteered that the law firm offices came across as stark, sterile, and harsh. She had an uneasy and uncomfortable feeling before ever meeting the partners. However, the CPA offices were warm, peaceful and relaxing. Without knowing anything about technical and professional qualifications, she had already become strongly predisposed, with a negative image in one case and a positive one in the other. Coincidentally, the law firm's layout, design, and decor were largely a function of the building's management. The CPA offices were carefully orchestrated and furnished by a well-known firm specializing in that field.

Why had the CPA firm taken that route? Because the managing partners had carefully considered information concerning the public's general negative image of the CPA. Some persons regard the CPA as a cold, aloof, figure-oriented technician, rather than someone who helps clients solve problems and increase profits. The decor, colors, textures, light levels, and background noise levels developed for these professional offices were designed to make people relaxed, to soften the environmental impact of "being in the CPA's office," and to set the stage for and encourage quiet and warm human interaction. I recognize that these variables are associated with certain costs. All I'm asking is that to the extent possible you give yourself every advantage in setting the stage for client contact.

A word about your own office is in order. A professional's office should be an extension of the image he or she wishes the prospect or client to perceive. Many professionals mistakenly make their personal offices extensions of themselves or of the concept they have of themselves. If you love to hunt elk, moose, and bear, that's fine, but keep your stuffed animals and trophy heads at home in your den unless your professional practice is located in a hunting-oriented town and your clients and prospects consists solely of the local hunting club members. I know a professional whose walls are lined with mounted fish. They bear no relationship to the rest of the office decor, which in my judgment is highly appropriate for his professional field and standing. I finally asked him, why all the fish? He said, "Because my wife won't let me keep them at home!"

Then there's the psychologist who had a huge professional practice dealing primarily with school-aged children. We'll call him simply the "pack rat." His office was a great warehouse. Nothing that came in the mail was thrown away. Pictures, awards, travel mementos, old files and filing cabinets gradually engulfed him and his clients. His office gave the impression of a totally overwhelmed, confused professional who was hopelessly behind. The office became not only uncomfortable, but embarrassing to his staff, the brunt of jokes from his young clients, and a source of wonderment and insecurity for the parents who were paying his professional fees. What finally happened? At my urging, his wife and staff attacked his office. Scores of cartons were required to cart away the years of accumulated litter. In addition, I invited the psychologist to my office so he could see the contrast. He got the point. Unfortunately, I see the litter beginning to accumulate once again.

What happens in these cases? Are professionals blind to such situations? Most professionals are extremely busy; their minds are engaged in important problems and solutions. They often just don't see the image-damaging cues that are so readily apparent to prospects and clients. As negative conditions persist, professionals even become used to them. When his wife and staff started to strip the litter from the psychologist's office, he protested: "But my office is so comfortable—it feels just like home." Well, the professional office is not supposed to be a home, it's supposed to be a place where prospects, clients, professionals, and staff come together to focus on client needs and desires and fulfillment of those needs and desires in such a way as to create and maintain client loyalty and practice growth.

Costuming

In Chapter 2 we discussed the essential differences between product and service marketing, the importance of costuming. We mentioned briefly the importance of costuming the staff to convey a proper image and to define the various roles the staff performed. Let's focus briefly on costuming the professional. MDs have largely solved the costuming problem. They wisely wear white uniforms. These outfits state very clearly who they are. Dr. X may wear a sports shirt under his uniform; Dr. Y may wear a Dior shirt and tie. No matter. In either case, the costuming is appropriate and basically professional.

In most professions, however, dress is left to the discretion of the individual. This is a mistake. Clothes do make the person, at least in terms of the initial impression, and in my opinion, far beyond that point. The way one dresses is thought to be a highly personal matter and none of anyone else's business. This sensitivity is alien to the marketing approach. In a sense, your apparel is the "packaging" in which you are "delivered." The field of packaging is a multibillion-dollar industry in which great attention is given to minute details that might make one product more appealing than another. I encourage you to apply the costuming/packaging approach to your own professional appearance and to the appearance of your entire staff.

How should you proceed? Remember, marketing is matching. There is no one standard formula that can be applied to each professional situation. In my judgment, to be well dressed is to be appropriately dressed. You have several guidelines to follow. What clients expect is largely defined by the norms of your profession. During business hours and periods in which you are in direct contact with or representing clients, it may be appropriate to wear a conservative suit and unobtrusive accessories. In after-hour or office working sessions with clients, the jacket may come off to differentiate the nature of the occasion. I'll pass along two generalizations I feel have been helpful to me and to my clients. First, buy the very best clothing and accessories you can afford. By best, I don't necessarily mean the most ostentatious. I refer here to quality. Quality ensures the appropriate cut, style, fit, wear, repeated cleaning potential, and recognition by the discerning prospect or client.

Second, when in doubt, make the conservative decision. If you find yourself in a quandary selecting clothing for a meeting with a prospective client, always select the more conservative of the options. Leave the ornamental watch in the jewelry case, select the blouse or shirt with soft, muted colors, leave the white shoes in the closet. You won't be sorry. Inappropriate attire can be distracting not only to the prospect, but to you. We've all had periods of discomfort when we knew we'd made the wrong choice. Yes, there may be times for that wild jacket or dress, crazy tie or blouse, or unusual jewelry, but generally these are limited to special social occasions such as parties. Clients ask, "Should I read the 'dress for success' books?" The answer is "absolutely yes"! I'm not advocating that you should be a fashion plate. I don't recommend that professionals be on the cutting edge of fashion or be the first with the newest styles. Conservatism is the rule.

Professionals who disagree with the costuming approach frequently comment: "People utilize our services based on what we do for them, what we know. Not how we look." I'm not suggesting that the tail should wag the dog, that all you have to do is program the costuming and atmospherics corectly and you'll be an instant success. I am adamant, however, that atmospherics and costuming must be part of your marketing professional services program.

Consider, for example, that some large law firms use wardrobe consultants. These consultants may be affiliated with a local apparel shop that features quality merchandise and an expert tailoring staff. These professionals are completely outfitted based on an image the *firm* believes is appropriate for its members. An important part of the staff training program in many major CPA firms involves the professional image. Books like *Dress for Success* are required reading. Alternative professional wardrobe development is carefully prescribed. Part of the evaluation of each staff member is based on professional image.

Finally, I'm familiar with a firm, and I'm sure there are many others, whose specialty is image wear. It markets a line of professional outfits and uniforms, and consulting services designed to handle the costuming situation. One of my clients was having great difficulty in achieving consistent professional appearance on the part of staff. The practice included several offices in different states. Image wear was the answer. Staff members were provided with conservative trousers or skirts, as appropriate, in several colors. They were also provided with the appropriate ties and conservatively colored blazer jackets. While this approach might not be appropriate in many professional settings, it seemed to work well for this group.

If you manage an existing professional practice, you may have a problem. Because of personal sensitivity, it may be difficult to approach and counsel professionals concerning the negative aspects of their image. Please consider establishing written guidelines for the personal aspects of professional practice. These should include dress and personal grooming. You will not be able to convert every staff member, but I'm confident you'll make progress. I'm also confident that staff members will appreciate what you're doing in cases where they were not aware of the opportunity to improve their own personal image.

Last week I addressed 18 professionals who all worked for the same firm. The founder of the practice was most upset that one of his three-year staff persons had begun to neglect his hair and personal appearance. He wanted me to "make an example" of this individual and "shape him up". My client was frustrated and had found it difficult to counsel a thirty-five-year-old professional who should know better. In investigating the situation, I found that the individual in question had recently gone through a divorce and also had had some personal financial reversals. He was in a low period of his life, and his personal appearance showed it. Rather than single this individual out, we waited until a day of staff training was planned. I gave a seminar as part of the day's activity entitled, "How You Look from the Client's Side of the Desk." By the way, the professional in question showed up with hair longer than ever before, shirt unbuttoned, and no socks! In addition to the discussion, written materials were provided for personal review. We're seeing a change in the professional, and key members of the staff are also attempting to give him strong moral support during this difficult time.

One to One

Before we discuss one of the many recommended structured approaches for conducting prospect of client interviews, I'd like you to consider two related topics.

These are listening and body language. Too often, personal persuasion is associated with talking. The talking technique may work selling magazines door to door, but it generally backfires in professional/client one-to-one situations. In discussing the behavior of consumers of professional services, I emphasized that it was critical to establish an emotional contact, to empathize and to demonstrate to the prospect or client that you truly understand his or her unique situation and needs. This can only be accomplished if you learn to listen in an attentive and sincere way.

Sales and Marketing Management magazine asked me to do an article on the relationship of listening to selling. In summarizing the article, the editor said: "The salesman who is too busy talking to hear what his customer actually says misses what the future holds for them both." During the last ten years, communications theorists, writers, and consultants appear to be giving more and more attention to the listening side of the interpersonal communications equation. What are the characteristics of an effective listener?

1. The underlying element of the entire approach is an attempt to understand the customer. This approach implies acceptance of people as they are, including respect and tolerance for each prospect's uniqueness and the conscious avoidance of value judgments and stereotyping.
2. A good listener is aware that his or her strongly held values and sensitivities will often be different from those of prospects. Before each interview, the listener consciously clears the mind of preconceptions and makes a conscious commitment to concentrate on the act of listening.
3. Be alert for your client's feelings and sentiments. These may be expressed not only in language, but in tone and body position. If you are attempting to follow only the logical content or the intellectual component of the conversation, you may be missing a key portion of the communication. This aspect of listening is best exemplified by the title of a popular book published in 1981, *Why Aren't You Listening to What I'm Not Saying?*
4. The professional listener knows his or her own professional image and the impact that image is likely to have on others.
5. The effective listener establishes an agreeable atmosphere, one free from distraction for both parties.
6. No matter how nervous, boring, or belligerent the speaker is, the listener listens to messages on the speaker's own terms.
7. The best listeners are always totally prepared concerning the speaker's situation and the subject to be discussed.
8. Make allowances for the speaker's circumstances. If a client has misplaced a memo that was going to be the topic of the meeting, don't concentrate on the confusion or irritation; focus on the content.
9. There are several communications sidetracks. Don't seize on minor or sore points. Listen to them carefully, but ask a nonthreatening question that brings the conversation back to its main purpose.
10. Give feedback signals: shaking the head; stating, "I understand"; changing your facial expression; summarizing basic points and repeating them back to the prospect or client. These steps allow the client to evaluate how well the message is getting through. If it isn't, the signals are clear and give the prospect a chance to make corrections or additions to the communication.

Unfortunately, our human passion for talking is more powerful and far more common than our desire to learn. Profitable marketing, however, is based on achieving an awareness of unsatisfied wants and desires by learning about our client's needs. We then, of course, provide the services that fill the void. The professional who develops and nurtures the skill of listening enhances his or her ability to learn and to market professional services effectively.

THE CLIENT INTERVIEW OR CONSULTATION

Should you attempt to structure and shape the prospect or client interview? Yes. Why? First, the prospect or client expects it. You are the professional, you should be in control. Second, gaining and maintaining control will enhance your ability to learn the prospect's needs and determine if and how you might assist. Equally important, if you're not able to help, you can make the appropriate referral. I am not an advocate of the so-called canned personal sales approach. It's simply not appropriate for professional marketing. Part of being professional is being yourself, letting your training and experience radiate and communicate the confidence and concern you have for your clients.

The canned approach carefully considers every component of the one-to-one sales interaction. Each component is carefully scripted. The script usually contains the exact words the "salesperson" is expected to say. In addition, gestures, voice inflection, and the use of selling aids and demonstrations are also carefully programmed. Although the highly structured canned approach is not appropriate for the marketing of professional services, there is nothing wrong with utilizing a set personal selling structure as a point of departure.

Please examine the following three approaches to the professional-prospect interview situation. All three assume that you've done your marketing homework. In other words, you know the prospect's situation and needs and are ready to convince him or her that you can fill these needs.

The Traditional Sales Approach

The first structured approach has been adapted from *The Textbook of Salesmanship* by Russell, Beach, and Buskirk.[2] This approach is fairly consistent throughout the literature of selling and includes the presentation, trial close, uncovering and meeting objections, and the close.

1. The presentation. To the extent possible, the interview should include dramatization, proof, visualization, and demonstration. In the professional setting, dramatization is designed to display sincere interest in the client's needs and situation. Enthusiasm on the part of the professional, good listening, feedback, and interchange are effective ways to demonstrate that the professional is emotionally tied in to the needs of the prospect. Another effective dramatization tactic is tele-

scoping. Telescoping is projecting the client's current problem into the future and assessing its consequences. What the professional does is to acknowledge the importance of the problem and to indicate what might happen if the situation is not handled promptly and effectively.

One way professionals can offer proof of the importance of the immediate purchase of services is through the use of comparative case examples. The professional might briefly recount the experiences of previous clients. For example, a client who declined to take action on needs may have been adversely affected due to the delay. Successful outcomes for clients who utilized the service could be enumerated. If appropriate, the prospect could be referred to current or past successful clients as a further form of proof.

The use of visualization and demonstrations in selling is fairly simple. A salesperson could show a cross-sectional model of a steel-belted radial tire. That tire could further be demonstrated in terms of its attributes against a standard nonradial. Can professionals utilize visualization and demonstration as part of their presentation techniques? Absolutely. Orthopedic surgeons utilize working models of joints and bone structure. They demonstrate to patients or clients considering surgery exactly what is wrong and what will be right after the surgical procedures have been performed. Financial analysts and pension planning specialists produce computer printouts simulating potential client financial outcomes, given certain investment strategies. CPAs provide literature concerning how their audit, tax, and management services staffs work. They might even produce a tentative engagement timetable and preliminary proposal to provide tangibility to the prospective client interview.

Slide presentations interspersed with comments by the professional and dialog might walk the prospect through a typical consulting or executive development engagement format. Copies of the professional's standard agreement or contract, where relevant, can be discussed to provide tangibility or demonstration to the proceedings. In my opinion, it is extremely important to provide tangible expression of the intangible components of quality, skill, concern, and experience that prospects can't see, taste, smell, feel, or touch. I don't advocate a canned approach. A full-fledged presentation may be overkill in specific one-to-one situations. I do think, however, that there are useful concepts to be borrowed from the field of professional selling.

2. The trial close. "Closing" a sale involves asking for and/or receiving the prospect's authorization to provide the service. The purpose of a trial close is not actually to ask for the order, but rather to take the pulse of your presentation. Sometimes prospects may be substantially presold before the consultation. In such cases, approval may be voiced early in the discussion. For example, a prospect might say: "I would like you to do a time and motion study in the boat production assembly section of our Los Angeles plant." At this point, the professional could shift inquiries directly to the specifics of the engagement and move quickly to a discussion of scheduling and fees. If the prospect had indeed already decided to use the industrial engineering consulting firm in question, an engagement contract

could be produced and probably signed at that first meeting. On the other hand, a prospect shopping for consulting services might make the following introductory remark: "We're trying to learn about alternative approaches to dealing with our rapidly increasing labor costs at our boat plant." In such a situation, a more detailed presentation might be in order.

Assuming that you have taken the longer route, the "trial close" concept will help you determine just what progress you are making toward turning the prospect into a client. The key to a trial close is asking questions. For example, you might outline two or three approaches to the consulting assignment given in the boat production example. You might then ask: "The method of observation on a sampling basis by your own supervisory personnel, whom we would train, seems to represent the best value in your case, doesn't it?" Or you might say: "Of the three alternative approaches I've outlined, which do you feel is more appropriate for your firm's situation?" Please note, you're not asking the prospect to sign a contract. However, if the prospect says, "Plan B seems better suited for us. How soon could you start?" you could immediately shift from delivering the remainder of your remarks and move directly into the close.

Professionals have the reputation for concentrating on the problem presented by a prospect without ever asking for the order. Most prospects expect the professional to take control, to prescribe. Prospects seem frustrated when the professional seems unwilling or unable to advance the plot and bring the consultation to a conclusion. The use of the trial close approach can provide valuable feedback concerning progress. In many cases, it can shorten an unnecessarily long consultation, resulting in the more efficient and profitable utilization of your professional time.

3. Uncovering objections. *The Textbook of Salesmanship* reminds us that "objections are an integral part of the sales process. Once you accept the idea that objections are to be expected and are a normal result of the sales process, you will have a much sounder philosophical attitude with which to approach them." Inexperienced professionals are often shocked and knocked off guard when prospects register objections. After all, "I am the professional." Today's consumer of professional services is more informed, more aggressive, more cost-conscious, and probably engages in more comparative shopping than ever before. Honest objections help the professional clarify the prospect's need and how well the professional is responding to that need.

There are a few golden rules in dealing with objections. First, don't argue. Second, never be defensive. There are several standard approaches. For example, you could accept blame by saying: "I guess I didn't get my message across very clearly on that particular point." Or you might concede to the prospect by saying: "I think you have a very good thought there; here's another way of looking at it." You could respond to a more strident objection by saying: "I identify with your enthusiasm on that point and I admire your candor in sharing it frankly with me." Regardless of the approach you adopt, the basic philosophy of uncovering objections involves questioning and proferring the trial close.

The basic philosophy in handling objections is acknowledgment, identifying with the prospect, and response. Generally, objections should be responded to immediately. There seem to be two general exceptions that call for postponing the handling of objections. First, if the price objection is raised too early ("I don't think we will be able to afford your fees"), the professional would be wise to respond: "Our fees depend on the alternative methods available and selected to provide you with a complete and lasting solution to your problem. We need to know more about your specific situation, and then I think we can address the fee question more effectively." Second, objections might be raised prematurely. Be sure to acknowledge the objections and express your understanding and acceptance. However, try not to be sidetracked. Let the prospect know that you'll be covering that point in detail in just a few minutes.

4. The close. Under the best of circumstances, the prospect takes care of this for you. The prospect might ask: "When can we begin?" or "Do you have a standard contract or agreement that we might execute today?" In other cases, the professional might have to proffer the close and seek binding confirmation of retention. When a prospect fails to respond to closing overtures, there are at least three possibilities. First, the prospect wasn't really a prospect to begin with. That is, the person really did not have the need for your services at the present time, the means to pay for them, or both. Second, the prospect may have already made a decision to buy at some date in the future and even though you are the first choice, simply will not make a commitment now. Third, there may be some hidden objections you have not uncovered or stated objections to which you have not responded adequately.

If a prospect seems to back away from a decision, you might say: "Let me run through this quickly one more time to be sure I understand your expectations." At that point, the professional would feed back statements of the prospect's problems, the methodology, the scheduling, the expected outcomes and fees. Typically, during this feedback period the professional would question the prospect carefully on each aspect of the proposed service. Generally, the factor that is responsible for the failure to close will surface. The professional should zero in on that area of objection, attempt to bring it to resolution, and then proffer the close again.

5. The hanging close. In marketing professional services, there is often a delay between the presentation and the actual close. For example, a health maintenance organization group might make a presentation to a county manager. The county manager does not have the authority to bind county employees to a health service contract without going through the proper channels. Similarly, a CPA might propose an estate tax planning program to a prospective client, but that client may wish to discuss the work with family prior to retaining the professional's services. It is essential that you follow up promptly and effectively all consultations that end in a "hanging close."

Sometimes the prospect will say: "I'll present it at our next executive meeting." In other cases, the prospect might simply say: "I'll need to take some time to think this over." In both cases, the professional should select and confirm a date for the next contact. For example, you might say: "Excellent—I'll give you a call next Thursday morning." Strike while the iron is hot; the prospect is there for a consultation. There must be a problem or at least the potential for rendering service. Don't beat around the bush on your follow-up call or visit; get right to the point. Don't ask the prospect, "Have you had time to consider our discussion the other day?" Be positive: "Which of the following dates would be more convenient for us to get together and begin our preliminary analysis?"

The Six-Step Approach

In their excellent chapter, "Your Firm's Personal Selling Program," Gilson, Cawley, and Schmidt offer their six-step approach for effective new prospect consultation.[3]

1. The rapport stage. This is primarily a listening operation. The professional attempts to establish rapport based on identifying and emphathizing with the client's problem. In addition, the professional must be alert to identify and alleviate underlying attitudes and anxieties.

2. The information-gathering stage. The professional does a lot of questioning. The attempt is to exhaust all the intricacies of the specific problem as well as the general situation. The professional probes deeply into each issue and attempts to identify exactly what will be involved on the part of the professional or the firm. As this discussion takes place, the professional is making physical or mental notes that will be used in giving an initial fee estimate. Impress your clients here by the number and types of questions you ask and by the concerned way in which the questions are posed and the responses acknowledged.

3. The points of agreement stage. Here discuss the general issues and specific points concerning areas of agreement between you and the prospect. Show how your expertise will match the prospect's needs.

4. The fee discussion. Only after you are fully aware of the work that will be required should you move to this stage of the consultation. Prospects who press for fee estimates early should be made aware that full information must come first. Assuming that you know the facts and want the engagement, put the fee in perspective by telling the prospect in great detail what will be involved. If this is a standard assignment, you may wish to quote a fixed fee. If you perceive contingencies, you may wish to quote a fee range. (We'll discuss fee setting and management in the next chapter.)

5. Countering objections. Once a fee is quoted, some prospects will become anxious and start asking additional questions or raising specific objections. As previously discussed, it's important to isolate, clarify, and deal with the objections immediately. If the objection is based on fees, you might review the work to be done and see if there is a way of reducing or transferring professionally performed work to the client or to others. If the fee is more than the client can handle right now, you might wish to consider some form of extended payment.

6. The closing. At this point, you can begin to ask the telling questions. They might include specific scheduling for the work, setting up the appointments needed to get the project under way, discussing and presenting your standard professional agreement form for signature, specifying the amount of retainer required, and so on. If the prospect does not act on your closing proposition, then it's time to determine what additional questions (objections) need further clarification.

The Three-Step Approach

James J. Mahon, CPA, offers still another approach to the professional-prospect consultation.[4] Mahon identifies three specific stages in the new client consultation.

The first is the appraisal stage. Here he recommends that the initial conversation not last more than several minutes. Small talk and getting to know each other are the appropriate goals for appraisal. In addition, silent language predominates. Personality and style set the tone. The object here is to open the channels of communication, to make the prospect feel relaxed and comfortable.

The second stage involves confidence building. The professional listens and gains knowledge of the prospect's problem and needs. Then two-way discussion ensues. The professional should convince the prospect that he or she or the firm has the technical competence, intelligence, and ability to do the job. As the professional clarifies and responds to the client's needs, some clients may feel compelled to show that they are knowledgeable. They may wish to query or challenge some of the professional's assumptions. Answers to these questions and objections should be straightforward, moderate in tone, and presented with quiet assurance based on the knowledge of the prospect's operations. Answers should be specific and quite detailed. In leading up to the close, the professional should give the impression that he or she has a definite plan for performing the engagement. In addition, starting and finishing schedules might be offered if appropriate.

The final stage is asking for the engagement. Mahon notes that professional salespersons are taught to ask for the order directly and forthrightly. He recommends the following type of closing approach: "Mr. Prospect, we have enjoyed meeting with you and are impressed with your company's growth. We want you to know that we would like to work with you and your people—we would be happy to serve you." At that point the professional should wait in silence for the prospect's reaction. At this time perhaps hidden objections may be raised, clarifying questions asked and answered, or approval for the engagement given.

We've looked at three approaches to the one-to-one personal selling situation. The literature of personal selling is rich in both approaches and examples. The specific approach you use is not as important as being aware of the importance of adopting an underlying structure that will move the consultation along productively and hopefully, with the desired result. You probably noted more similarities in the three approaches presented here than differences. How does your own client consultation approach measure up?

EXTERNAL COMMUNICATIONS PROGRAMS

Professionals have an excellent and often wasted opportunity to gain visibility through external personal appearances. Much of what professionals do is of inherent interest to a wide variety of potential audiences. These audiences include professional peers, referral sources, local opinion leaders, potential clients, existing clients, and the community at large. Opportunities for external communication present themselves in the form of speeches, seminars, and workshops. The marketing objective of all these activities is to gain visibility for the professional and to communicate to all types of audiences the fact that the professional is deeply knowledgeable in the area of his or her expertise. In addition, it's important to convey the impression that you and the members of your organization are warm, concerned, friendly, helpful individuals. Every time a professional speaks before a group, the group receives two distinct impressions. The first is the emotional or attitudinal impression; the second is the competency impression. Clients do retain professionals with whom they may not have specific personal rapport. However, it is more likely that prospects will retain and remain loyal to professionals they both like and respect.

If you or your practice are well known and established, you probably have to turn down offers for external personal appearances. You've already established your reputation and visibility in your professional environment. However, if you're a new professional or if you're seeking to improve practice development and retention, an external personal communications program should be part of your marketing professional services plan. I'd like to touch briefly on the steps I've found productive in establishing and implementing such programs. They include the audience, the means, and the technique.

The Audience

As a first step, you should identify and describe each potential target audience. For example, audiences might include your direct professional peers, individuals in exactly the same professional specialty as yourself. Additionally, there may be important related professional audiences. For example, a trial attorney specializing in commercial practice may find that nonlitigating attorneys in related fields such as real estate have potential as referral sources. Outside referral sources make another worthwhile target group. These typically include professionals and laypersons who come in regular contact with individuals who might be clients for your own services. For a financial counselor, these might include attorneys, bankers, CPAs, and insurance professionals. Opinion leaders include those who plan an indirect role in the referral process or in the regulatory or approval process for your own profession. They might include leading community figures; members of boards, commissions, and governments; and members of the media. The community at large includes members of civic, social, service, religious, recreational, and other types of clubs and organizations. You might also consider existing clients where opportunity exists to group clients with similar needs together for speeches, seminars, workshops, or courses.

Once you have identified the various types of audiences, you should rank them in priority order according to their importance and potential for helping you reach your marketing objectives. Next, you need to do the research and develop the information that will let you carefully describe each target group. For example, if your peers are critical in your objective to position your firm as the "professionals' professional," then you need to know something about the committees, groups, and organizations within that peer designation. You'll need to know membership, meeting times and places, typical program content, current areas of interest or assignment. If you are a single practicing professional or a member of a small organization, you might select only one or two audiences per year to pursue and penetrate.

The Means

Basically you have four alternatives: the speech, the seminar, the workshop, and the short course. Speeches are typically short in duration. They are in essence monologues where you talk and the audience listens. Seminars imply a more interactive environment. Frequently there will be more than one speaker. This approach is often referred to as a panel discussion. The objective is to have short statements by the speakers and then at least 50 percent of the time devoted to questions and discussion between audience and speakers. Seminars and panel discussions are typically more effective when the audience is small enough that effective interaction can take place.

A workshop normally involves doing. By that I mean that participants are expected to work. They typically apply what has been presented or discussed by the speaker(s) or workshop leader. The workshop is usually longer in duration, with a day being the normal minimum time. The workshop format implies small-group activities, the provision and use of materials, and the participant taking away something tangible as a result of the activity. Courses are usually long term in nature. They involve several meetings. Characteristics include a written syllabus and detailed schedule, teaching and learning materials, outside readings and assignments, examinations or projects, and some certification of attendance, completion, or performance. Course format usually involves one of two approaches. First, the so-called intensive approach, where participants might attend the class for three straight days of twenty-four contact hours. The second approach might involve four or more meetings, once a week over several weeks.

Few professionals offer courses strictly on their own. However, you could target a course instructorship in a program being offered by your professional organization or local chapter. Many professions today require continuing professional education credits. This presents several opportunities for the professional to become an instructor. In addition, local high schools, community colleges, colleges, and universities may offer special evening programs or continuing education courses. Becoming an instructor in the right course could put you in touch with and audience of interest. Often, however, long, regularly scheduled courses are not compatible with the travel and schedule demands of some professionals.

The Technique

Regardless of the format or audience, there are several important points to be considered when the professional becomes the speaker/panel member/workshop leader/instructor. Even if you are the most skilled orator in your field, you can quickly be done in by factors beyond your control. For most of us who are average speakers, much more is required. In the following checklist, I've attempted to hit the highlights. Each item is based upon real situations in which I've been asked to observe and evaluate professional presentations.

1. Does the professional's introduction develop the best image? Here we are often at fault. We may fail to provide adequate advance information in concise, clear form. Often the individual introducing you would be grateful to receive a three-by-five card triple-spaced and typewritten and would read word for word exactly what you had put on the card. If you are representing a professional firm, be sure your introductory remarks include a brief description of the organization you represent. Never send a copy of your résumé unless it is specifically requested.

Frequently, busy program chairpersons are overwhelmed by a long list of professional credits. They simply say: "Here is Ed Wheatley. His resumé is lengthy and impressive. It contains far too many honors and publications for me to discuss in detail—Ed." Wonderful introduction, isn't it! After that happened the first time, I handed the program chairperson a three-by-five card that read: "Dr. Edward W. Wheatley is a professor of Marketing at East Carolina University. His bachelors, masters, and Ph.D. degree fields include advertising, marketing, and business administration. He is the author of over two dozen published articles and monographs and three books. Ed is a member of several professional and honorary groups. He's a marketing management consultant to a wide variety of business and professional organizations. His topic for today is "Marketing Professional Services." Invariably, that type of introduction will be read word for word.

2. Has the presentation been reduced to writing? At the very minimum, your presentation should be carefully drafted in outline form, including major topics and

subtopics to be covered. Ideally, the presentation should be prepared in a complete, fully developed draft. This has several advantages. First, other members of your organization can review, evaluate, and assist you in refining the presentation. Second, you will be more confident and aware of what it is you wish to say. And finally, you may lever the presentation into a publication. Sometimes you might wish to provide copies of your written remarks to audience participants for their future reference and use. These all have marketing advantages. If a member of your professional staff is speaking, it is essential that you understand what that person intends to say and have confidence in thorough preparation prior to delivery.

3. Is the language of the presentation appropriate? If you are speaking to a professional peer group, the use of jargon, private jokes, and current phrases may be totally appropriate. It can be deadly, however, if you're talking to a group of outsiders. The best protection for the inexperienced speaker is to have a representative audience member read and react to the proposed remarks. In addition, be sure to define all your terms; and don't use acronyms and initials.

4. Has your presentation been thoroughly rehearsed and timed? Most speakers underestimate the speed at which time passes. They typically run over their allotted time. This results in the cardinal sin of no time for interaction and audience response. If you've been given 30 minutes for a speech, I suggest you prepare one that lasts roughly 15 minutes. Your own nervousness and extraneous expansion on comments and remarks will probably add another 5 minutes or more to the prepared statement. The remaining time should be allotted for questions and discussion.

5. What if there are no questions? For one reason or another, audiences are sometimes cold. You should be prepared to ask the audience several questions or to propose hypothetical, challenging situations that could galvanize the audience to action. Sometimes, we just strike out. Under these circumstances, it's best to say thank you and terminate the program. Sometimes, however, silence at the end of your presentation may be due simply to a reluctance on the part of the audience to begin interacting with the professional. If I know audience members or if my clients are speaking to groups where they have acquaintances, I always plant questions. If questions from the floor are slow to come, my plants quickly raise their hands. Friends in the audience may also get other individuals with whom they are acquainted involved by citing examples that apply to their friend's particular situations.

6. Do you know what your presentation sounds like? Prior to your appearance, tape the live delivery of your remarks. Ask a colleague to listen to and critique the presentation. Ideally, this colleague should be a person who is familiar with the type of audience you will be addressing. You'll be surprised how many helpful hints will emanate from such practice.

7. How are you leveraging your personal communications skills? Is full use being made of audiovisual techniques, of graphics, of handouts? The use of media forces a change in attention level or boredom level in the audience. I'm not suggesting that you should dim the lights and start pushing the advance button on a Carousel slide projector. However, alternative stimuli, including your voice, a flip chart, film materials, a recording, do help keep the audience interested and require their constantly refocusing attention.

8. Have you carefully checked the physical environment? It's essential that you have the advantage of a good environment, with proper accoustics, lighting, electrical outlets, seating, lectern for your notes, and so on. Would you wish to retain a professional who didn't have the presence of mind to ensure that everything required for a professional presentation was in place and working? I know one professional who carries his own slide projector, tray, screen, extension cord, and small lectern in the trunk of his car. He's been caught short and embarrassed too many times by program chairpersons who have not done their jobs.

9. Can you turn personal communications into written communications? Is there an opportunity for the content of your presentation to be reproduced, bound in a high-quality binder with your organization's logo on the outside, and distributed to every individual attending the presentation? In addition, you can use this opportunity as an opening to mail these materials to individuals who were members but were not in attendance. Participating members will love it, because it demonstrates to members who were not present that something worthwhile went on at the meeting.

10. What about the issue of applied versus theoretical? Select topics that have to do with current controversies and how-to applications. Don't go into deep theoretical and abstract arguments unless you're presenting to a peer group in meeting for just that purpose.

11. Does your presentation contain a commercial? It's very easy to remind the audience that you are on the professional staff of a particular organization, to tell briefly what your organization does and where it's located. Most audiences do not resent a *short* commercial. In fact, more often than not, they expect it.

12. Do you leave the door open for further contact? One professional I know arrives early for any luncheon speech. She places her materials at the side of each luncheon plate with her business card stapled neatly to the front. She then briefly refers to this package and suggests that the audience may wish to look at these materials at their leisure and/or pass them along to anyone who might have the need for her particular type of service.

Sometimes you may not have a sufficient number of materials or individuals may have to leave your presentation early for personal or professional reasons.

Also, you may run overtime and not have the opportunity for the questions and discussion you had planned. One way to solve this problem is with a preprinted form. The bottom of the form can be torn off and become a mailer. The form says: "I am sorry that the press of our schedule made it impossible for us to visit during the meeting. I appreciate very much your attendance and interest in the topic. Please take a moment to complete this form so that we can continue our communication at a later date." The mail-back section of the form might read: "Dear (your name): (1) Please send me _____ copies of your report and additional information on the topic. (2) I have a specific question; please call or write me at _____ . (3) Please have the individual in charge of _____ in your organization contact me. My address and phone number follow."

13. Thank you letter and rescheduling. Be sure to thank your host organization for the opportunity of being with them. If appropriate, be sure to let members know of your willingness to participate in the future. Be sure to schedule a follow-up call, should later appearances be appropriate. Where deep and intensive interest existed in parts of your presentation, you may wish to suggest specialized seminars or workshops addressed to those specific topics.

If group presentations are an integral part of your marketing program, these remarks should be regarded as only a beginning. Locate and study books concerning group communication, giving effective presentations, group selling, the use of graphics in communications, and so on. Be sure to share your knowledge with the members of your staff. There are few personal sales techniques stronger or more successful than effective interpersonal communication and presentations. But an ill-prepared, badly staged and presented professional personal appearance can seriously damage an otherwise sound MPS program.

Chapter 10
Your Professional Fees

Even the professional with the most philanthropic and humanistic motivation imaginable must earn adequate compensation. If the professsional is not adequately compensated for services, then sooner or later, that professional is simply out of business. From a marketing management point of view, there are only two basic elements in determining professional fees—supply and demand. The supply side of the equation deals with the costs incurred in offering and providing service to clients. The demand side of the equation concerns the number of potential buyers and the prices they are willing to pay for services they consume. When professionals get into economic trouble, you can be sure they have failed to consider the supply or demand factors of their practice adequately. Of course, it's a real red letter day—both literally and figuratively—when both problems occur simultaneously.

    The topic of fee setting and management is one regarded in many different ways, depending on the professional field in question and the individual professional. However, regardless of the public pronouncements, all professionals agree that adequate return for their efforts is a basic necessity for continuing their professional practice.

    In this chapter, we'll examine professional fees from several viewpoints. The importance of establishing fee objectives will be discussed. Three alternative approaches to developing objectives will be presented and related to your practice positioning statement. Next, alternative fee strategies will be suggested to help you structure the pursuit of your pricing objectives. The question of determining specific professional fees will be addressed and developed. Ways to positively and effectively communicate fee policies to clients will be discussed. Problems and potential solutions in the area of client billing and particularly collections will be treated. Finally, certain special fee situations will be considered. These include contract fees, retainers, interprofessional fees, and the changing legal and ethical environment.

ESTABLISHING FEE OBJECTIVES

In marketing management, price is always one of the key strategic variables. In *Basic Marketing—A Managerial Approach*, Jerome McCarthy gave a classic definition of the term price.[1] He stated that *price* is basically money for something else. As a marketer, one can decide to be a price competitor or to compete more along nonprice lines. Where price competition is used, major emphasis is given to offering lower competitive prices and communicating them actively to the market. In nonprice competition, the marketer focuses on other aspects of the product or service. The attempt here is to use nonprice attributes of the product or service to sell. The nonprice competitor seeks to maintain stability in prices for individual items or services. In addition, in a multiproduct or service situation, the non price competitor seeks to maintain a balance among the various high, medium, and low price offerings in the line.

Pricing objectives and strategy must be congruent with professional positioning. If you're positioning yourself as the Rolls-Royce in your competitive spectrum, bargain-style pricing, price cutting, and the use of heavily publicized loss leaders can result in a confusing and damaging professional image. Conversely, if you want a high-volume, low per-client financial return, no-frills organization, all aspects of your marketing program must follow suit. Prospective clients might be suspicious of plush locations, abundant staff, and rich selection of alternative service items. If you seek to establish and communicate a position as the leader in your area, clients will expect to pay for your expertise. Since volume will be lower, fees will probably be at the higher end of the scale. On the other hand, if you are a clinic or store-type basic services operation, your fee ranges will more appropriately be at the lower end of the competitive spectrum.

Alternative fee objectives usually take one of three forms—profits, volume, or market stability.

Profit Objectives

On of the most frequently discussed versions of this objective is "profit maximization." Before you adopt this objective, consider carefully the difference between the short-term and longer-term implications. Setting fees to maximize profits in the short run could lead to forms of professional behavior and consumer response that may diminish your opportunity to continue to earn such profits in the future. Major corporations have modified profit maximization objectives to state specifically that profit maximization should be pursued in the long run—that is, over a period of years. In the short run, survival, breakeven, and market position objectives can be as important as maximizing profits. Underlying these approaches is the development and delivery of professional service in such a manner as to warrant repeat purchase, referral, and growing consumer loyalty. Another approach to this objective is to establish fees based on a certain return on investment. For example, the professional might specify a 15 percent yield on a $100,000 investment in professional education, equipment, and location. Fees are then set so that the gross revenue of the practice minus the costs, including salary, yields the desired return on investment, in this case $15,000.

Share/Volume Objectives

Many professionals establish an annual revenue target based on their experience and/or norms for the profession. They work backward from that projection and alternative fee schedules to chart the number of engagements necessary to reach the objective. The assumption is that the higher the practice volume, the better. The conclusion is that higher volume will lead to higher profits or return on investment.

Be careful: This may or may not be true. If higher volume is attained through fee reduction, and if costs are not carefully controlled, the professional can be in the unenviable high volume-low profit situation, or worse, high volume and loss position. We'll examine these factors in a bit more detail when we consider the economics of fee setting later in the chapter. Where volume objectives are utilized on a regular basis, the figure finally selected should receive careful scrutiny. In speaking with the managing senior partners of a professional firm recently, I was surprised to see how proud they were of the fact that they had maintained an average 10 percent increase in revenues over the last three years. Their enthusiasm quickly faded when I pointed out that their fee increases and volume were not even keeping pace with inflation. In fact, costs were increasing much more rapidly than revenues, and the firm was losing ground.

Firms in the consumer products and services field frequently pursue a variant of the volume objective—that is, market share. Market share is the percentage of the total market being serviced by any one competitor. The total potential market in terms of sales volume is estimated. This figure becomes 100 percent and the basis for market share computations. For example, Heineken Beer currently enjoys a market share in excess of 50 percent of the U.S. for imported beer. The 60 or more other competitors share the remaining market with several firms able to obtain only fractions of 1 percent of total potential. In certain consumer goods and services industries, sales and market information are regularly collected and commercially available.

The advantage of market share is primarily economy of scale. Large firms with major distribution systems can react more effectively to take advantage of market opportunity. Major market share competitors enjoy lower costs in several aspects of the business. These include production, distribution, and promotion. In the professional arena, market share has its advantages. In a *Barron's* article entitled "Profit or Loss?"[2] it was noted that the Big 8 accounting firms have clients among 95 percent of the New York Stock Exchange listed corporations. Fewer than 1000 firms audit 10,000 corporate clients who file reports with the Securities and Exchange Commission. Concerning the pursuit of market share objectives, one Big 8 CPA pointed out that the only way a firm could make it work is to lower profits. This would be unacceptable to many partners. Another method would be to cut corners, which means professional service could suffer. Another problem with market share related fee objectives is the difficulty in measuring total market potential. Even where that is possible, it is often difficult to assess your individual share of the market compared to that of your professional competitors. Data are frequently closely held and not available.

Market Stability

What does your professional firm have in common with U.S. Steel? Perhaps, an affinity for market stability pricing. Author Joseph P. Guiltinan calls market stability fee setting "risk-aversive."[3] In such situations, industries like coal, steel, copper, and oil opt for less competitive and more stable pricing structures. The reason seems to be the potential for wildly fluctuating commodities and product cost and demand factors. Rather than ride a roller coaster of high and low demand and high and low prices, market stability pricers seek to provide an acceptable average return in good times and bad. Shorter-term profits may be subordinated to the longer term. In such situations there may be an industrywide price or set of price schedules for basic products. You may also find a "price leader"—that is, an individual firm who usually makes the first move in increasing or decreasing basic prices. In steel, we might be talking about U.S. Steel, in banking about Chase Manhatten, and so on.

How does this relate to the professional? Rates for specific services, hourly rates, or per diem rates may already prevail in your profession. This fee structure provides a basis or a norm to establish fees, depending upon positioning objectives, special skills, market opportunities, and other factors. Professionals might charge at, or above, or below the norm. However, within reasonably comparable groups of professionals, fees remain stable within the established range.

FEE STRATEGIES

Once you have selected a basic approach to pricing your professional services, there are several fee strategies you may wish to consider. These strategies may be used singly or in combination, as your positioning and market opportunities indicate.

Fee Segmentation

If clients fit neatly into homogeneous subgroups or segments, you should consider carefully whether differences among segments justify differing fee structures. For example, an actuarial consultant is frequently asked to develop actuarial tables based on certain data and assumptions for clients developing or modifying pension plans. This is a fairly standard service involving known and tested statistical methodology. However, one client segment might be composed of large business corporations whose pension programs have been well developed and documented. Another client segment might consist of small organizations who are just beginning to establish pension programs. In the first case, the consulting professional could work swiftly and efficiently with good data and a knowledgeable client. In the second example, a much greater effort may be required to produce the actuarial tables desired.

Sometimes the end product is the same, but the level of effort and difficulty involved in achieving the result is markedly different. Where such differences exist, you should investigate the strategy of differentiating fees by segment. There are two important conditions: First, that you are able to demonstrate the basis for such fee differentials if they are challenged by a client or prospect; and second, that clients or client organizations don't frequently or freely move from one segment to another.

Price Lining

This strategy is commonly seen in retailing. In men's shirts, for example, we've come to expect the $8 to $12 shirt, the $13 to $20 shirt, and the $21 to $30 shirt. All three shirts are adequate as appropriate apparel for the office. However, as we move from the low to the medium to the high price line, we expect to find greater product differentiation to justify the price differential. Similarly, a dental clinic has the opportunity to establish price lines for the dental examination. For example, the clinic might offer "basic," "regular," and "full service" examinations. The basic exam might cover examination only. The regular exam could include examination and cleaning. The full service exam could include examination, cleaning, X-ray, and fluoride treatment. Once price lines are set, the pricing process is simplified. Price lining is helpful to consumers because it helps them become familiar with the variety and quality within a particular service class. The grouping of related services into distinctive fee patterns also helps the professional to become more precise in cost analysis and revenue forecasting.

A key disadvantage to the price lining approach is that clients continue to expect a fee to which they have become accustomed. Modifying price lines to meet changing cost or market conditions too frequently can destroy some of the advantages derived from the strategy. In the consumer marketplace for manufactured products, this is a particularly difficult problem. However, consumers purchase manufactured goods and nonprofessional personal services on a rather frequent basis. So they remain in more constant touch with price lines. Noninstitutional buyers of professional services—that is, individual users—consume on a less frequent basis. In addition, inflation-driven fee adjustments have become the rule rather than the exception since the mid-1970s. This reduces some of the difficulties normally associated with price lining in professional service applications.

Leader Pricing

Leader pricing typically involves the substantial reduction in a price charged for a frequently demanded, regularly consumed product or service. The marketer engages in leader pricing to build volume and to introduce as many consumers as possible to the firm. The objective is to market additional products or service at full price to those consumers responding to the leader priced item. A familiar example is the supermarket chain that has consistently low regular or weekend prices on bread, milk, eggs, beer, cigarettes or some other frequently purchased staple. Experience indicates that the supermarket customer buys additional items during the visit made to take advantage of the special. In addition, the marketer may sell impulse items or expand the purchase to include other unplanned consumption.

Mass marketers of professional services such as franchised tax preparers, law stores, and dental clinics utilize the leader pricing strategy. H&R Block has advertized a flat-rate $10 fee for the preparation of a simple tax return for the individual taxpayer. Jefferson's/Ward's dental clinic promotes the $13 basic dental examination. Many law stores offer to prepare a simple will for a flat fee of $25. Careful analysis would probably indicate the these services are offered at or below cost. However, the leader pricing professional is hoping to generate a loyal customer base that will utilize higher-fee services over time.

There are three major dangers in leader pricing. First, clients may purchase only the leader service. The more sophisticated clients are able to understand and appreciate a bargain when they see one. In such cases, your competitor gets the business with a reasonable rate of return, while you provide a basic service with little or no return. Second, leader pricing may not be congruent with certain positioning strategies. To be most effective, leader pricing must be widely communicated and promoted. This sort of vigorous price appeal may not fit your positioning decision. Finally, leader pricing can set off price wars. The field of public accounting is a perfect example. Today, many corporate clients regard the financial audit as a necessary evil. They believe their books and records are accurate. However, the law may require an independent audit by an accounting professional. Prospective clients put pressure on the accounting firm to perform the work as cheaply as possible. Full-service firms often approach the audit as the key to open the door to additional business in the area of taxes and management consulting services.

In the *Barron's* article cited earlier, the head of a Big 8 accounting firm allegedly complained to a colleague that one multinational client was solicited on a no-fee basis for the first year. The article cites an instance in Cincinnati where a major auditor has offered to do the work of local country clubs for a token fee of $100.

In the same city, a university put up a systems study for bid and expected to pay about $250,000 for the work. However, the award went to a Big 8 firm that offered to do it gratis. The use of the audit as a leader pricing item is blamed by some of the growth-at-any-cost syndrome. Other analysts contend that leader pricing is a consequence of the reduction in the chargeable hours as the supply of new clients dwindles.

Competitive-Based Strategies

A sophisticated manager always considers possible and probable competitive reactions to decisions. This is especially true when the manager is operating in a price-sensitive environment. Pricing strategies related to competition typically take three forms: to beat, meet, or lead competition. In that order, they infer lower, similar, or higher competitive fees. Pricing to beat, meet, or lead competition is based on one fundamental assumption—competitive equality. As a general rule, I try to avoid competitive-based fee strategies. Yes, from time to time it is necessary to compete head-on. Sometimes institutional buyers will produce copies of a competitor's proposal with a fee clearly indicated. In other instances, open bidding may be solicited. These exceptions should be handled on an incident by incident basis.

Competitive-based fee strategies can be particularly dangerous when there is heterogeneity among the competitors. The assumption that your cost structure, expertise, productivity, and areas of opportunity are essentially the same as those of a competitor should be vigorously questioned. I have seen instances where professionals have purposely submitted a low proposal, prompting a competitor to submit one that was even lower. When trying to deliver on the proposal, the low-priced competitor was not able to provide the quantity or quality of service anticipated. The stronger competitor patiently waited. The client finally discharged the lower-priced firm and retained the higher-priced firm on a three-year contract.

Often professionals would simply be better off to say: "I'm sorry. We simply cannot provide the level of quality that we believe this assignment requires below our quoted rates." It may be foolish for a firm of litigating attorneys to offer cost-competitive will preparation. It would be equally foolish for a sophisticated public accounting firm to attempt to be price competitive in the area of bookkeeping services. Generally, I do not have a high regard for competitive pricing as the sole strategy for professionals. Certainly, fees are important, but professionals should be able to demonstrate other client benefits to offset competitive fee differences. These include service, expertise, dependability, and sincere personal concern and identification with the client and client problems.

Prestige Pricing

Prestige pricing has its basis in the oft-repeated economic concept, "You get what you pay for." While a Rolls-Royce and a Chevrolet Chevette may both get you from point A to point B, the way in which you are transported differs greatly. Earlier we talked about two dimensions of products and services—the functional attributes vs. the emotional or psychological attributes. A recent medical school graduate may perform an appendectomy utilizing perfect medical technique. However, some clients would "feel better" having their appendix removed by an experienced senior surgeon.

The concept that "you get what you pay for" is based primarily on the theory of our market system. Individuals who are more meritorious will rise to the top of their professions. Their records and reputations will grow. Responding to the basic law of economics that there is an inverse relationship between price and the supply and demand for a service, certain clients will be willing to pay more to secure the services of these prestigious professionals. In some instances, these higher fees are based on improving the probability that the professional will solve the client's problem more effectively than a less experienced or renowned professional. In some cases, certain clients, particularly the wealthy, simply wish to be associated with a certain level of professional practitioner. Here the fee is not an item of major economic consequence; more important is the prestige of having Doctor X perform the operation or attorney Y handle their legal matters.

If your practice positioning places you in pursuit of prestige and status, please remember our discussion of consumer behavior. Fee reductions or price competition in a prestige-oriented marketplace will cause some clients to become suspicious of value. They will wonder if they're still getting the same top-level service. Others experience the loss of the psychological statisfaction of being associated with a prestigious firm whose fee structure placed its services out of the reach of many clients. Don't confuse prestige pricing with the what-the-traffic-will-bear approach, or as I like to describe it, the Robin Hood pricing strategy—robbing from the rich in order to serve the poor. Prestige pricing involves a consistent set of fees that are simply higher than average competitive levels. The prestige firm may actually handle a smaller number of clients. However, the return realized from each account is usually higher than the norm for that professional specialty.

Discounts and Allowances

A recurring fee strategy question involves fixed fees versus variable fees. If a variable fee approach is utilized, the next question usually involves the degree of variance and the reasons why variance should be granted. In consumer and industrial service marketing, it is not uncommon to find list prices or pricing schedules that do not vary one penny from one pricing period to the next. However, these prices are almost always adjusted to reflect certain discounts and allowances, depending upon the individual purchasing situation. As a general rule, marketers should not offer discounts unless there is a shift in a marketing function. A common example would be the discounting of swimwear during the late summer and early fall. This discount is granted with the recognition that the consumer will perform the storage function. In addition, the consumer may be assuming a fashion risk concerning the acceptability of this year's style during next year's season.

Before you modify fees through discounts and allowances, put your idea to the litmus test. The basis for a reduction of a bona fide fee, one that recovers costs and earns an adequate return, should be the transfer of some functional responsibility from the professional to the client. Examples of functional shifts include these:

1. Assumption of greater involvement by the client. I was asked to analyze a professional marketing plan development project and submit a proposal. The work recommended priced out at $15,000. The prospective client's management committee had been given a $10,000 budget maximum for the assignment. I suggested that the client might be able to substitute its staff work, computer time, and clerical resources for those of my own staff. The project was redefined so that client staff were working under my supervision, and a substantial fee allowance was possible.

2. Seasonal factors. Some professionals experience definite seasonal peaks and troughs in level of activity. If professional clients are willing to postpone services to a lower activity period, a fee adjustment may be warranted.

3. Quantity discounts. Doing business in high volume over time produces economies of scale for the well-managed professional firm. Clients who are willing to sign service contracts and engage in multiservice utilization should share in the economies of scale through appropriate fee adjustment.

4. Interprofessional fee allowances. In some fields, including medicine, law, accounting, management consulting, engineering, and architecture, professionals may share an assignment with other professionals or firms. In most cases, this takes the form of a prime contractor and subcontractors. In cases where an assignment is too large for a single professional or firm to handle, other professionals may be called in or it may be that a special type of limited expertise is called for, and one must go outside one's own organization to secure that talent. Firms offering participation to nonfirm professionals usually expect a lower interprofessional fee. I'll use a personal example. I was contracted by an international consulting firm. They were doing a national study concerning energy consumption patterns. It required someone familiar with a particular state environment who also had contacts with major developers in the area. I proposed a $7,000 fee to do the work that was required. The consulting firm placed my segment of the study in their proposal at $10,000. In this case, the consulting firm was the prime contractor and I was the subcontractor.

Why should I be willing to grant a 30 percent discount on my professional services to the prime contractor? The prime contractor had taken all the risks and borne all the administrative and overhead costs in developing and gaining the assignment. Certainly that is worth a considerable allowance. In addition, when one works with other professionals, it is usually possible to work more efficiently. Why? Because the professionals in question typically have a more structured, organized, and standard approach to problem formulation, data collection, and analysis.

Interprofessional discounts are much more than simply professional courtesy. They are based on the transfer of functions from one individual or firm to another. Individual professionals and smaller professional organizations may find subcontracting a useful way to augment income, gain experience, and grow. In such cases, prime contractors become a major market segment and target. The economics and practices involved in interprofessional discounts should become an important item of managerial analysis and control.

5. Cash discounts. In manufacturing, retailing and wholesaling companies typically receive small discounts if their bills are paid promptly. For example, an invoice for $1000 with discount terms of "2%, 10 days; net, 30 days" translates as follows: The total balance of $1000 is due within 30 days; however, if the bill is paid within ten days of date of the invoice, then the buyer is entitled to deduct 2 percent from the amount due. If the buyer takes advantage of the discount terms, a remittance of $980 rather than $1000 would be sent. All things being equal, which they seldom are, a buyer not taking advantage of the savings is borrowing money for 20 days at an interest rate of 37 percent. This assumes a 365-day year and roughly 18 twenty-day periods at 2 percent each.

In business situations where the size of the purchase is typically high and repurchase occurs frequently, the impact of not taking cash discounts can be significant. Therefore, you'll find cash discount terms customarily offered in a variety of business settings. Generally speaking, however, professionals do not utilize cash discount strategies to encourage early or prompt payment. If collections and cash flow are a problem for you, you may wish to experiment with the cash or early payment approach.

FEES FOR NEW SERVICES

Before you determine your fee strategy for a new professional service, give considerable attention to the question, "What do we mean by new?" In most cases, we find that "new" services usually fit into three categories:

1. Repackaged or positioned. This is basically the same service dressed in new clothes or offered to a new market segment.
2. Improved or modified. Through some change, the service has become better. The level of improvement can range from very small to quite significant.
3. A breakthrough. This represents a quantum leap in service improvement. It could be a significant modification of existing procedure—for example, a high speed, water-cooled drill in dentistry—to a newly available service, such as computer auditing of computerized recordkeeping systems.

Remember our definition of price? "Money for something else." In setting new service fees, a realistic appraisal and understanding of the something else is crucial to adopting an appropriate strategy. Alternative strategies include *skimming* and *penetration*. If the service is unique and innovative and a large unmet demand exists, the initial fee might be set relatively high to skim the market. This traditional terminology in marketing management was based on the analogy of skimming the rich cream from the top of bottled milk. Skimming allows professionals to recover service development costs quickly and to earn a reward for their developmental time, costs, and risks. Skimming offers the professional attractive, entrepreneurial reward for innovation and risk taking, but there are also dangers. First, clients may not react well to the high fee differential for the new service. This can be offset by targeting only new clients who really need and will pay for your unique offering. Second, if the service is really innovative or even if it is merely popular, competing professionals may get wind of the higher fees. This will encourage competition, copying, and price cutting, particularly in the more competitive professional service areas. Although knowledge of the innovation is impossible to prevent, you should be aware of the importance of preserving the uniqueness of the new service to your organization's advantage as long as possible.

Finally, as the new service becomes more widely available and known, supply may catch up with demand. This inevitably means some form of fee competition. Clients who paid the higher fees during the skimming phase may feel they were unfairly treated. Should this occur, it is essential to point out that lower costs are made possible by higher volume and greater efficiency in service delivery.

A penetration fee is designed to create trial, rapid acceptance, and high volume for the professional. The service may be priced slightly above the breakeven point. If you see the service as a leader item, you may wish to consider offering it at cost or even below if the offsetting benefit of increased clients and revenues from other full-fee services is envisioned. In the professional setting, establishing an extremely low penetration fee can make prospects suspicious of quality. Unless fees from other areas of your practice are providing the needed return, you'll soon face a thorny problem with penetration. Few professionals can afford to follow a penetration strategy over the long term. If it is successful, clients will drain professional time away from full-fee activities to satisfy the high-volume demand for low-priced service.

Sooner or later, penetration fees must be increased unless the new item is destined to be the perennial leader pricing service. The trick is to demonstrate to the penetration clients that you are indeed the professional to handle all client problems. In this way, you might convert the economically motivated prospect who has growth potential to a full-time, full-service client. I've known professionals who have done just the opposite. Since it was a low-fee penetration service, an obviously lower level of professional care, concern, and quality was exhibited. As soon as fees were raised, the penetration clients left. Penetration offers a unique way for prospective clients to become familiar with you and your organization. However, the strategy must be carefully managed and implemented.

Penetration fees reduce competitive interest and may allow you to make inroads and capture market share. In the consumer goods and services marketplace, the strategy is most often used for staple products such as beer, cigarettes, toothpaste, soft drinks, and bread. Skimming, on the other hand, is more often used for new shopping and specialty items such as handheld calculators, CB radios, in-home video communcation systems, household computers, and microwave ovens.

DETERMINING PROFESSIONAL FEES

Professionals frequently ask me: "What can the field of economic theory teach us about fee setting?" At that point, I'm tempted to leap to the chalkboard, draw demand and supply curves, compute coefficients of elasticity, talk about marginal analysis, and produce an indifference curve. However, to temper my enthusiasm for theory, I think of a colleague at the university. When I ask him if he has the time, he proceeds to tell me how to build a watch! The point is, fee setting in the professions operates within some very definite economic parameters.

Types of Costs

I prefer to begin any analysis of professional fees on the cost side of the equation. Why? Because cost can generally be accurately determined or reasonably estimated. In addition, there may be administrative records from which cost estimates can be derived. Finally, many professions have excellent national and regional associations. These groups commission periodic or annual studies concerning the economic and managerial aspects of the profession. Even the most poorly organized professional can learn something from examining the cost norm for professionals in the same gross revenue range. Another thing I like about costs is that they are somewhat subject to your control. Certainly, you may not like to contemplate certain tough cost decisions; however, at least in the area of variable costs, you have the power to do so. Controlling new client demand, on the other hand, may be much more difficult. Finally, when I've seen professional and commercial organizations in trouble, I'm frequently appalled to find how little they know about the actual costs of offering their respective products and services.

It's not possible, nor is it desirable, for you to become a cost accountant or an economist. There are, however, experts in these areas who assist professionals of every type in documenting and understanding costs. I urge you to consider having this basic information developed and maintained in a updated fashion. Before you can assess alternative fee levels or your rate of return from prevailing or traditional, established fees, you must understand both the fixed and variable cost aspects of your practice.

Fixed costs are those that do not vary appreciably with level of practice activity. These include location rental, utility charges, mortgage payments, insurance, office equipment and furnishings, and the staff support and administrative personnel necessary for you to remain open for clients. These types of costs are often called uncontrollable costs or administrative and overhead expenses. The variables costs are those that do change with level of activity. For example, direct materials and supplies used in a particular engagement, travel time and costs, time of professional staff who work directly with clients. Variable costs are sometimes called direct or controllable costs. Ideally, each professional should know the variable cost of providing each type of service offered. In addition, a portion of the fixed cost of practice operation has to be allocated to each service on some consistent basis related to the justifiable portion of overhead attributable to that service.

While the allocation of fixed expenses is as much an art as it is a science, there are some objective measures. For example, the charging of space costs to a tax attorney in a multiprofessional law firm could be based on the number of square feet that professional and related staff and reference materials occupy. Similarly, charges for clerical staff, paralegals and any firm administrative personnel could be allocated based upon the percentage of time they spent on tax practice matters. Please don't be upset if these allocations are not precise—they seldom are. However, they will help you gain a clearer picture of the costs of operating your own practice or of each segment of a multiperson firm.

Breakeven Analysis

Once fixed and variable costs have been determined or estimated, breakeven analysis may be utilized. Breakeven analysis basically determines the quantity or number of engagements that have to be sold at given fee levels if the professional's total revenue is to equal total costs. Every engagement sold above that breakeven figure represents a contribution to profit. If the professional does not achieve the breakeven figure, obviously the practice is operating at a loss.

I recently worked with a young professional who was intent on leaving his firm to set up a management consulting firm of his own. He was tempted by the high hourly fees charged by his firm's principals. He stated that his fee levels were much more modest, and he therefore expected to do quite well. I asked him what he thought his breakeven point would be for the first year of operation. I was retained to assist him in developing a new business plan he was going to present to 12 interested investors. After analyzing the fixed and variable costs necessary to place him in practice at a competitive level, he found that his breakeven point would have required total revenues far in excess of what seemed to be possible during the first year. His investors were unwilling to wait indefinitely for a return on their investment. The project was ultimately abandoned, but unfortunately, the professional in question had already left his firm and was now unemployed. Being a marketer, I am optimistic by nature. However, before I get too excited about the possibility of increasing sales, I thoroughly investigate the cost implications and breakeven requirements for each venture.

Cost-Plus

Cost-plus fee setting is another well known and widely practiced technique. It assumes, of course, that costs are known and their behavior well understood. The professional makes a decision as to what return level is satisfactory and tacks that onto the service cost base; hence the name *cost-plus*. I have an acquaintance who is the chief executive officer of an advertising agency. He utilizes cost-plus pricing exclusively. In all his proposals, he outlines the cost estimates for all services to be provided. He then adds a figure of 20 percent for entrepreneurial return (profit). He refuses to budge from that figure. In addition, he cautions prospects about retaining professionals who do not understand their costs or are not earning an adequate profit. His point is that "something has to give," and in most cases, he asserts it's the quality of the project. This simple, yet compelling approach to fee setting, along with the high level of professional skill of he and his staff, have made this agency stable and successful.

Other Cost Approaches

Other cost-oriented fee-setting approaches include contribution pricing and return on investment pricing. These techniques, as well as demand-oriented techniques, are widely discussed in the literature of accounting, finance, marketing, and managerial economics. It is beyond the scope of this book to provide an in-depth treatment and analysis of each technique, nor should you feel less than adequate in this area. One of my own personal crusades is the more complete preparation of professionals in the area of management and marketing during their professional training. I hope this will begin to occur as a result broadened professional education. At this point, you should now be challenged to learn more about this area and to question the availability and accuracy of cost information for your own practice.

COMMUNICATING FEES

Picture this. You're with a group of friends at lunch. Everything goes fine, the lunch is delightful, the conversation refreshing. Suddenly, the check arrives. That same lighthearted group may become quiet. People stop to remember and think in earnest about what they had and what share of the tip they ought to contribute. Take another situation. You shop and shop for that new car. You finally find a product you like and a dealer you like. After the fun of discussion and the test drive, the atmosphere changes. It's time to bargain, it's time to negotiate. It's only natural that payment is often associated with conflict in the consumer's mind. To conceptualize, to theorize, to plan, to think ahead, to analyze, to diagnose, that's all a lot of fun. To pay is something else again. Professionals often fail to consider a client's or prospect's feelings concerning fees. I suspect that unvocalized fee objections account for a large number of unclosed engagements and client turnover.

Earlier we discussed some of the essential differences between products and services. The intensely personal nature of the service marketplace and the intangibility aspect of performance measurement create some unique needs in the management of service fees. To compound the problem, many professionals seem to have woven a web of mystery around their fee structures. Indeed, it appears almost beneath the dignity of some more conservative and prestigious professional personages and firms to engage in direct fee discussions. Professionals operating in a monopolistic environment may indeed be able to follow this mode. However, if you believe, as do I, that market economics, disclosure, and public scrutiny will become increasing influences in the professional service field, you may wish to adopt a more modern approach concerning fees. This approach can be summarized in one word: "communicate."

Tell your clients and prospects what your fees are and how they are derived. Explain that adequate fees are necessary to ensure the proper level and quality of professional service. Consumer fear and uncertainty concerning fees leads them to suppress their questions. This failure to consider one of the most important aspects of the professional service purchase can waste precious time for both prospect and professional. How can fee policies and procedures be communicated?

A highly regarded orthopedic surgeon I know operates at the high end of the fee schedule. In his waiting room, clearly displayed, is a tasteful printed and framed statement that says, in effect: "We would be pleased to discuss any questions you have regarding professional fees." In another professional practice, prospects receive written material about the firm. There is a specific section dealing with fee policies, billing, and collection. Prospects are set at ease that the important topic of fees will be included on the agenda of the first consultation once the client's requirements are clearly understood.

As a general rule, it is wise to include fee policies and practices as a standard part of any firm brochure. The level of specificity will vary by type of profession and type of prospect. For example, a law store or legal clinic may be happy to mail the current fee schedule to anyone who inquires. Indeed, specific fees are frequently featured as part of media advertising for this type of professional organization. A less direct approach would involve clearly posting a fee inquiry piece in the waiting room. It might read: "We welcome your questions concerning our professional fees. Please ask our receptionist for a copy of our fee policy and practices." Such policy statements might discuss alternative fee arrangements, such as hourly rate, contract fee, retainer. Prospects can be made aware of the advantages and disadvantages of each type of arrangement.

The important thing is to get the fee question out in the open for prospects or clients who are concerned about it. There will be less surprise, resistance, disappointment, and perhaps uncollectible fees when the fee question is positioned to be simply a natural part of the overall engagement.

If you or your organization utilize some form of contract or standard agreement, this will be the place in which the actual fee for a particular engagement will be documented. Let the prospect know that discussion of the specific fee for this engagement will depend upon the factors relevant to his or her particular requirements. Before quoting a final fee, be certain to enumerate the steps that will be taken on the client's behalf. This ensures that the client has a full understanding and appreciation of the work that will be performed for the fee about to be quoted.

Some professsionals feel comfortable quoting fee ranges in their in-office fee policy statements. This may be a helpful device for prospects. If a person looking for a $25 will finds out that the law firm that he has walked into prepares wills for a range of $250 to $500, he knows he has come to the wrong professional. Preliminary information concerning fee ranges helps eliminate unqualified prospective clients. In these times of increasing costs and soaring inflation, please be sure to use the word "current" liberally in any fee quotation or estimate you might publish. Propspective and current clients should be placed on gentle notice that fee levels will not remain unchanged indefinitely.

There are, of course, exceptions to the previous discussion. Professionals with leading national reputations who are in a seller's market may simply set a flat fee based on what the market will pay. At the other end of the spectrum are professionals who are bound to serve anyone, regardless of the clients's ability to pay. But as one professional said to me, "You know since I've started being more communicative about fees, my collection percentage has increased. I guess I've scared away a lot of deadbeats who realized that I was concerned about the income side of my practice."

Gilsen, Cawley, and Schmidt[4] suggest that all clients feel reassured if fees are discussed upfront, based on preliminary estimates of the amount of time a billable service is likely to take. They recommend that the professional be very specific as to all the work that will be involved. They further state: "It doesn't hurt to draw it out a bit, either, to make perfectly clear all the benefits that the client will receive. Point out, for example, the problems that will arise in time, money, and opportunity lost on the client's part if your services are not performed. Don't get trapped into answering the question, 'Just tell me what it's going to cost me,' with a hefty sounding fee that isn't placed in the context of all the service you will provide and all the benefits the client will enjoy."[5]

GETTING PAID!

However, there's a funny thing that happens on the trip between selling the client and collecting the fee. Sometimes, they don't pay! The field of credit and collection is an extremely well-developed specialty area. It is replete with national associations, special publications, workshops, books, courses, and conventional wisdom. For our purposes, however, it is sufficient to focus on a few basic and enduring principles of billing and collecting for professional services:

1. Develop, document, an implement a billing and collection system. Don't be frightened by the word "system" if you're an individual professional. A system doesn't have to be complex and cumbersome. It can consist of a few simple policies followed by action and follow-up utilizing predefined communcations pieces with predetermined time and rules. The large professional firm will have a more complex system, but it will be based on the same principles. Figure 10-1 illustrates a collection system model for a large medical group. Please note that this system contains owner-manager developed objectives, credit policies, collection procedures, and performance monitoring. In this situation, patients are encouraged to pay for services at the time of receipt in non-insurance-covered treatment. For clients who are billed, two statements are sent, then a series of nonrespondent letters in cases

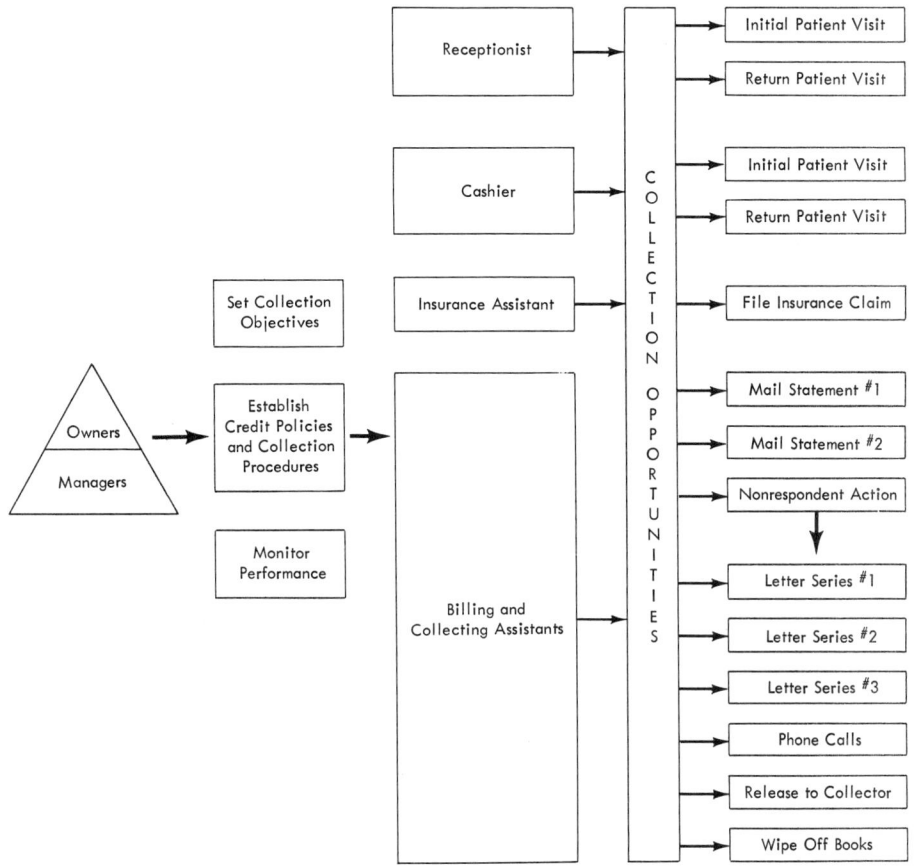

FIGURE 10-1 A collection model

Source: Robert L. Harrison, "Anatomy of a Collection System," *Medical Group Management*, 27 (November-December 1980), p. 55. Reprinted with permission by the Medical Group Management Association, 4101 E. Louisiana Ave., Denver, CO 80222.

where payment is not received. The first letter is a "gentle reminder," the second a "firm, but helping hand," and the third is a "last resort" notice. Some credit and collection managers would suggest that the phone call in the model be placed earlier in the sequence. Whichever form you prefer, a structured and consistently applied billing and collection system will help minimize uncollectible fees.

2. Professional service statements should be sent promptly. Many professional services are consumed at the time they are rendered. There seems to be a direct relationship between the promptness of billing and the promptness of payment. Over time, client appreciation of the service rendered may diminish. In addition, clients may feel that the professional doesn't need the money, since the bill took so long to arrive!

3. Itemize, itemize, itemize. A bill that reads, "for professional services" doesn't do much to resolve the client's cognitive dissonance. This is particularly true when the fee is large. The bill should describe in detail exactly what work was performed and by whom. Where hourly rates are utilized, computations and extensions used to arrive at the final total should be shown on the bill. The client will be reminded that you did indeed do work on his or her behalf.

4. Progress payments. Rather than send one large bill at the end of an engagement, split the bill into several progress payments. The number and size of the payments will vary with each professional and type of client. There are many valuable benefits to progress reporting and payment systems. From the collection point of view, clients may be better able to afford immediate settlement of the smaller bill. They get into the habit of paying as the service is being rendered. Finally, problems and misunderstandings arise early, and if necessary the professional can interrupt service until the problem has been solved or payment received. Obviously, where ethical codes preclude such tactics, client cooperation by moral suasion must be sought.

5. Overruns or underruns. There will be occasions when actual fees will be higher than estimated fees or vice versa. As soon as this can be verified, the client should be contacted directly. The problem or the good news should be explained fully, and a follow-up letter sent. It's not a bad idea to request written acknowledgment of a fee overrun and approval for the additional billing to make it a matter of record in the client's file. Where costs have been overestimated or special circumstances resulted in increased efficiency or productivity, tell the client exactly what happened. Small underruns due to better-managed engagements make clients disproportionately happy. First of all, it demonstrates that you are honest! Second, it shows that you are indeed shepherding their resources in addition to servicing their needs.

ETHICAL AND LEGAL ISSUES

Professionals who collude to fix fees, who pay referral fees, or who engage in fee discrimination will come under tougher regulatory scrutiny during the 1980s. During the mid- and late 1970s, the Federal Trade Commission gave considerable attention to anticompetitive practices in the professions. The interest of the federal government and the several states who have enacted their own versions of the Federal Trade Commission Act stems from the Sherman-Antitrust Act, passed in 1890. The major thrust of Sherman Act is to prohibit contracts, conspiracies, or monopolies that restrain trade. The Clayton Act of 1914 and the Robinson-Patman Act of 1936 helped clarify and apply the Sherman Act. The Clayton Act prohibits specific practices that substantially lessen competition. The Robinson-Patman Act attempts to regulate buyers and sellers in areas of price discrimination, commissions, allowances, and trade discounts. Not only the letter of these acts but their spirit has been used to mirror professional practices. It is one thing to allege collusion or price discrimination, and still another to prove it. However, actions against professionals receive wide national publicity. They are extremely damaging to the confidence placed in professionals by the general public. In my judgment, it is within the enlightened self-interest of the several professional associations to take steps to identify potential anticompetitive practices and to work to bring them more in line with the developing professional service market environment.

One recent Federal Trade Commission complaint against the American Society of Anesthesiologists (ASA) alleged that their relative value guides concerning fees were illegal under Section 1 of the Sherman Act. Judge Kevin Duffy of the United States Court in Manhattan threw out the complaint. James E. Brian, *American Family Physician's* Washington correspondent, stated:[6]

> Judge Duffy's statement, I think, may be useful in discrediting the FTC's attempt to outlaw other good faith enterprises by the professions which are intended to "restrain" bad practices, to "combine"—or even to "conspire"—in various self-disciplinary activities. . . . I feel that all of medicine is confronted with a "clear and present danger," and it should resist—far more obstreperously than it has thus far—every one of the various incursions of the FTC in such areas as the enforcement of ethical principles, collective self-regulation and self-improvement, and other programs designed to improve the quality and availability of medical care.
>
> Brian further stated that the elemental fallacy on which the FTC bases so many of its jousts with the medical profession is the treatment of medicine as a business and the attempt to make medicine respond to the same marketplace influences as industry. When you mix one part professional ethics with one part commercial law and one part market economics, you're sure to get a volatile brew regardless of who's right or wrong. It's becoming clear that many areas of professional practice, particularly professional fees, will be more closely scrutinized in the future.

Notes

Chapter 1

1. Philip Kotler, *Marketing Management* (Englewood Cliffs, N.J.: Prentice-Hall, Inc., 1976), p.5.
2. Aubrey Wilson, *The Marketing of Professional Services* (London: McGraw-Hill, 1972), p. 15.

Chapter 2

1. Professor Lovelock's remarks were delivered at the American Marketing Association "Special Conference on Service Marketing," Orlando, Florida, February 1981, where he was a guest speaker.
2. Everett B. Turner, "Marketing Professional Services," *Journal of Marketing*, 33 (October 1969), p. 58.
3. Warren J. Wittreich, "How to Buy/Sell Professional Services," *Harvard Business Review*, March-April 1966, p. 128.
4. Ibid., pp. 127-128.
5. James E. Bell and David Appel, "Marketing Crisis in the 70's," *The Southern Journal of Business*, 5, 3 (July 1970), 9.

Chapter 3

1. Eugene J. Kelly and William Lazer, *Managerial Marketing: Perspectives and Viewpoint*, 3rd ed. (Homewood, Ill.: Irwin, 1967), p. 386.
2. Ibid., p. 388.
3. Philip Kotler, *Marketing Management: Analysis, Planning and Control* (Englewood Cliffs, N.J.: Prentice-Hall, 1976), p. 448.

Chapter 4

1. E. J. Fox and E. W. Wheatley, *Modern Marketing–Principles and Practice* (Glenview, Ill.: Scott, Foresman, 1978), pp. 370-91.
2. Ibid., p. 174.
3. Edward W. Wheatley, "Generalities to Ruin a Marketing Plan," *Sales Management*, January 1, 1971, pp. 18-25.
4. Ibid., p. 46.
5. Mark L. Stern, *Marketing Planning: A Systems Approach* (New York: McGraw-Hill, 1966), p. 13.
6. Martin L. Bell, *Marketing Concepts and Strategy*, 3rd ed. (Boston: Houghton Mifflin, 1979).

Chapter 5

1. Christopher C. Gilson, Linda C. Cawley, William R. Schmidt III, *How to Market Your Law Practice* (Germantown, Md.: Aspen Systems Corporation, 1979), p. 43.

Chapter 6

1. E. J. Fox and E. W. Wheatley, *Modern Marketing: Principles and Practice* (Glenview, Ill.: Scott, Foresman and Co., 1978), p. 98.
2. Philip Kotler, *Marketing for Nonprofit Organizations* (Englewood Cliffs, N.J.: Prentice-Hall, Inc., 1975), pp. 103-104.

Chapter 7

1. James L. Heskett, *Marketing* (New York, Macmillan, 1976), p. 52.
2. Christopher Gilson and Harold W. Berkman, *Advertising: Concepts and Strategies* (New York: Random House, 1980), pp. 45-50.
3. Jack Trout and Al Rise, "The Positioning Era Cometh," (New York: Rise Cappiello Colwell, Inc., 1972), pp. 38-41.
4. Jonathan Kwitney, "Why Is Schaefer Beer the One Beer to Have When Having More...?" *The Wall Street Journal*, December 13, 1972, p. 1.

Chapter 8

1. Norman Rachlin, CPA, "Using a Printed Image to Expand Your Practice," Florida State University Accounting Conference, May 13-15, 1981, Tallahassee.
2. Christopher C. Gilson, Linda C. Cawley, and William R. Schmidt III, *How to Market Your Law Practice*. (Germantown, Md.: Aspen Systems Corporation, 1979).

Chapter 9

1. Robert W. Denney, "How to Develop—and Implement—a Marketing Plan For Your Firm," *The Practical Accountant*, 14, 7 (July 1981), 18-30.
2. Frederick A. Russell, Frank H. Beach, and Richard A. Buskirk, *The Textbook of Salesmanship*, 10th ed. (New York: McGraw-Hill, 1978), pp. 266-365.
3. Christopher C. Gilsen, Linda C. Cawley, and William R. Schmidt III, *How To Market Your Law Practice* (Germantown, Md.: Aspen Systems Corporation, 1979), pp. 244-49.
4. James J. Mahon, *The Marketing of Professional Accounting Services* (New York: Ronald Press, 1978), pp. 178-81.

Chapter 10

1. Jerome McCarthy, *Basic Marketing—A Managerial Approach* (Homewood, Ill.: Irwin, 1978), p. 491.
2. "Profit or Loss?" *Barron's*, March 12, 1979, p. 18.
3. Joseph P. Guiltinan, "Risk-Aversive Pricing Policies: Problems and Alternatives," *Journal of Marketing*, January 1976, pp. 10-15.
4. Ibid., pp. 94-96.
5. Ibid., p. 95.
6. "View from the Hill," *American Family Physician*, January 1980, p. 225.

Index

A

Administrative communication, 152-53
Advertising, 4, 17, 18, 23, 136-47
  agencies, 140-42
  campaign approach, 138-40
  classic mistakes, 143-47
  definition of, 136
  institutional, 136
  professional help, 140-42
  short-term and long-term effects of, 136-38
  (*see also* Positioning)
American Advertising Federation, 144
American Cancer Society, 14, 16
American Marketing Association, 2
American Medical Association (AMA), 18
American Oil Corporation, 14
American Society of Anesthesiologists (ASA), 195
Appel, David, 31
Atmospherics, 159-61
Avis Rent A Car, 114

B

Basic Marketing—A Managerial Approach (McCarthy), 178
Beach, Frank H., 165
Behavior mapping, 96-99
Bell, James E., 31
Bell, Martin L., 9, 62, 64
Benefit segmentation, 101, 103
Berkman, Harold, 112
Billing, 192-94
Body language, 164
Borden, Inc., 8, 20
Branching questions in MPS audit, 37-38
Breakeven analysis, 189
Brian, James E., 195

Budget, advertising, 139
Burger King Corporation, 3
Buskirk, Richard A., 165

C

Campaign approach to advertising, 138-40
Canned personal sales approach, 165
Cash discounts, 186
Caterpillar Tractor Corporation, 15
Cawley, Linda C., 81-82, 140, 169, 192
Century 21, 17
Citgo, 15
Classification, market, 100-101, 110
Clayton Act of 1914, 194
Client analysis and targeting, 92-110
   behavior mapping, 96-99
   classification, 100-101, 110
   identification, 100, 110
   market research (*see* Market research)
   MPS audit and, 37, 40-41
   segmentation, 101, 102, 103, 110
   targeting, 101, 103, 110
Client interview or consultation, 165-71
   six-step approach, 169-70
   three-step approach, 170-71
   traditional sales approach, 165-69
Client mix, 84
Client services brochures, 130-31
Closing, 168-69, 170
Coca-Cola Company, 114
Collection system, 192-94
Collusion, 194-95
Commitment, 49
Committee format, MPS program and, 55
Communication (*see* Personal communication; Written communication program)
Communication flows, development of informative and persuasive, 3, 4-5
Community relations, 23

Competition, 7, 91
Competitive-based fee strategies, 183
Competitive communication, 136-52
   advertising (*see* Advertising)
   proposals, 147-49
   reports, 149-51
   seminar materials, 151-52
Competitive environment, 81-86
Comprehensive scope of MPS audit, 34
Confidentiality, 36
Congruence of objectives, 51-52
Conscious versus subconscious cues, 124
Consultants, 56-57, 140-42
Consumer orientation, 11
Consumer panels, 26
Consumer perception, 123-24
Contingency planning, 73-74
Contribution pricing, 190
Coordination, 49-50
Cost-plus fee setting, 189-90
Costs, types of, 188-89
Costuming, 161-63
Courses, 172-73
Cultural environment, 79-81
Customer loyalty, 4, 5-6

D

Datsun Z-car, 112
Demand estimation dilemma, 24
Demarketing, 15
Demonstrations, 166
Denney, Robert W., 155, 156
Director of marketing, MPS program and, 55-56
Directory listings, 135-36
Discounts and allowances, 184-86
Distribution, directness of, 26
Do it yourself method, MPS program and, 57-58
Do it yourself syndrome, 29
Dramatization, 165-66
Duffy, Kevin, 195
Durability of services, 23-24

E

Economic variables, 71-74
Emotional needs, 23
Energy business, 14-15
Ethics, 78-79
   professional fees and, 194-95
Evaluation:
   of advertising, 140
   elusiveness of, 25-26
Experimental research, 3
External communications programs, 171-76
EXXON Corporation, 14

F

"Fantastic-frustration syndrome," 50
Feasibility of objectives, 51-52
Federal Trade Commission (FTC), 18, 194, 195
Fees (*see* Professional fees)
Fee segmentation, 181
Financial auditing, 33
Fixed costs, 188-89
Flexible objectives, 52-53
Focus groups, 3, 26, 109
Foote, Nelson, 31
Ford, Henry, 7
Fox, E. J., 15, 31, 51, 96, 97
Front-office management, 157-58
Functional versus emotional impressions, 124

G

General Electric Company, 8, 20
General Foods Corporation, 4, 20
Generalizations, marketing, 58-60
Gibbs, Christopher, 86
Gilson, Christopher C., 81-82, 112, 140, 169, 192
God syndrome, 28-29
Gross national product, 20
Guiltinan, Joseph P., 180

H

Hanging close, 168-69
Harvard Business Review, 30
Heineken Beer, 179
Hertz Rent A Car, 114
Heskett, James L., 112
How to Market Your Law Practice (Gilson, Cawley, and Schmidt), 81-82, 140, 169

I

Identification, market, 100, 110
Image, 15, 156-64
   atmospherics, 159-61
   costuming, 161-63
   institutional contact, 157-59
   printed, 123-26, 156, 157
Implementation schedule, 52
Inflation, 5
Institutional advertising, 136
Institutional communication, 129-36
   client services brochures, 130-31
   directory listings, 135-36
   functions of, 129-30
   newsletters, 133-34
   partners, associates, or principals brochures, 131-32
   publications, 134-35
   special topics brochures, 129, 132-33
   updates, 134
Institutional contact, 157-59
Intangibility of services, 23
Interprofessional fee allowance, 185-86
Interviews (*see* Client interview or consultation)
Inventory problem, 24

J

Jones, Deborah, 158
Jordan, Jim, 113-14

K

Kelly, Eugene J., 33
Kotler, Philip, 2, 33, 34, 62, 101, 102, 159
Kwitney, Jonathan, 113

L

Lazer, William, 33
Leader pricing, 182-83
Learning curve, 50
Legal environment, 76-78
Legal issues, 18
   professional fees and, 194-95
Letter of transmittal, 150
Levitt, Theodore, 28
Listening, 164-65
Location, 159-60
Logos, 126-29
Long-term advertising, 136-38
Lovelock, Christopher H., 26
Loyalty, customer, 4, 5-6

M

McCarthy, Jerome, 178
McDonalds, 4
Mahon, James J., 170
Malpractice, 77-78
Management letters, 33
Managerial environment, 89-91
Managing partner, MPS program and, 54
Mandatory-formal approach to implementing MPS program, 66
Marketing:
   basic functions of, 3-6
   concept, 8, 10-13
   definitions of, 2
   evolution of, 6-8
   meta, 14-16
   negative bias towards, 1, 7
   scope of, 1-2
Marketing Concepts and Strategy (Bell), 64
Marketing executive, 11-12
Marketing for Nonprofit Organizations (Kotler), 101, 102
Marketing Management: Analysis, Planning, and Control (Kotler), 62, 159
Marketing mix, 12
Marketing of Professional Services, The (Wilson), 105
Marketing Planning: A Systems Approach (Stern), 63
Marketing professional services (MPS) audit, 31, 32-45
   client analysis and opportunities, 37, 40-41
   control and evaluation, 45
   criteria for good, 33-34
   definitions of, 32-33
   limitations of, 35-37
   mechanics of taking, 38
   personal communication, 37, 43-44
   practice environment, 37, 38-39
   practice philosophy, positioning, and targeting, 37, 41
   professional fees, 37, 42-43
   service mix, 37, 41-42
   written communication, 37, 44-45
Marketing professional services (MPS) program, 31, 46-69
   definition of, 47-48
   desirable characteristics of, 51-53
   generalizations, 58-60
   implementation and control, 62, 66-69
   importance of, 48-51
   organizing, 53-58
   structuring of, 60-65
Market research, 21
   focus groups, 3, 26, 109
   objectives, 105
   observation, 3, 109
   process, 106-9
   specialists, use of, 104, 106
   surveys, 3, 108
   tests and experiments, 106-8
Market share, 179-80
Market stability, 180
Market tests and experiments, 106-8
Measurement of progress, 50
Media reps, 140-42

Meta marketing, 14-16
Midas Mufflers, 24
Modern Marketing—Principles and Practice (Fox and Wheatley), 31, 51, 96, 97
MPS audit (*see* Marketing professional services (MPS) audit)
MPS program (*see* Marketing professional services (MPS) program)

N

National Cash Register Company, 113
Natural environment, 79-81
Needs and desires, understanding, 3-4, 29-31
Need-satisfying products and services, development of, 3, 4
Negative bias toward marketing, 1, 7
New client letter, 153
New services, fees for, 186-88
Newsletters, 133-34
Nissan Motors, 112

O

Objections, dealing with, 167-68, 170
Objectives, 51-52
Objectivity of MPS audit, 34
Observation, 3, 109
Organizational chart, 8, 9, 10

P

Panacea syndrome, 35
Panel discussions, 172
Partners, associates, or principals brochures, 131-32
Peak-load problem, 24-25
Penetration fee, 186, 187
Periodic basis of MPS audit, 34
Personal appearances, 171-76
Personal communication, 154-76
    body language, 164
    client interviews (*see* Client interview or consultation)
    external communications programs, 171-76
    image (*see* Image)
    listening, 164-65
    MPS audit and, 37, 43-44
Personal contacts, 82, 84
Personal element in service marketing, 25
Personal selling, 4, 23
Planning (*see* Marketing professional services (MPS) program)
Political environment, 75-76
Positioning, 84-85, 111-21
    definitions of, 111-13
    examples of, 113-14
    expanding concept, 114-16
    statements, 116-21
"Positioning Era Cometh, The" (Trout and Rise), 113
Postpurchase customer relationship, 5-6
Practice environment, 70-91
    competitive environment, 81-86
    economic variables, 71-74
    ethics, 78-79
    legal environment, 76-78
    managerial environment, 89-91
    MPS audit and, 37, 38-39
    natural and cultural environment, 79-81
    political environment, 75-76
    technology, 86-89
Practice management plans, 47-48
Practice philosophy, positioning and targeting, 37, 41
Presentation, 165-66, 173-76
Prestige pricing, 183-84
Price discrimination, 194-95
Price lining, 181-82
Pricing strategies (*see* Professional fees)
Printed image, 123-26, 156, 157
Probing questions in MPS audit, 37, 38
Procter & Gamble Company, 4, 20, 139
Producer/service unity, 87

Product marketing:
  differences between service marketing and, 21-26
  typical process of, 21, 22
Professional cards, 152-53
Professional fees, 84, 177-95
  breakeven analysis, 189
  collection of, 192-94
  communicating, 168, 169, 190-92
  competitive-based strategies, 183
  contribution pricing, 190
  cost-plus fee setting, 189-90
  discounts and allowances, 184-86
  ethical and legal issues, 194-95
  fee segmentation, 181
  leader pricing, 182-83
  market stability, 180
  MPS audit, 37, 42-43
  new services and, 186-88
  prestige pricing, 183-84
  price lining, 181-82
  profit objectives, 178-79
  return on investment pricing, 190
  share/volume objectives, 179-80
  types of costs and, 188-89
Professional regulations, 76-77
Professionals, definitions of, 16-17
Profit objectives, 178-79
Promotions, 4
Proposals, 147-49
Publications, 134-35
Publicity, 4, 5, 23
Public laws, 76
Public relations, 23
Public relations firms, 140-42

Q

Quantity discounts, 185

R

Rachlin, Norman, 123, 131
RCA Corporation, 5-6
Receptionists, 157-58
Referral fees, 194

Reports, 149-51
Resistance, 66-67
Return on investment pricing, 190
Revson, Peter, 27
Rise, Al, 113, 114
Robber barons, 7
Robinson-Patman Act of 1936, 194
Russell, Frederick A., 165

S

Sales and Marketing Management magazine, 164
Sales era, 7
Sales promotion, 4, 17, 23
Schaefer beer, 113-14
Schmidt, William R., III., 81-82, 140, 169, 192
Segmentation, market, 101, 102, 103, 110
Selective perception, 36
Seminars, 151-52, 172
Senior professional, MPS program and, 53-54
Service gap, 31
Service marketing:
  differences between product marketing and, 21-26
  growth of, 20-21
  roles of marketers, 26-27
Service mix, 37, 41-42, 84
7-Up, 114
Share/volume objectives, 179-80
Shell Oil Corporation, 14
Sherman-Antitrust Act of 1890, 194
Short-term advertising, 136-38
Six-step approach to client interview or consultation, 170-71
Skimming, 186-88
Slide presentations, 166
Society of Consumer Affairs Professionals, 6
Spastic syndrome, 138, 144
Special help, 90
Specialization, 90, 125
Special topics brochures, 129, 132-33
Specificity of objectives, 51-52, 53

Speeches, 172
Stationery, 152-53
Steele, Irving, 159
Stern, Mark E., 62, 63
Structure of MPS program, 60-65
Supreme Court of the United States, 18
Surveys, 3, 108
Switchboard operator, 157-58

T

Targeting, market, 101, 103, 110
Task force (MPS program), 54-55
Technology, 86-89
Telescoping, 166
Textbook of Salesmanship, The (Russell, Beach and Buskirk), 165, 167
Three-step approach to client interview or consultation, 170-71
Traditional sales approach, 165-69
Trial close, 166-67
Trout, Jack, 113, 114
Turner, Everett B., 29

U

Uncertainty, reduction of, 30
Updates, 134

V

Variable costs, 189
Variable fee approach, 184-86
VIP approach to communication, 129
Visualization, 166
Voltaire, 6
Voluntary-informal approach to implementing MPS program, 66-67

W

Warranty programs, 26
Westinghouse Electric Corporation, 8, 20
Wheatley, Edward W., 15, 31, 51, 59, 96, 97
Whirlpool Corporation, 5-6
Wilson, Aubrey, 18, 105, 106
Wittreich, Warren J., 30
Workshops, 172
Written communication program, 122-53
  administrative communication, 152-53
  competitive communication (*see* Competitive communication)
  image and, 123-26
  institutional communication (*see* Institutional communication)
  logos, 126-29
  MPS audit, 37, 44-45